Praise for *Simple Prosperity*

"This is a valuable and concise digest of much that we've figured out in recent years, about health, stress, joy, community. The only thing it won't tell you how to do is make more money; instead, it will let you see that you may already have enough."—Bill McKibben, author *of Deep Economy: The Wealth of Communities and the Durable Future*

"Perhaps the highest compliment one writer can give another is 'I wish I'd said that!' David Wann has woven together all the right stuff to make a compelling and appealing case for the abundance of enough and the poverty of more. He stands firmly with one foot in the intimate details of daily life and the other in the shocking details of the degradation of healthy ecosystems and communities. Both the appeal of a better personal life and the horror of what will be upon us if we don't act should get us all on the Simple Prosperity bandwagon."—Vicki Robin, coauthor of *Your Money or Your Life* and cofounder of Conversation Cafés

"Dave Wann's recipes from his own experience in *Simple Prosperity* are a breath of fresh air, and just what we need for a saner future. They include ideas, sound research, and down-to-earth advice we can all use. This book is also much more: a friendly, personal guidebook for living a more enjoyable, healthy, loving life."—Hazel Henderson, author of *Ethical Markets: Growing the Green Economy*

"If ever there was a right book at the right time, *Simple Prosperity* is it. This country needs this book."—Lester R. Brown, president of Earth Policy Institute and author of *Plan B 2.0: Rescuing a Planet Under Stress and a Civilization in Trouble*

The New Normal

Also by David Wann

Coauthor

Affluenza: The All-Consuming Epidemic
(Berrett-Koehler)

Nonfiction

Simple Prosperity: Finding Real Wealth in a Sustainable Lifestyle
(St. Martin's Press)
Biologic: Environmental Protection by Design
(Johnson Books)
Deep Design: Pathways to a Livable Future
(Island Press)
Superbia: 31 Ways to Create Sustainable Neighborhoods
(New Society Publishers)
The Zen of Gardening in the High & Arid West
(Fulcrum Publishing)
Reinventing Community: Stories from the Walkways of Cohousing
(Fulcrum Publishing)

Contributor

Take Back Your Time
(Berrett-Koehler)
*Less is More: Embracing Simplicity for a Healthy Planet,
a Caring Economy, and Lasting Happiness*
(New Society Publishers)

Poetry

Log Rhythms
(North Atlantic Books)

The New Normal

An Agenda for
Responsible Living

David Wann

St. Martin's Griffin ⚞ New York

www.stmartins.com

Library of Congress Cataloging-in-Publication Data

Wann, David.
   The new normal : an agenda for responsible living / David Wann. — 1st ed.
      p. cm.
   ISBN 978-0-312-57543-4
  1. Social values—United States.   2. Sustainable living—United States.
3. Lifestyles—United States.   4. Quality of life.   5. Conduct of life.
I. Title.
   HN90.M6W357 2011
   306.0973—dc22

                                2010037913

First Edition: January 2011

10 9 8 7 6 5 4 3 2 1

Contents

Acknowledgments

This book could never have been written without the thorough, self-directed work of people who are truly champions of change and guardians of the future. In particular, I drew on the research of the Earth Policy Institute and the Worldwatch Institute for data that reveal where we are as a civilization and where we need to go. My sincerest thanks to Lester Brown, Christopher Flavin, and their colleagues for clearheaded, tireless reporting and advocacy. I also relied heavily on stories in *Yes!* magazine, *Ode* magazine, the *New York Times,* and *Time* magazine, and on *60 Minutes* and National Public Radio. Online resources like *Daily Grist,* the Environmental News Network, and *Worldchanging* are incredible sources, too.

There are many other visionaries whose lives and work have especially inspired me over the years. Wendell Berry, Dana Meadows, Amory Lovins, Paul Hawken, Bill McKibben, Hazel Henderson, and David Korten are a few of this generation's superheroes—lantern bearers whose work has long been powered by generosity, hope, and a tenacious belief in humanity's talents and instincts. I encourage readers to peruse my short list of recommended readings at the end of this book, but of course what converts ideas to reality is the hands-on work of activists and practitioners: human rights, peace, and environmental activists; biologists and bioneers; green engineers and entrepreneurs; policy makers, teachers, spiritual mentors, artists, and web weavers in all walks of life.

Thank you!

David Wann

Preface

The cultural framework we live in—our way of thinking—will either save the day or drop the fragile egg that rightfully belongs to the future. We usually assume that huge challenges can only be finessed with technical, political, and economic fixes, but we forget that all three are programmed by human culture, and it is there that we can leverage change most quickly and effectively. What do we really mean by this fuzzy term "culture"? It's not just paintings and music, not just opinions, values, and styles; it's nothing less than the lens through which we perceive reality—the customs, traditions, symbols, norms, motivators, and direction that constitute a way of life. Right now, our culture is confused, trapped between the old paradigm—in which economic growth is king—and a new paradigm that correctly perceives limits to growth and acknowledges its potentially catastrophic social and environmental costs. We are looking for a new identity—a new normal that is more secure, stable, and sensible.

Our most influential institutions—schools, family, government, business, and the media—instruct and insist that the shortest route to meaning, happiness, and equality is through the marketplace: a bustling, bumbling universe of production, transaction, and consumption. Centuries ago, economies of the developed world geared up to produce more than we need to be happy, and we obediently bent our way of life out of shape to keep up with overproduction. Although this worn-out paradigm continues to accelerate, we ask ourselves, nervously, "Where is this sports car taking us? Does it have dependable brakes?"

A primary source of cultural dissonance is the disparity between institutions and intuitions. A harnessed, institutional mind-set says, "Full speed ahead—look what we've created!" But our intuition—with the full force of evolution behind it—cautions, "Slow down—look what we are destroying!" This duality is very familiar to those who study nature. Successful living systems (including humans) typically progress from being highly productive yet wasteful to being highly protective and efficient. In their most mature, climax stages, biological systems have learned how to optimize diversity, resourcefulness, and resilience, weaving partnerships among species to make use of each scrap of resource, and to survive threats from outside the system (such as climate changes). This book maps a pathway to cultural maturity, a natural and achievable destination.

The overall theme of nature is not bloodthirsty competition, but functional, celebratory interdependence and cooperation. Ecosystems—and civilizations—succeed by building on the accomplishments of preceding systems. For example, shade-loving Douglas fir trees take root in the shadow of Ponderosa pines, which in turn get their start in soil built by grass roots and microbes. A mature civilization does not violate natural realities and laws; however, there is more than enough evidence to charge our civilization with planet-slaughter. To clear our name, our generation's pivotal assignment is to design a systemically more mature way of fitting in. Our intuition tells us that it's not higher profits and faster transactions we crave but greater *value*. If we get more use out of each electron and each cubic foot of soil, if we learn to meet our needs squarely for health, food, social connection, and shelter, then we won't need *or want* as much money—individually or collectively. At that point, our way of life can be less expensive, less destructive—and more satisfying. It isn't sacrifice, and it isn't threatening, if everyone does it together—if rich and poor (people and nations) meet somewhere in the middle, in terms of material wealth. Rather than enduring lives of debt, doubt, fear, and stress, we can create a lifestyle and culture filled with the affluence of time, health, and stimulation. But first we have to come out of denial, acknowledging that our excessive, wasteful way of life can't and won't continue. Game over. Like participants in a 12-step program, we need to confess that our way of life isn't working. Only then can we make appropriate course corrections in policies, technologies, and everyday habits—all contained within the rich matrix we call culture.

If at first the idea is not absurd, there is no hope for it.
—Albert Einstein

It always seems impossible until it's done.
—Nelson Mandela

Introduction

Once Upon a Paradigm, When Growth Was King

A s writers approach the finish line in a book project, which is typically when we write the introduction, we of course have high hopes that readers and reviewers will connect with the message and commit scarce time to the book. I can save some of your time right up front—and possibly entice others to take a chance. This book is not for those who assume our familiar way of life can remain much as it has been. It's not for those who expect things to "get back to normal" once the recession is finally over, or after inevitable price spikes in oil, water, and grain hit. After all, normal wasn't realistic. We desperately need to create a bright *new* normal, and that's precisely what this book is about. Cultures and economies coevolve with existing conditions such as climate, population, and availability of resources, and when those conditions change, so must a culture. That's the way life works. We need to reprogram the software of our civilization, nothing less, because the norms that have been drummed into us over the past eight or ten generations are no longer relevant. Our current agreements congealed centuries ago, when conditions were radically different. There was only one-tenth the number of people in the world, and the planet's reaches and resources seemed infinite. There was no need to assign value to living systems—they were essentially free, and exploiting them was likewise thought to be *risk*-free.

Now we see how wrong we were, through a zoomed-in lens of explosively converging events. Just since 1960, global consumption has grown sixfold. Metals production also has grown sixfold; and oil consumption, eightfold. Meanwhile, human population and water consumption have doubled, as expectations of higher consumption have spread like an epidemic around the globe. But how can this economic paradigm of excess possibly survive in an age of dwindling resources? Life has seemed effortless in our times for one simple reason: we've been mindlessly spending our natural endowment as if we'd won a Powerball lottery. In 2008 alone, global consumers bought 69 million vehicles, 85 million refrigerators, 297 million computers, and 1.2 billion cell phones. Every day, the global economy extracts the equivalent of about 112 Empire State Buildings from the earth, disrupting the nests, seedbeds, roots, and hunting grounds of gazillions of living things. Yet the dogma of hyperproduction and throwaway consumption teaches us to ignore the holocaust of the living systems that support us. Once mainstream culture accepted a calculated and dubious link between high levels of consumption and well-being/success, everything else became secondary. It's time to vigorously and heroically challenge this aggressive paradigm, which has already hit the planet's living systems like dozens of nuclear bombs.

➤ A Few Little Glitches

But wait a minute—this is *not* a "disaster" book, so busy trying to be an alarming bestseller that it neglects in-depth, point-by-point solutions. The whole idea here is to stimulate rapid change by debunking our current way of life and proposing something better. In this book, I will present an agenda including thirty-three high-leverage actions that can take us to a more affordable, more admirable era. Americans often ask, "What can I do to help make the world more sustainable?" I believe the first step is to be informed, and in this book I've provided a primer regarding basic issues and solutions for the challenges that lie ahead. With the knowledge that I've compiled, a citizen can be part of the world forum about systemic change, and a student might be stimulated to pursue a career in new-paradigm fields ranging from politics to "bioneering"—designing with nature. Because we are a forecasting species, we create the future; so let's picture an equitable, moderate, highly successful civilization, and go there. In this book, and in my own life, I see the future as a glass not only half full, but half full of sparkling cider. Imaging anything else is a waste of time.

Admittedly, there are a few little glitches. For starters, as the organizing principle of a civilization, unlimited material growth on a finite planet is and always has been a fairy tale, plain and simple. We believed it like little kids believe in Santa Claus or Superman. We need a more realistic organizing principle that pursues qualities that *are* infinitely renewable, such as the continuous cycling of nutrients, weather, and water through the biosphere—the planet's real economy; the ongoing search for efficient and equitable ways of meeting core needs; and ageless values like trust, curiosity, and community. Gandhi's words should be a beacon: "Speed is irrelevant if you're traveling in the wrong direction," he warned, calling for economic balance as the world's industrial pace began to exceed what nature could provide and culture could moderate. We're playing our game expertly, he was saying, but it's the wrong game. "No matter how far you've gone down the wrong road, turn back," echoes an old Turkish proverb. There is enough wealth for everyone—even on a crowded planet—if we coordinate our energies and efforts, redesign our social software, and change direction. There's unimaginable trauma ahead if we don't.

➤ Recycling the Western Paradigm

Physicist and systems thinker Donella Meadows believed that the creation of sweeping change involves scrapping one paradigm and putting another into service. "A paradigm is a shared idea in the mind of society that constitutes that society's deepest set of beliefs about how the world works," she explained in her online article "Leverage Points." She listed a few tenets of our current, dogmatic paradigm: "People who are paid less are worth less. Growth is always good. Nature is a stock of resources to be converted to human purposes." Though she was completely aware of the pervasiveness of these flawed beliefs, she knew that they can dissolve in the blink of an eye. "There's nothing physical or expensive or even slow about paradigm change," she writes. "In a single individual it can happen in a millisecond. All it takes is a click in the mind, a new way of seeing. It is in the space of mastery over paradigms that people throw off addictions, bring down empires, and have impacts that last for millennia."[1]

The time has come for such a paradigm shift. We are truly at the end of an era, sorely in need of systemic change that can and must be a turning point in history. We've worn nature out and ourselves, too, trying to comply with mandates for constantly increasing profits, productivity, speed, and mobility. Now it is time for a restorative era, rich in nature-friendly, ingenious design and ways of enriching and redirecting our most valuable achievement of all: human culture. It's time for a renaissance of human values.

The choices we are making are so much bigger than one kind of detergent or another, one lightbulb or another. Putting it bluntly, the editors of *Worldchanging* e-zine write, "There are no simple steps worth caring about. We'll only head off disaster by taking steps—together—that are massive, societal and thorough. Most of what needs to be done involves political engagement, systems redesign, and cultural change. It can't be done in an afternoon and then forgotten about."[2]

Beneath the media's radar screen—so focused on scandals, crimes, and movie stars—we are choosing a new way of being in the world. More than we consciously realize, our culture is choosing how much weight we will give to the public sector—including commonly held assets like climatic stability and the prosperity of species, and culturally rich assets like parks, libraries, fire departments, arts, and education—and how much to the private sector, with its familiar emphasis on individual gratification. There are tensions between being consumers and being producers of our lifestyle; between rational and intuitive decision making; between being comfortable with change and being unwilling to budge.

We are exploring whether to give a higher priority to discretionary time, which would necessarily mean choosing less work; whether we truly want convenience or a more vigorous self-reliance that uses our unique hands and brains; whether we want centralized or decentralized patterns of living and governance; and whether we want to democratically shape technology rather than passively letting it shape us. (If we're smart—and vigilant—only emerging technologies that match the rhythms of nature will be socially and politically acceptable.)

This may seem obvious, but why not reprogram human civilization to fit our genome? The way we typically design suburban development isolates us from one another, granting higher status to wheels than to legs and lungs. This just doesn't fit who and what we are. Why should we put up with designs that make computers and a few shareholders happy, but confuse the hell out of the rest of us? We concentrate sugar in processed foods, fooling our taste buds into thinking we've found a whole hillside of blueberries, when really all we've found is forty pounds of excess weight. We build doomsday bombs that are useful only if we don't use them, and conduct wars to teach other people how not to kill—by killing them. It's up to us to change the rules of a game whose end point is collapse.

In a cultural revolution like the one that's now taking shape, citizens have had enough. With little left to lose, they vehemently oppose the ransacking of nature and the unequal treatment of people. They propose new symbols of success, new ways of expressing who we are and how we should behave. Various movements of the past century—the human rights, environmental, and peace movements among them—demonstrate that we are ready for heroic, historic, just-in-time change. The megachallenges we confront demand a culturally cohesive response—a social tsunami—because they threaten our *collective* safety and security.

For example, humans have long been defenders of our territories, in an instinctual bid to favor the strongest gene pools. Now the territory is the earth itself, and the human population needs to manifest a new survival ethic—we might call it "biospirituality"—that ritualizes respect for all living things, making destruction of nature unthinkable and unforgivable. In combination with consensus policies that reward what we need and penalize what we *don't* need, this bright new ethic will enable even the aging boomer generation to see the first glimpses of the turnaround, to have a window on the welcome regeneration of watersheds and forests, of hope, determination, and purpose. Together, those now living can establish a viable *action plan* for restoring and preserving the climate, habitats, and traditions with which humanity evolved. The twenty-first century will see the emergence of significantly different ways of thinking, some of which are summarized in the following table. Some things we *know* to be true will sink to the bottom of our culture, while others will rise buoyantly to the top, within a new normal. Knowing that cultural changes are coming can help us make timelier and wiser decisions.

· Choosing a New Normal ·

Old Paradigm	New Paradigm
Perpetual growth of capital is the goal.	Sustainable yield; preservation of systems and good quality of life are the goals.
Products and profit as outputs.	People and culture as outputs.
Emphasis on quantity, appearance, force.	Emphasis on quality, durability, precision, flexibility.
Throwaway mentality: onetime use, products not repairable.	Closed-loop, continuous-recycling mentality, products easily repaired and reused.
Disruption of natural balance acceptable if profit justifies it.	Natural systems must remain intact and functional.
Biologically oblivious.	Function and value are enriched by understanding nature.
Understandable only by experts	Easily understood by anyone.
Generates hazards and requires protective equipment, guards, or defensive spending.	Increases security and safety, doesn't require vigilance or monitoring.
Operates with inflexible, standard operating procedures.	Offers innovative, diverse solutions to both technical and social problems.

Old Paradigm	New Paradigm
Centralizes authority, limits access.	Empowers individuals and communities, broadens and decentralizes authority.
Uses non-renewable energy and materials from distant sources.	Uses renewable energy sources and recycled materials, obtained locally.
Extends supply lines and process steps to deliver goods and services.	Shortens supply lines and process steps, saving energy and preserving culture.
Causes unforeseen health effects, limits wellness, and dominates nature.	Nature-compatible, proven over the course of billions of years.
Nature seen as a warehouse of resources to be extracted and exploited	Nature has intrinsic, quantifiable values when left in place.
Promotes and fosters exclusiveness and isolation of people from what they need.	Meets needs precisely and inclusively with rich, local networks that enable accountability and participation.

➤ Tipping Point

Despite an almost limitless, sometimes comical capacity for denial, most humans sense that these kinds of changes are coming, and that they are something on the order of humanity's shift from strictly hunting and gathering to the predominance of agriculture. The underlying purpose of that shift that happened about ten thousand years ago was to provide greater stability and security. With agriculture and community as a way of life, humans could enrich their home territories and store up food supplies in good years, increasing their odds of surviving the lean years. The coming megashift, away from the industrialized depletion of the planet's resources and toward their regeneration, is also about stability, security, and survival.

Although our current lifestyle still seems all too normal, it's become crystal clear that the half-millennium-long Industrial Revolution is running on empty. The lifestyle it spawned may be familiar, may tickle our taste buds and play our brain cells like a pinball machine, but is it sustainable? No way. There's not enough rich industrial ore, topsoil, or biological habitat left; not enough natural resilience to absorb our wastes and provide immunity; not enough climatic stability; not enough psychological stamina, or cheap energy, timber, or potable water, for the same old hyperconsumption game to continue—especially as human population and expectations continue to swell. The overall goal in the new era will no longer be indiscriminate growth, but rather incremental, qualitative improvement—like a well-practiced concerto or a basketball team that keeps getting better (not bigger!).

To save our civilization, we'll need to rethink the way we farm, fish, and harvest wood; the way we design buildings and make energy; the way we manufacture products, deliver goods, and provide mobility. There's a lot of work to be done, and a lot of jobs, sustenance, and satisfaction in going in the right direction, at the right speed. Shifting these massive, global industries in a more sustainable direction will require a more sustainable paradigm for agriculture—that recognizes the farm itself as the most important product; higher standards in the construction of buildings and neighborhoods; and achievable, affordable ways to optimize energy efficiency and clean energy flows.

➤ Trashing the Throwaway Mind

As I began writing this book, I knew there were specific targets I'd go after, like coal-fired power plants, poorly designed packaging, out-of-season fruit from distant continents, feedlot rather than grass-fed beef, suburbs without stores, communities without recycling services, 30 million acres of thirsty, hungry lawn in America, the abuse of prescription drugs, and processed food. The book's intent is to evaluate and guide decisions that can steer us clear of both personal and planetary bankruptcy. As Thomas Friedman argued in a recent *New York Times* editorial, "We must grow in a different way. Economies need to transition to the concept of net-zero, whereby buildings, cars, factories and homes are designed to generate as much energy as they use and be infinitely recyclable in as many parts as possible."

I agree completely with Friedman's words. It seems obvious that good decisions provide the greatest good for the greatest number of people, over the longest period of time. Although this is a very general, fuzzy concept, it's our first checkpoint for evaluating decisions. How can industrial energy and food systems that deplete the resilience of natural wealth provide the greatest good for the longest period? Urges Friedman, "Let's grow by creating flows rather than plundering more stocks." He asks a question that resonates with this book's central message: "What if the crisis of 2008 represents something much more fundamental than a deep recession? What if it's telling us that the whole growth model we created over the last 50 years is simply unsustainable economically and ecologically and that 2008 was when we hit the wall—when Mother Nature and the market both said: 'No more.'"[3]

Knowing that most readers are already treading water in an ocean of information, I've limited this book's content to high-leverage changes that will make the biggest difference. Expanding on thirty years of research in many areas, I've presented new-paradigm solutions in these all-important categories:

- where we live and how we build

- what we eat and how we grow

- how we interact with, and protect, nature

- what we buy, and how we design and make it

- how we provide power, mobility, and access

- how we prioritize and budget both private and public capital

If we look at these key leverage points in a context of preventing climate change, habitat destruction, and "culture cancer," these are the sectors with the highest immediate potential. As I researched and wrote, I kept a list of "paradigm principles" that provide guidelines for a new, more affordable way of life.

The Twelve New Normal Paradigm Principles

1. The challenges we face are not just technical—they are social, biological, political, and even spiritual challenges. For example, green technologies won't be sufficient if our current value system keeps pumping out too much stuff and settling for sloppy services. Even green overconsumption is overconsumption, which results in more transactions and "throughput" than the planet's living systems can handle without collapse.

2. Technology is no longer the limiting factor of productivity—resources are. Deeper wells can't pump water that's no longer there; larger boats and nets can't harvest more fish when fish populations have been wiped out.

3. Major historical shifts occur when a majority of the population understands that it is easier to adopt a new way of life than to prop up the broken one. Therefore, the "bad news" we've heard over the past three decades is not really negative, but rather useful evidence that systemic change is necessary.

4. In our search for a new way of life and the products that will help achieve it, we are exploring whole new ways of thinking and designing. We are choosing not just hybrid cars, but hybrid systems that provide food, mobility, wellness, shelter, energy, and employment synergistically. The overall goal is not arbitrary, anything-goes growth—often burdened with dysfunction, illness, and waste—but growth and improvements that meet essential needs *fully*.

5. New systems of accounting will track productivity in terms of quality, not just quantity. For example, exemplary companies now track tons of cement or sheets of paper produced *per unit of energy* (not just per dollar invested). Similarly, to evaluate the overall productivity of farming, the new metrics will track the nutritional value of the food and the health of the farms it came from, not simply bushels of grain or pounds of beef.

6. Decisions will be made and priorities will be set using far wider criteria than price, profit, and prestige. For example, living capital—life itself—should unquestionably have a higher priority in decision making than transitory material capital.

7. We can't change the realities of resource scarcity and population increase, so we need to change our way of life instead. For example, we are a social species that uses status to organize the group, but there are many other ways of awarding status besides material acquisition, such as trustworthiness, knowledge, kindness, and integrity. The new normal reminds us that a leaner way of life is healthier.

8. Designers can't assume that energy will be abundant, or that discretionary time will continue to be scarce. In the future, we will use more human time and energy and less fossil-fuel energy. We will once again participate physically, by walking rather than driving, or operating window covers to maintain desired temperatures in homes and offices. "Totally automatic" may be a desirable goal for robots, but not for humans.

9. A sustainable economy maximizes the productivity of resources as well as of people. Writes Paul Hawken, "When you maximize the productivity of people, you use fewer people, but we have more people than there are jobs. Basically we are using less and less of what we have more of, and with natural capital, using more and more of what we have less of."[4] That kind of economy doesn't make

sense. Why not move toward full employment of a *part-time* work-force, giving us enough income as well as more time for living? To fund public services and infrastructure, why not tax fossil fuels and pollution, not work?

10. Some products and resources—such as food, water, and gasoline—need to be priced *higher* to ensure both full cost accounting and minimal waste. For example, gasoline should rightfully cost much more because its environmental and health effects are not currently accounted for.

11. Saving a civilization is not effortless and convenient; it takes focus, strategy, and engagement. Our generation's mission should be to create and maintain an economy based on fully satisfying finite needs rather than chasing insatiable, market-driven wants. Let's slow down and meet needs directly, delivering more value per life-time.

12. Democracy may be our greatest social invention to date, but it can't work unless citizens are informed and have both political access and sufficient time to exercise their shared power.

➤ Changing the Channel

Let's face it, we Americans are in the habit of expecting easy solutions. Just give us lists of products we can buy and small decisions we can make that will enable us to feel less guilty and less responsible. Just give us warm and fuzzy economic indicators like "home sales are up" and "consumer confidence is up." We keep hoping, naively, that it will be simple and automatic to "save the planet," that if we're just more dutiful recyclers and car-tire inflators, our frenzied yet familiar routines can continue—no real change necessary. If we screw in a few more compact fluorescent or LED bulbs, maybe we can avoid the need to rethink our civilization's combative relationship with nature? Not exactly. Until we change the *direction* of our plug-and-play, no-effort-required lifestyle, we'll continue to be an endangered as well as a dangerous civilization. We'll continue to generate game-ending carbon dioxide as we convert ecosystems to must-have, easily broken gadgets and nutrition-free, processed food. Our most important mission is to get beyond a "simple" mentality and take part in creating a more mature culture. We need universal endorsement of a more sensible, sustainable value system that doesn't reward corporate or governmental exploitation but does revalue living systems. We need policies that support enlightened new goals. Here's the good news: the most effective way to save our civilization is also quite simple if *most people* do it; we just need to start talking about different things. "Voting with our dollars" is not as powerful as ongoing, stimulating discussions about value-driven ways to prevent collapse. *We just need to change the subject (and the channel) to something that matters.* We need to report back from small groups, "This is what we came up with." We're far more than consumers; we're voters, teachers, employees, churchgoers, discussion group members, menu planners, city planners, product designers, investors, union members, members of food co-ops, farmers market attendees, recyclers, politicians, and writers. Most important, we are people who talk, e-mail, twitter, text, and otherwise communicate with other people, constantly building opinion and culture the way humans have always done. Each one of these many roles can be guided by the new-paradigm ethic outlined in this book—an ethic that has been coming into focus for at least half a century.

Every civilization has a collective identity, and ours is now obsolete, agreed upon when conditions were radically different. We need to reach new social agreements, quickly. For example, houses large enough to get lost in and sky-high salaries for playing sports or managing companies are no longer useful symbols of success. This is not to say that a person's life accomplishments don't have value, just that we need to agree on new ways to express and reward those accomplishments. We want the respect of our peers, but let's earn it by being authentic, service-oriented, and fair. From here on, status symbols should express who we are and what we do with our time and energy, rather than just what we earn and own. If we simply change the meaning of this one word—"success"—we can steer the civilization in a completely different direction. Bloated stock portfolios and yachts the size of battleships won't win our respect in the new era, but reliability and honesty will.

In the book *Born to Be Good: The Science of a Meaningful Life,* University of California, Berkeley, psychologist Dacher Keltner challenges the familiar interpretation of natural selection as based on dog-eat-dog competition, arguing that humans are successful as a species because of our traits of nurturing, altruism, and compassion. His own interpretation of evolution? "Survival of the kindest."[5] As our transition unfolds, competition will become less of a dogma and cooperation more of a mantra. (Anthropology and genes, after all, trump returns on investment.). As an analogy for our whole culture, consider the popular game of Scrabble—typically played as a nail-biting competition. It's still Scrabble and just as much fun if its goal is to use all the tiles in the set, cooperatively. Players are still challenged to create the best possible words, but keeping score becomes unnecessary. It's the skill, challenge, and teamwork that count, not the ego boost and the stinging defeat. Our culture can and should reward people for teamwork that makes equality as well as efficiency easier to accomplish. Humans are hardwired to cooperate. In fact, the act of cooperation actually stimulates the pleasure center in our brains. (We can prove this with real-time brain scans.) This defining characteristic—cooperation—can help us create a more sensible civilization.

➤ Outside the Comfort Zone, but No Longer Afraid

As I was researching and writing this book, friends asked me what it was about, and I began to tell them, "systemic change." I would tell them what I was discovering in each chapter—for example, that deforestation emits more greenhouse gases than all the world's trains, planes, buses, and automobiles combined. The restoration of forests is a collective decision, based on an ethic that considers the greatest good. However, we can participate as individuals by using less paper per capita, eating lower on the food chain, and devising more efficient ways to cook food in developing countries. Changes like these aren't self-righteous, moralistic actions but logical and unselfish. They are not sacrifices, but simply pragmatic and profitable ways of meeting needs. Forests are being cut down primarily to make paper, to provide pasture and feed for meat production, and to provide fuel. Collectively, we can distribute information and package food with far less paper; reduce heart disease and obesity by eating less meat; and invent vehicles that are exponentially more efficient. If everyone works together toward objectives like these, we can break our addiction to a destructive—and not really very satisfying—way of life.

As I talked with friends and colleagues about deforestation or the need to change the way we farm, plan cities, or design products, their eyes would sometimes glaze over, and I knew what they were thinking: Really, how can individuals affect these huge systems? "We can't change the way farmers grow food, or planners plan cities," they would say. "And we can't just move to smaller houses or change to more eco-friendly jobs. We can only make small, unthreatening changes because we have families, we have certain routines, and because we are up for promotions."

That response is reasonable and familiar, but I believe we *can* make changes that are much more than "simple," no matter who or where we are—if we agree to leave our comfort zones just a little, until a "new normal" becomes comfortable and routine. It is the people, not just government or big business, who should issue powerful, explicit guidelines to food retailers, designers, and planners: "We want affordable grass-fed beef because it makes biological sense: herbivores eat grass, a storehouse of energy that humans can't digest. Health and environment are higher priorities now—we want manufactured products that are not toxic. And we want cities that are built for people, not cars. We want these things NOW." We can wake up and become citizens again, signing petitions, shifting our investments, voting for candidates who champion sustainable solutions; becoming bloggers and blog readers; and joining sustainability teams where we work. With a different way of thinking about our lifestyle—and more time—we can also produce some of our own food (even if just by growing a fruit tree or an herb garden), and we can create balanced meals that give us health and hope. We can entertain ourselves, take part in our own preventive health care, and educate ourselves on subjects of interest. The more active, engaged, and passionate we are in our daily lives, the less vulnerable we'll be to the call of the mall.

As our culture continues to mature, the odd person out will be the one who doesn't keep up with the "green" Joneses who use far less packaging, eat less meat, recycle almost everything, and volunteer in the community to restore a creek or mentor a student who's fallen behind. It will be normal to take responsibility for our own eco-footprints, and at last, the debt we sweep under the carpet will be revealed as a fool's paradise. Many aspects in our future won't look familiar—how can they when the whole idea of change is to behave differently?

Duane Elgin, author of the classic book *Voluntary Simplicity,* imagines two different people who ride bikes to work to save gasoline. The first person gets great satisfaction from the exercise, the contact with nature, and the knowledge that she is using carbon-neutral energy. The second person does not *prefer* to commute by bicycle, but is forced to for financial reasons. Each revolution of the bike chain entails mental as well as physical exertion because he feels ashamed and powerless. The point is that choosing a more sustainable alternative is far more comfortable than feeling stuck with it. Since so many of our individual decisions are based on what others think of us, a more moderate way of life will enable fewer people to feel stuck.

➤ Free to Choose

In a recent poll, nearly half of Americans said that protecting the environment should be a higher priority than economic growth. A full 78 percent said they would pay $2,000 more for a car that gets 35 miles per gallon

rather than only 25 miles per gallon. This kind of choice will not only deliver warm, fuzzy eco-feelings, but also save far more than $2,000 in the
long run—a strong, rational decision. But the fact is, we make choices based
not just on facts and finances but on values, emotions, social rewards, and
essential needs like safety, security, and meaning. So even if the car didn't
eventually save money, it might still be worth it if it met essential needs.
Emotional, intangible rewards are multidimensional and sometimes hard
to quantify, or even identify. For example, one of the strongest motivators
in our species is the conversion of shame into pride, yet this alchemy is an
emotion, not a fact. Furthermore, it's hard to show it to other people. Evaluating the benefits of specific actions is almost as challenging because they,
too, are not readily visible. For example, eating less meat confers benefits
like health, environmental stewardship, and empathy for fellow species.
There are many financial benefits, too, and some of them are also not obvious. The amount of meat our civilization cumulatively consumes will have
a direct effect on utility bills and insurance premiums. If meat's share of
greenhouse gases (roughly 18 percent of the global total) is reduced, there
will be fewer catastrophic weather events that cause spikes in food prices
and that force insurance companies to pass costs along to policyholders.
Temperatures will remain moderate, and so will our use of costly air-
conditioning.

If we take care of our communities with continued fiscal support for
parks, water quality, and museums, the benefits may be both obvious (a
higher quality of life) and not so obvious (increased tourism that makes our
whole city more prosperous). Property values will go up, while property
taxes may well go down, since other sources of revenue are increasing. As
we begin to use public transit, sidewalks, and bicycles, the costs of maintaining and repairing roads will go down because the roads will last longer.
The health of bikers and walkers will go up, but medical expenditures will
go down.

In the new era, instead of treating nature as a limitless warehouse of
industrial booty, we will acknowledge its primordial value as a *sacred garden* that for very pragmatic reasons must not be abused. This decision is
inevitable; either we can make it intentionally, or eventually government
regulations will force us to make it as resources become scarce and pantry
shelves empty, causing populations to revolt. Unless we come out of denial, the environment will continue to degrade and hundreds of millions of
people will become environmental refugees, as tens of millions already
have. The functions that nature performs—from the production of oxygen
to the regulation of climate—can continue only if nature remains intact or
is regenerating.

In the new era, we'll be far more sensitive to the needs of nature and society at large, realizing at last that, as Marcus Aurelius wrote in the second century, "that which is not good for the beehive cannot be good for the bee." Once again, we'll design and craft products the way bees produce honey—without harming the flower.

The big picture is that production and consumption will no longer be the defining characteristics of the next civilization—cultural richness, efficiency, cooperation, expression, ecological design, and biological restoration will be.

1

The Software of Civilization

I n the seven chapters that follow this one, I will present and discuss in depth an agenda of thirty-three public and personal choices: political, economic, technical, and social actions to create a more sensible way of life. In this first chapter, I want to explore the historical context, social framework, and value system in which these levers of change are embedded. We're social animals, and we need to tackle the large challenges we face together. Whether we like it or not, change happens, and the truth is, it will be far less painful to move to a new historical era now than to wait nervously for another generation, passing unsolved challenges on to our children and grandchildren. Our new-millennium mission is to take responsibility now, choosing a sustainable, anthropologically appropriate pathway for humanity, nothing less. Because of converging historical currents, the awesome responsibility to be catalysts of a new era falls to us. The ball is in our court, and that ball is the earth itself.

➤ Beyond the Industrial Revolution

Paradigm shifts occur during periods when significant cultural and natural factors converge. What we think of as the Industrial Revolution unofficially began with the invention of the mechanical clock way back in the thirteenth century, which enabled time to become a measurement of productivity. But our present era came into full swing after the Renaissance, in the sixteenth century. The world—and our understanding of it—was expanding. A new way of life was emerging from the shadows of plague, superstition, and oppression. Leading thinkers perceived the world in a more mechanical, less spiritual way. The focus of human energy shifted from the afterlife to the more profitable, "enlightened" present. The most significant change of all was the liberation of the individual—free now to strive for mastery over miraculous new machinery and financial systems. Encouraged by social norms to be "industrious," the individual could now make choices within the context of this stimulating, outward-looking, materialistic way of life, rising to the limits of his or her talents and aptitudes—at least in theory.

· Factors That Enabled the Industrial Era ·

1. A rethinking of land ownership, including the closing of the commons, and the consolidation of fiefdoms into kingdoms and nations

2. Intellectual, religious, and scientific revolutions in the Renaissance period (fourteenth to seventeenth centuries)

3. Emergence of modern ship technology, merchant navies, and global exploration, creating a frenzy of demand for imported luxuries

4. Development of the plow and other advances in agricultural productivity, freeing agrarian populations from a bare-bones, subsistence lifestyle

5. Introduction of banking, common currencies, and the factory system of production

6. Increased social mobility and personal freedom, awakening in the individual aspirations of financial success

It all seemed to fit together so well: one technology was bolted onto another and one custom merged with many others to shape a civilization whose central mission became making and having more, and having it faster. Although the symptoms of decline are increasingly urgent, many still believe obsolete concepts that are embedded in this paradigm: that the earth's resources are limitless and that nature is *inside* the economy, at our disposal. Many still fervently believe that individual acquisition is the best way to create social good, and that God will shield us from all harm if we simply "keep our noses to the grindstone" (ouch). It hasn't fully sunk in yet that the human population is geometrically expanding while many keystone species are declining and while natural resources and cultural wealth are being plundered. The idea that we can damage huge natural systems and alter the planet's climate still doesn't seem real to many, even after decades of focused debate and vivid, discomforting early warnings like drought, melting glaciers and ice sheets, and monster hurricanes.

But the pages of history are turning. What once seemed like an ingenious, equitable strategy for collective prosperity is increasingly coming under fire. When our current paradigm was first shaped, species were abundant, and nature could easily absorb the comparatively harmless wastes we generated. The world was not centralized, and people had more direct access to things they needed, like food, social support, and the abundance of nature. Things are radically different now.

• Factors That Make the Emerging Restoration • Era Inevitable

1. Emerging scarcity of key resources like oil, water, minerals, fish, soil, grain

2. Expanding understanding of biology and ecology

3. Completed exploration and mapping of the planet (we know what's here)

4. Expanding understanding of how the mind and body work

5. Development of computer technology and nature-based chemistry

6. Increasing interest in nondenominational spirituality

7. Growth of human and livestock populations beyond sustainable limits

8. Strong trend toward relocalization, quality, and craft

9. Changing attitudes about meaning, authenticity, expression, and creativity

➤ Grim Fairy Tales

There are at least a billion people on the planet who worry constantly about getting enough food, and another billion who worry about eating too much food; a billion who can't find clean water, and another billion who drink bottled water at least sometimes even if their tap water is just as pure. We in the industrialized world are overfed but undernourished in many ways. Socially, psychologically, physically, and spiritually, we are not fully meeting human needs. We've become susceptible to a virus of dependency, passive consumption: working, watching, waiting, and wasting (in another book, I and my coauthors called this virus "affluenza"). Although the TV commercials would have us believe that every itch can be scratched with a trip to the mall, the truth is we're consuming more now but enjoying it less. According to surveys taken by the National Science Foundation over the past thirty years, even with steady increases in per capita income, our level of overall happiness has actually tapered off.

Why? Many believe it's because a lifestyle of overconsumption creates deficiencies in things that we really need, like health, social connections, security, and discretionary time. How can we really expect a money-distracted culture to create trust, loyalty, inspiration, calmness, and meaningful traditions? The evidence indicates that the quest for more, both personally and commercially, often strips these essential qualities away, leaving us borrowing, buying, and selling rather than being. The truth is, the current industrialized lifestyle is designed for maximum consumption and "tolerable" amounts of waste and destruction. That's our creed. In good faith, we structured an economy around extractive technologies, cheap labor, new individual freedoms, hard work, and consumer spending. This cultural story is now so woven into our psyches that it's hard to imagine how else society might work. In our world, reality has become perception. It's considered shameful to have a below-average income or a beat-up car, unless one is actively *struggling* to acquire more.

So ingrained is the story that we rarely question its overall meaning and implications: the faster the global economy grows, the faster the world's fragile living systems decline. Each American now requires an average of thirty acres of prime land and sea to satisfy both the needs and wants of our excessive lifestyle—a national total of roughly 9 billion acres. This is more than three times the acreage of the United States, which is a primary reason the United States is currently more than $12 trillion in debt. To continue consuming at current levels, Americans will have to be aggressive and opportunistic with other countries' rightful wealth. We'll have to allocate more to the military; work even harder and longer at jobs that often don't stimulate us; carry more stress, debt, doubt, and shame. We'll have to react obediently to crises like 9/11 and the current financial meltdown with "patriotic" shopping—that is, unless we decide to change the story we live by, to change what we mean by the word "success."

➣ The Anthropology of Success

According to one *New York Times* article, after the financial meltdown of 2008 even some wealthy homeowners cut back to two meals a day rather than trade in their Lexus or Jaguar. This secretive belt-tightening measure helps them save face because it's not visible to their neighbors and friends. On other, middle-class driveways, more than a few SUV owners who can't afford to fill their tanks have been convicted of torching the vehicles to collect the insurance. Meanwhile, in low-income households, as much as 40 percent of the household budget goes to purchase, operate, and maintain vehicles.

What do we want our vehicles and other possessions to express? We are a story-telling, lesson-learning species whose stunning success is largely the result of highly evolved social skills. Our ever-expanding brains enable the interpretation of complex facial expressions; speech and language; a strong sense of fairness and social organization; and the complex social relationships that make cooperation, group decisions, and advantageous mate selection possible.

The overall mission, hardwired in our genes, is to survive long enough to have offspring, protect the territory they will live in, and perpetuate the social structure of the people who will take care of them. This strategy is starkly pragmatic: we need to take care of one another and act cooperatively or we won't make it. Therefore, we've always valued trust, resourcefulness, authenticity, and the integrity of our leaders. Security, safety, and social connections are as valuable now as they were sixty thousand years ago, when our genetic ancestors left Africa and began to explore and settle the rest of the planet.

One of the primary mechanisms for maintaining social cohesion is status: the relative standing of an individual within the group, and that individual's ability to obtain and retain respect and make positive social contributions. Individual status helps organize the group and make it more functional. However, status as a social mechanism developed in small, relatively stable, face-to-face groups, in which people knew one another over the course of a lifetime. Now our social world is shuffled, fragmented, in constant flux. The evolution of our brains and instincts hasn't kept pace with sweeping changes in our way of life over the last five hundred generations. Author Jim Rubens characterizes our current lifestyle: "unceasingly fluid relationships, constant challenges to our status within new groups, the geographic dispersion of extended family, the message that only we are responsible for our life's outcome, the barrage of status comparisons we see in mass media, and the incessant modeling of unattainable, stratospherically high goals."[1] All these conditions pit the individual *against* the group, resulting in an epidemic of depression because of what Rubens terms "social defeat."

Yet, to make collective, world-changing decisions, we need social coherence, organized by networks of trust and respect. In other times, status has been awarded to hunters, fighters, storytellers, healers, elders, and priests—not just the person with the most tools, furs, or cars. Sociologists have proven that status is critical to our health, because lower social status correlates with higher stress levels and mortality rates, lower birth weight, obesity, heart disease, lung disease, incidence of smoking, asthma, cancer, diabetes, number of sick days taken on the job, accident rates, suicide, exposure to physical violence, and compromised mental health. No wonder we are status seekers! We need recognition and respect to be healthy. However, this recognition doesn't have to center on material symbols. *A cultural shift to other ways of earning and rewarding respect is a central theme in creating a sustainable future.*

It's clear that in the United States, possessions and consumption have become a shorthand to communicate status, and it's also clear that in our headlong pursuit of goods and services, we're making an unprecedented mess. Why not just change the way our civilization achieves and confers status? To meet an urgent need—to reduce the volume of consumption and accompanying destruction—why not confer *social* rewards in place of material rewards?

Instead of honoring bank CEOs who fluff their own pillows with fairy-tale bonuses and take catastrophic risks with our money, why not respect and reward people of service, people who have gained our trust, people intent on making the world safer and more sane? Why not agree—by means of cultural mechanisms like art and innovative policy making—to think about personal worth in a different way? What must change are the *symbols* of success. It's not large, expensive, hard-to-maintain houses we truly want but large *lives* that contain enough discretionary time and generosity to share with those we love and respect. In an era less obsessed with status through consumption, it will be not exotic vacations we'll cherish but rather a contentedness that makes life an adventure no matter where we are. In the near future, there will be less energy-intensive travel and more focus on creating great communities where we want to be. Instead of accumulating just monetary wealth, we will accumulate calmness and wellness as our lifestyle becomes less confusing, more equitable, and more affordable.

➤ Avoiding Status Anxiety

In a less stressful lifestyle, there will be more options for attaining status. If we slow down and cultivate a wider appreciation of one another's unique passions and accomplishments, everyone wins. Says Robert Sapolsky, who studies the social aspects of baboon behavior, "We are capable of social sup-ports that no other primate can even dream of. For example, I might say, 'This job, where I'm a lowly mailroom clerk, really doesn't matter. What really matters is that I'm the captain of my softball team or deacon of my church.'" In other words, we can opt out of confining, stress-inducing social expecta-tions and instead, by the strength of healthy self-concepts, help lead the cul-ture in a completely new direction.[2]

A great example of the tangible benefits of avoiding status anxiety is the community of Roseto, Pennsylvania. In the 1890s, hundreds of Rose-tans migrated to America from Italy, building stone houses with slate roofs and a church. They grew fruit trees and vegetables in their long backyards, and grapes for homemade wine. Their village culture remained strong; shops and restaurants flourished on Garibaldi Avenue.

When several local physicians noticed how few residents of Roseto had heart disease, an in-depth study was performed, with astonishing results: for men over sixty-five, the death rate from heart disease was about half that of the United States as a whole. In fact, the composite death rate was 30 to 35 percent lower than the U.S. average. A sociologist reported that there was no suicide, no alcoholism or drug addiction, and very little crime. There were no peptic ulcers, no welfare recipients. The physicians and scientists concluded that the secret of the health and vitality of Roseto residents was the community itself, with many civic organizations, a strong religious con-gregation, and extended family clans. It was not merely genes and individual choices that made a person healthy, but the culture he or she was part of. One of the factors that led to the comparative health of Roseto, Pennsylva-nia, residents was a sense of equality in the local culture, which downplayed material success and awarded status based on skill, trustworthiness, and authenticity.[3]

➢ Changing the Symbols of Success

What about that quintessential symbol of success, the polished and powerful automobile? In the social language we now speak, cars symbolize a wide variety of human desires; not just status, but personal power, sexual prowess, freedom, and expression. We'll pay half a year's salary or more to symbolize these qualities, yet in the coming era, we may be seeking dif-ferent qualities altogether. For example, a well-crafted, well-used Volvo may not make the neighbors envious, and maybe that's a good thing. That old car meets a core need—safety—because of the way it's designed. Dura-bility is also a central part of the car's value; it's fairly common to get half a million miles out of one of these cars. It also confers security because there are no payments to be made—and who would ever steal such a well-worn car in a parking lot? In making his or her goal miles per vehicle rather than miles per gallon, the car's owner defers the energy-intensive manufacture of another vehicle (up to a fourth of the car's life-cycle energy occurs in its manufacture), thereby participating in a culturally critical movement to reduce carbon emissions. By deliberately unplugging from stressful social expectations, the owner feels a sense of freedom and liberation—another essential human need. That frumpy old station wagon might even convey status after all, in a new era whose core values now reward moderate, productive, unpretentious lifestyles.

The suit has also been a status symbol for a century or more, yet in a changing era, many people feel more successful sitting at their home desks in T-shirts and sweatpants, earning a paycheck without having to fight traffic or endure endlessly repetitive staff meetings.

While our core needs have remained much the same over the millennia (self-esteem, security, social support, status, clean water, nutritious food), the way we meet these needs has changed radically in the age of machines. In a new era—more conscious of living things and less focused on products—our habits and practices will shift once again. Chilean economist Manfred Max-Neef classifies human needs into nine essential categories, arguing that the most valuable choices are those that meet the most needs at a time.

- subsistence

- protection

- affection

- understanding

- participation

- leisure

- creation

- identity

- freedom

So, in his view, breast-feeding is far superior to formula feeding because it not only meets subsistence needs perfectly but also meets core needs for affection, participation, protection, and identity. Similarly, gardening is a jackpot activity because it meets needs better than careless industrial farming with its flawed products. Gardens provide subsistence, leisure, creation, understanding, participation, and protection, and maybe even affection. And a great neighborhood is superior to an isolated house because it not only provides shelter—a subsistence need—but protection, affection, leisure, identity, and participation.

This matrix of needs can be applied to just about any decision: What essential needs is the object or action meeting? Who benefits from this choice? Is it good for other people and the environment, or just me? In today's world, there are many ways that the unbounded rights of the individual conflict with the collective good: for example, when individual economic gain is perceived as a higher priority than the preservation of a stable, survivable climate or the preservation of a beautiful town (think Potter, the evil banker in *It's a Wonderful Life*). Ironically, survival itself is not deemed a worthy pursuit in our current, broken paradigm, because it's not profitable—an absurdly bizarre and poignant perception. Somehow, in our mainstream mind-set, individual rights trump social good, which means that it's time for a less self-centered way of life—a new normal.

➤ Getting What We Really Want

When we say we "want" a certain thing, aren't we subconsciously saying that we hope it will meet as many essential needs as possible, for example, recognition by others or a better feeling about ourselves? When 60 percent of Americans say they would trade one day's pay for one fewer workday a week, they are effectively saying that with more discretionary time, they could better meet their needs for leisure, time spent with friends and family, being an active citizen, and taking care of their health. In fact, the polls say that about 60 percent would trade a high salary for better health.

Pollster John Zogby's book *The Way We'll Be* presents key findings about shifting values in America. In one poll, respondents chose qualities that define the American Dream. While 34 percent thought that it was best defined in terms of material possessions and aspirations, an equal percentage thought it was more about freedom, equality, and spirituality. Like Gandhi, this latter group felt that there's "more to life than increasing its speed."

In another recent Zogby poll, qualities that our children need to learn were identified. "Achieve a better life," the most materialistic category, ranked below health and hygiene, self-respect, responsibility, and respect for others. It's sinking in throughout industrial cultures that the quest for money is really a quest for unmet needs like health, trust, respect, and authenticity—and that money delivers these qualities only indirectly.

When asked which traits were most important in a partner, "authentic" ranked way up at the top with 58 percent, ahead of "intelligent" (22 percent), "witty" (4 percent), and "good-looking" (only 1 percent). It seems we are giving greater value to what psychologists call intrinsic qualities, and less to the extrinsic, self-conscious, outward-looking traits. There are similar shifts in consciousness at the social level. For the 50 million Americans sociologist Paul Ray calls the "Integral Culture," the rebuilding of neighborhoods and communities is high on the list of priorities, followed by concern about violence and abuse of women and children. The sanctity of nature and the need to actively protect it is also a high priority among these "cultural creatives," who might be thought of as scouts exploring trails to a more sensible era.

Author Margaret Wheatley shared what she heard in an informal seminar with thirteen teenagers who are friends of her son:

> They want less hate. They fear for the planet. They want robots to do the dull work. They want schools to stop being so awful. They want to stop violence. They want to stop being desensitized by the media to violence, suffering, warfare. They want families and they want to be loving, supportive parents. They want to stop taking America for granted.
>
> I ask them, what do you hope for? They reply: I want to know I've given my best, no matter what. I want a lot less negativity. I want to know that I've encouraged another human being. I want something to happen that will unite us as humans—maybe that will happen if we make contact with extraterrestrials. I want to end the greed of corporations. I believe one person can make a difference, like Gandhi did. I want us to stop being hypocrites and take responsibility for our own behavior.[4]

These are intelligent kids!

· A Wish List We Can All Agree On ·

Healthy, low-stress lives, with more leisure time

Happy kids

Real security in our neighborhoods

An environment with a stable, sustainable "immune system"

Places we can go to experience and be renewed by nature

Genuine, nonpretentious connections with friends

Contentedness rather than anxiety as a starting point for each day

A sense that life has purpose and meaning

As a society, are we achieving these qualities? Clearly, no—we are falling painfully short, in troubled times that require better of us. The big questions remain on the table: Do we want a society that treats people fairly, or a latter-day form of feudalism, in which a small minority holds most of the wealth and power? Do we want a world in which species are on the rebound, or one in which habitats are being swallowed up by poorly planned development and machinery that's controlled by computer logic alone? Do we want a world we hurry through stressfully and fearfully, or one worth slowing down for? There's one especially critical course correction we are making as we usher in a new era: choosing a more holistic way to define and value success.

➤ Stuck in the Birth Canal: Three Barriers to a New Normal

There are many reasons why civilizations resist megachanges that could make life more satisfying, equitable, and secure. Three obstacles are especially relevant to this book's discussion: cultural crisis, hyperindividuality, and overproductivity. In today's world, we are often unable to access our own instinctual values; an obsessive economy is trampling our historically effective instincts. We've become separated from nature and isolated from the eternal flame of core values that humans have carried for ages. This isolation is a lonely scenario, often explored by (probably lonely) existential thinkers. Fortunately, it is correctable. Our values will wait for us to return, and they will guide us toward benefits we've forgotten we can have. First, let's look at what's holding us back.

1. CANCER OF THE CULTURE

Mainstream economists argue vehemently that the market is logical, so we should leave it alone; the problem is, *humans* are not always logical. We respond to many cues and stimuli emotionally, not rationally. Some of our emotions revolve around fear and insecurity, which make us shrink from change. We want to be proud—individually and culturally—but we're often stuck in the muck of shame. In many more instances than we realize, we follow the crowd and the incessant instructions of media under contract to corporations. When faced with a decision, we often succumb to habit, convenience, and familiarity—just to be safe.

The most pressing choice of all right now is whether to focus on social priorities and cultural direction or on individual gratification. Individuals can't make the huge changes that are necessary. It's that simple. Until we stitch our culture back together, individuals will be dazed and confused, lacking direction, generosity, and humility. The fact that the economy has in large part *become* our culture is disturbing because the economy undervalues the most important resources of all, from social trust through climatic stability. The free market can't find a way to sell collectively held assets like biodiversity or contiguous stretches of habitat that are so critical for all living things. The market isn't much interested in cultural richness, either. Writes author and change agent Paul Hawken, "What makes life worthy and allows civilizations to endure are all the things that have bad payback under commercial rules: infrastructure, universities, temples, poetry, choirs, literature, language, museums, terraced fields, long marriages, line dancing, and art."[5] Culture is devalued in our world because it's difficult to sell prevention, tradition, resilience, and restoration. Their intrinsic value, durability, stability, and "biologic" actually compete with the shoddy products that make shareholders rich. As we find ways to change our priorities and value these timeless qualities, we'll have a different kind of economy that will require less extraction of materials and a less frantic pace. Either we will choose this more moderate pathway or converging factors will choose it for us.

One of the main purposes of culture is to restrain and moderate individual excess, but our collective identity is itself excessive, in crisis. To paraphrase psychologist Erich Fromm, the fact that millions of people share the same forms of mental pathology does not make them sane. We're like a family whose parents do not set clear, healthy guidelines for their children. Anything goes—drugs, weapons, junk food by the supermarket cartload—as long as it's profitable. Our global family desperately needs to set sensible guidelines that can produce better results: less crime, waste, war, and illness, and more respect for living beings. For example, we need to retrieve proven, traditional diets that prevent illness, and we must actively promote them, head-to-head with junk-food commercials. When the basic food groups and recipes of a particular culture are lost in the shuffle, our confusion is easily measured by an increase in our medical expenses. The traditional Mediterranean diet—based on a healthy balance of fresh produce, nuts, grains, olive oil, red wine, and fish—is disappearing in the blink of an eye, historically speaking. Towns in culturally ancient places like Crete are now overflowing with pizza joints, ice-cream parlors, chocolate shops, and soda machines. As a result, three-quarters of Greece's adult population is overweight or obese, and there is an epidemic of diabetes, high blood pressure, and skyrocketing cholesterol, even in children.[6] The Greek culture is losing its center, where its core values reside.

Seducing the Reward Center

Another distracting yet very compelling barrier to cultural change takes place in a small bundle in our brain, the nucleus accumbens, also called the reward center or pleasure center. This high-activity hub evaluates a continuing stream of experiences, registering hits of pleasure like a pinball machine registers points. The underlying purpose of the reward center is to seek out and secure essential needs like food, water, sex, and social connection. So irresistible are the chemical rewards (such as dopamine) given by the reward center that in several experiments, laboratory rats preferred self-induced electric stimulation of the reward center to eating. They lost 40 percent of their body weight, and died.[7] Humans have reported that continued stimulation of the reward center is "orgasmic." Is this why we can't get up and turn off the TV? Why bother to save the planet when a constant stream of stimulating illusion—images of what we want to see: sexuality, food, conquest, and happy faces—flows out of the tube and into our hollow heads?

The hopeful news is that using MRI technology, neurologists observe that altruism, generosity, and cooperation register as strongly in the pleasure center as gambling, drugs, shopping, chocolate, or gratuitous sex. One of the very strongest, most rewarding stimuli of all is the maternal bond of love and affection.

"In a recent brain-imaging experiment," writes author Jonah Lehrer in *How We Decide,* "a few dozen people were given $128 of real money and asked to choose between keeping the money and donating it to charity. When they chose to give away the money, the reward center of their brains became active and they experienced the delightful glow of unselfishness."[8] So the science is in: it will feel great to act unselfishly as a generation and win accolades from our descendants as superheroes and paradigm shifters. Maybe the nucleus accumbens, in a pinch, will learn to score beneficial actions higher, rewarding them more generously than nicotine, online fantasy football, and narcissism. Part of me is skeptical that such an evolutionary coup can happen quickly enough. So it's up to a reconditioned culture to step up the pace.

2. HYPERINDIVIDUALITY

Students are taught in Economics 101 that rational, individual decisions automatically (magically) result in collective good, as Adam Smith hypothesized in the eighteenth century: "By pursuing his own interest an individual frequently promotes that of the society more effectually than when he really intends to promote it."[9] Yet, ecologists remind us about biological limits to growth. The concept of continuous, consumer-fueled growth in a world of 7 billion people is simply not synonymous with "common good." In addition, many social scientists challenge the economic mantra of "consumer sovereignty." Says sociologist Tim Jackson, "Consumption is embedded within routine and normative practices which are as much collective as individual. We need to take a fresh look at how to accomplish social transformation."[10]

To change individual behavior, we need to rediscover the highest values of the culture, and use these as behavioral guidelines. The classic economic postulate of rational, individual choice as a basis for a free-market economy is wishful thinking. The model doesn't fit the species. Human behavior is grounded in a social alter ego—a cultural repository of ethics, standard practices, and evolutionary experience. To prevent megaproblems like global warming and water shortages, we need to decide collectively that we want sustainable communities; better ways of farming, fishing, and logging; and changes in the balance between work and life. Then, we must pool our efforts and our capital to actualize these new goals.

Scores of little guidebooks earnestly urge us to make small, effortless changes to "save the planet," and these simple choices are undeniably useful—if we do them. But if nobody else is doing them, why should I? For thirty years, we asked ourselves, over and over, "Paper or plastic?" when the correct answer was neither. It's taking us too long to make the small, personal changes. Our preoccupation with the individual ego and its gratification will no doubt become a subject of satire in the future. The truth is, we can't change the realities of resource scarcity and population increases, so we must change our minds and our way of life instead. We'll need no-nonsense policies that are bold enough to change our no-limits behavior. And we can't let these policies fall short of their intended goals. For example, between 1980 and 1990, mandated upgrades in automobile efficiency held transportation's share of oil consumption steady; but the pampered American psyche demanded larger and more powerful vehicles, erasing the efficiency gains and increasing oil demand. As a result, in 2010, one-sixth of all the oil consumed globally currently goes into the comparatively inefficient American fleet of cars.

Similarly, household appliances steadily became more efficient, but those gains were literally overpowered when huge-screen TVs, computers, and PlayStations began to define what we do indoors. Looking into the near future, renewable energies like solar, wind, and geothermal *can* meet the needs of a moderate, no-waste economy—but not of a careless, hyperconsumptive one. Since 1950, the average American home doubled in size, miles traveled per capita (on the road and in the air) more than tripled, and U.S. per capita consumption of energy-intensive meat increased by more than half. Since 1975, U.S. consumption of plastic-bottled water skyrocketed more than 2,000 percent, as Americans pursued a false symbol of health, stylishness, and purity. Our economy won't be sustainable until we curb our appetites for energy hogs like throwaway packaging, expansive green lawns; suburbs without stores, and airfreight shipping of produce. Simply finding substitutes for today's fuels and technologies won't break the ongoing fever of overproduction and overconsumption.

In *How Much Is Enough?* author Alan Durning points us toward true north: "In the final analysis, accepting and living by sufficiency rather than excess offers a return to what is, culturally speaking, the human home: the ancient order of family, community, good work and good life; a reverence for skill, creativity, and creation; a daily cadence slow enough to let us watch the sunset and stroll by the water's edge; communities worth spending a lifetime in; and local places pregnant with the memories of generations."[11]

Buy or Be Where?

"I don't ever let my gas tank get empty, so I won't have to see that '$100' on the pump meter dial when I fill up," confessed Bob Hammond of Chesterland, Ohio, when gas prices hovered near $4 a gallon. "It's a mental thing." Like so many of us, Hammond sometimes makes choices that are more about identity than about the full costs and benefits of a decision. He's the guy who loves his Avalanche, partly because it helps tell the world who he is, or wants to be.

The dominant cultural story is that the individual is completely free to choose what he wants in the market, and that these choices will meet his or her needs. But is this true? Our freedoms extend only as far as the choices available. Furthermore, individual choices are woven into a social fabric consisting of everyday routines and practices. We really have no choice but to consume if we want to participate fully in a group or society.[12] If a person wants to find a mate, get a job, or be included in a certain circle of friends, there are specific consumer goods—clothes, laptop computers, stylish cars, magazines—he or she must buy and display. The individual is largely powerless to resist giving gifts during the holiday season unless his name is Scrooge, and if he is invited to a dinner party, it's customary to bring a bottle of wine or a loaf of designer bread. If his kids want to play sports at school, he and his partner need to buy the needed equipment and also consume many tanks of gasoline to get them to practices and games. If he wants to make a telephone call at an airport or a shopping mall, he'd better have a cell phone, because public pay phones have all but disappeared. He may prefer to have a durable windup watch and alarm clock to avoid buying batteries, but they aren't available anymore. Though he is skillful at repairing things, he has trouble getting into the workings of the typical appliance when it gets sick—after all, manufacturers want to sell *new* products.

Try living in a suburban community without a car. Or try going on strike in your neighborhood—refusing to keep your lawn glossy green and your house freshly painted. Try hanging your laundry on a clothesline instead of using an energy-hungry dryer. In some neighborhoods, your homeowners association will fine you. When a little cluster of neighborhood Girl Scouts walks up your front walk, you pretty much have to buy cookies, even if you're on a diet or don't eat sugar. What you're really buying is social connection with the neighbors. In our current culture, you'll take a shower every single day, and of course your hair must have "body." If you want to feel safe, you need security alarm systems in your house and car, implanted computer chips for your pets, and sensor lights that go off and on—and off and on—as pedestrians walk by. If you drive quite a bit, you'll need a GPS system to tell you where you are and where you are going, and better bring your iPod and BlackBerry along, too. If you're a medical doctor, you'd better have multimillions of medical liability coverage. As a patient, you'll consume whatever prescription drug your doctor prescribes, even though by some estimates, up to fifty thousand Americans die every year from misprescribed medicine—more than die in car crashes.

Our household budgets are rising and so is the aggregate cost of our lifestyle. Our way of life is too expensive, both monetarily and ecologically. Here's the problem: a society of hyperindividuals ignores critical lessons that culture has learned and stored over the millennia. Without being taught to value cultural guidelines, individuals are less capable of restraint, and without restraint, we'll consume the planet itself.

We take our marching orders from social norms consisting of both software (social expectations, ethics and values, economic practices, and policies) and hardware (product design, technologies, and infrastructure). Since the instructions are out of date, so are the choices we make as individuals. The only way to create real consumer sovereignty is to change the way our culture thinks and the way society functions.

3. TRAPPED INSIDE AN IDEA: OVERPRODUCTIVITY

American society grew up in an age of surging productivity, and we shaped our personal lives to accommodate this industrialized way of life. We were trained to accept this economic postulate: unparalleled levels of production require proportional levels of consumption. In an all-you-can-eat economy, we literally bent ourselves out of shape to keep up—not just with the Joneses, but with Jones Inc. We stepped further and further into a way of life that gradually stripped us of our ability to feed ourselves, entertain ourselves, or even have original thoughts.

It didn't happen overnight. In 1776, two very influential books were written: Thomas Paine's *Common Sense,* which was read by more than a third of all American colonists; and Adam Smith's *Wealth of Nations,* which launched an economic paradigm. Paine's thoughts focused on freedom as a democratic, egalitarian idea. Smith's were more about making money; the newly liberated citizen could become a soldier in a crusade for continuous growth. The two ideas essentially merged into one, and with a sparsely populated and richly endowed continent at the citizen-soldiers' disposal, a logical idea—capitalism—eventually spun off megacities and megacompanies that control the world's most precious resources.

Capitalism, American-style, relies on the conversion of resources into goods and services, as well as the maintenance of legions of consumers to buy them. Over the centuries, although the technologies to make this idea work have constantly changed, the fundamental idea of continuous growth has remained in place. The American economy first commandeered land from Native Americans, then brought slaves from Africa and technology from Europe to create a factory system of production. Homesteaders cleared the land, loggers cleared the forests, and factory workers made products by the gazillion. At first, only men worked long hours; then women came into the workforce too, increasing both production and consumption. When the money we earned was not enough to keep up, we borrowed, and borrowed more. But productivity always outpaced consumption, and gross domestic product continued to climb.

Between 1900 and 2000, worker productivity per hour increased eightfold while the volume of products increased eighteenfold. The U.S. economy was on a roll, selling not only products to the rest of the world, but also a way of life. (It worked: China, India, and Brazil must have that way of life, right now.) Huge subsidies to build roads, bridges, railroad tracks, harbors, and airports all reinforced the idea of growth. In 1910, there were roughly 144 miles of roads and only about ten thousand cars in the United States, while in 2010, there are almost 4 million miles of roads and highways, with 250 million cars on them. Productively what?

➤ Diminishing Returns

Here's an essential message we should all take heed of: A paradigm shift is imminent because in various critical sectors, *technology and the resources that feed it have reached the point of diminishing returns.* The limits are no longer technical; they're biological and geological. We're running out. The United States spends about $300 billion every year to subsidize commercial ventures, but yields of water, fish, logs, and grain continue to fall. We're paddling faster but falling further behind. For example, the federal government subsidizes fishing boats and nets for an industry that has passed the point of sustainable yield in some parts of the world's oceans. No matter how much new technology is brought on line by the fishing industry, the catch of certain species won't increase. To make matters worse, as the fish get more scarce and therefore more expensive, it becomes all the more profitable to go out and catch them—a good example of how the free market often receives scrambled feedback.

Tangible proof of both declining resources and rising demand is cited in the book *Bad Money* by Kevin Phillips:

- In 1930, we discovered 10 billion new barrels of oil globally, and consumed 1.5 billion.

- In 1988, we found 23 billion, used 23 billion.

- In 2005, we found between 5 billion and 6 billion, consumed 30 billion.[13]

Similarly, data compiled by the U.S. Geological Survey indicate that at a projected 2 percent annual extraction rate, the world has mere decades left of economically recoverable reserves of lead (seventeen years), tin (nineteen years), copper (twenty-five years), iron ore (fifty-four years), and bauxite (sixty-eight years).[14] One of the major challenges the global economy faces is that industries receive more than $700 billion in global subsidies to extract or consume oil, minerals, water, trees, and soil. Agricultural subsidies support more than two dozen crops in the United States, with a large percentage going to corn, wheat, and soybeans. These subsidies are based on volume of yield rather than on how well the crop is grown and how sustainable the farm is—resulting in soil erosion and depletion of soil nutrients. Subsidies also support clear-cutting forests and drawing down ancient aquifers. Alarmingly, farmers, factories, and municipalities receive incentives to drill deeper and deeper wells to get less water. We still operate in the dig-it-up mode, rewarding ourselves for more output when efficiency and recycling all materials is the only sensible approach.

When stocks of fish are depleted, we resort to fish farming with its heavy doses of antibiotics and toxic releases of waste. Factory forests are a poor substitute for selectively harvested stands of forest, diverse in species and the age of trees, yet the market for wood continues to grow, and so do the tree plantations. In the food system, when produce coming from depleted soil fails to provide essential vitamins and minerals, we resort to vitamin popping; and when the quality of tap water becomes questionable, we resort to bottled water. How much less capital would the global economy need if natural systems were brought back into balance?

2

Why Not a Nonprofit Economy?

After years of writing about a more moderate lifestyle with less throughput in the global economy, I'm often asked, "Won't less production and consumption radically alter the economy as we know it?" Yes, it will, but the current economy *needs* to be recycled because it doesn't work. It contains too much waste and poor design, and it's not programmed to preserve the *source* of wealth. We need a different kind of economy that emphasizes forgotten practices like saving money and donating it, practical skills, time affluence, protection of nature, amateur art and self-expression. Right now, like the Munchkins in *The Wizard of Oz,* we are under the spell of a lifestyle support system that commands our obedience. We don't even know how to relight the pilot on our furnaces or spend a solitary hour in the park without a buzzing, ring-toning fleet of electronic gadgets.

Our economy's primary measurement of "progress" is the gross domestic product, which is very much a toxic loaf of bread because *all* economic activities are folded into it, whether beneficial or destructive. Waste, corruption, destruction of habitats, and preventable illness are all part of the index we use to measure success. Even though the bread is toxic, the superficial fact that it rises is good enough for mainstream economists. We need a new economic yardstick that tells us how we're really doing, such as the genuine progress indicator developed by the nonprofit organization Redefining Progress. The GPI subtracts "bads," including all these: the costs of crime, family breakdown, loss of leisure time, underemployment, dangerous or flawed consumer products, commuting, household pollution, automobile accidents, water pollution, air pollution, noise pollution, loss of wetlands, loss of farmland, depletion of nonrenewable resources, long-term environmental damage, ozone depletion, and loss of old-growth forests.

It's quite possible that the familiar U.S. GDP could be smaller in the future but contain greater real value overall, if the negatives decrease while positive values like social relationships, renewable energy, bike trails, small farms, preventive health care, and compact communities with vital town centers increase. In the emerging, more mindful economy, we'll be better attuned to what nature needs and what it can provide. For example, one of the most effective ways to counter global warming is to plant millions of trees, an adventure our society needs to find time for. The camaraderie of planting trees makes watching TV sitcoms seem passive and lonely. Aren't there tens of thousands of volunteer tree planters among the retiring baby-boomer generation of 70 million or more? There was a story on the Web recently about a boy who had orchestrated the planting of a million trees. This is the type of activity that can characterize a new economy that has many characteristics of a nonprofit organization.

The new economy of, let's say, 2050 will look and feel significantly different from our current, inefficient economy. Food systems will be more local and responsive to the nutritional needs of people, not just the monetary needs of companies. We'll be designing communities and using resources much more carefully and efficiently. Manufacturing and materials will function differently, as will health care, transportation, and the job market. All these systems will be guided by values beyond price and profit, enabling the economy to deliver more real wealth with fewer transactions, and less energy per product or service. We'll make better use of our lawns, streets, school buildings, even rooftops. The Worldwatch Institute estimates that there are more than eight thousand square miles of roof and building facade area suitable for solar cells, capable of supplying more than a third of U.S. electrical needs.

The specter of global warming will drive many of our decisions, making public enemies of carbon fuels, industrial farming, and deforestation—all major contributors to climate change. The Earth Policy Institute (EPI), directed by Lester Brown, has more than a few ideas about choices we can make, collectively, to avert apocalypse. Replacing fossil fuels with renewable sources of energy (mostly solar, wind, geothermal, and hydroelectric) constitutes more than a third of the EPI's so-called Plan B for reducing carbon dioxide. Planting trees, ending net deforestation, and managing soils to store carbon (i.e., increasing organic content and doing less plowing) constitute about an equal amount. Yet, as the Environmental Defense Fund documents, there is significant opposition to these urgently necessary responses. In 2008 alone, opponents of measures against global warming spent $450 million on lobbying and political contributions to block forward motion on climate change initiatives. "Fifty-two public spokespersons are engaged by polluters and the political right to spread disinformation about global warming," reports an Environmental Defense Fund bulletin. "2,340 paid lobbyists worked in Washington on climate change in 2008."

➤ Solving for Sustainability

To create an affordable economy we will need to slow the metabolism of human civilization itself by, for example, improving the usefulness and even questioning the necessity of certain manufactured goods. Beverage containers are a good example. Writes Brown, "A refillable glass bottle used over and over requires about 10 percent as much energy per use as an aluminum can that's recycled. Cleaning, sterilizing, and re-labeling a used bottle requires little energy, but recycling cans made from aluminum, which requires a melting point of 1,220 degrees Fahrenheit, is an energy-intensive process. Banning non-refillable containers is a win-win-win option—cutting material and energy use, garbage flow, and air and water pollution."[1] In other words, when efficiency and great design combine with inspired policy making, we can "make money" by never having to spend it.

Here are a few more shifts in the way we meet daily needs that will make the future more affordable:

The Shape of an Affordable Economy

- As our collective demand for products falls, so will prices, as we've seen recently with gasoline after the recession hit.

- As material wealth declines, other forms of wealth typically increase, such as time affluence, more time to care for children and the elderly, and connections with people and nature. These kinds of assets are tangible yet don't require money.

- When we design communities to fit human needs rather than developer or automobile needs, our whole lifestyle requires less money. Public transit will be far less expensive per capita than America's current, inefficient fleet of cars. (Even Ford's Model A went just as far on a gallon of gas as the average passenger car does in 2010.)

- Protecting and restoring nature delivers for free services like water purification, pollination, and recreation that we now pay for.

- Getting rid of packaging, glossy green lawns, and food waste also takes a huge chunk out of the collective cost of our lifestyle. So does reducing advertising; we currently spend $900 per capita to be shelled with unsolicited information, which of course is embedded in the cost of products and services. Less consumption means less advertising as well as less debt. And less debt means less interest on the debt.

- Reasonable reductions in meat consumption, air travel, and energy-intensive materials like cement, aluminum, paper, and synthetic chemicals increase personal and national income because producing these products and services uses a lot of expensive energy.

- War will finally be seen as the epitome of waste and futility, the costs of which remain significant even when the war is over (for reconstruction, ongoing medical treatment, etc.).

- Green chemistry, which shortens the steps and softens the environmental cost of making chemicals, in turn lowers the cost of everything manufactured.

- Credit unions can lend capital at lower interest rates, and already save borrowers $8 billion a year in interest on loans.

- Preventive health approaches and more empathetic, service-oriented doctors and nurses lower the cost of maintaining our health, and better industrial design prevents unhealthy pollution.

- Eliminating subsidies that result in the destruction of ecosystems would save the world about $700 billion annually, about a third of that in the United States. Rather than drawing down aquifers, letting soil erode, clear-cutting forests, and overfishing the world's fish species, we will learn how best to use each resource, and how to harvest only a sustainable yield.

- In the new economy, recycling will become a ritualized, standard practice, embedded in design and policy, so less costly extraction will be required.

- In a world with fewer materialistic goals and priorities, there will be less need for crime control, lawsuits, and security systems. Emphasizing social support and greater equality nurtures a society that is more trusting and less fearful and that has less status anxiety, a direct cause of crime.

These savings arise not because we are doing without but because we're tuning up our value system, getting rid of waste, creating and adopting more sustainable ways of getting things done. Rather than requiring 100,000 hours of work and commuting per lifetime, a more affordable lifestyle enables each citizen to work less and pay closer attention to things that deliver genuine wealth and health.

➤ New Normal Agenda Point #1: Changing the Speed and Direction of Business

Old Perspective: The mission of business is to compete with rivals to give consumers and investors better prices and returns. Business should do everything the law allows (and more) to provide a high volume of goods and services. Externalize environmental and other costs to the public. Use money to make more money for those who already have money. Cooperate among competitors to fix prices. All's fair in love, war, and business.

New Perspective: The mission of business is to produce quality goods and services to meet the basic needs of everyone. Corporations exist not only to make profits but also to provide stimulating jobs, high-quality products, trustworthy links with communities, a sense of purpose and meaning for both producers and consumers, and a respectful alliance with living systems. A central goal is to optimize the use of all resources to minimize pollution and waste.

THE HEAVY LIFTING

- Support citizen activism that holds business accountable for environmental and social impacts.

- Invest in socially responsible companies.

- If you are in a management position, become a boardroom activist to align the company with changing values and circumstances

While many economists, investors, and corporate kingpins fervently believe that the U.S. and other industrial economies will come barreling back from the deepest recession since the 1930s, many others are not at all sure. We're damned if it doesn't, damned if it does, say alternative thinkers. Given current rules, assumptions, and blind spots, our economic paradigm will be deadly for many of the vehicle's passengers. What can we do to avoid depleting our economic and cultural wealth, as well as the world's living systems? Who's leading the way toward a less violent, more realistic economy? These urgent questions hang over our times like dark thunderclouds.

WHAT NEW-PARADIGM THINKERS ARE SAYING

Commenting on the Great Recession, trend tracker Faith Popcorn stated bluntly, "This is not a momentary correction, nor a down cycle—it's the end of the world as we know it. What we are deciding is whether, through new Rules of Engagement, we'll find a new way to set our priorities."[2]

David Korten, a onetime consultant with the U.S. Agency for International Development, is equally pessimistic about the continuation of business as usual: "Our economic institutions and rules, even the indicators by which we measure economic performance, consistently place financial values ahead of life values. . . . Our economic crisis is, at its core, a moral crisis. . . . If the world is to work for any of us, it must work for all of us."[3] Economist and attorney Robert Reich, who was labor secretary in the Clinton administration, also calls for a completely new paradigm: "It is illogical to criticize companies for playing by the current rules of the game. If we want them to play differently, we have to change the rules."

Reich continues, "The mission of business is to compete with rivals to give consumers and investors better and better deals. However, good deals depend on filling the airwaves with sex and violence, filling our stomachs with junk food, trampling human rights, and putting children to work." To deliver "good deals," corporations routinely take what Reich calls moral shortcuts:

- moving jobs overseas to lower wages

- substituting computers for people

- resisting unions

- pushing small businesses out of communities

- deserting communities for better incentives elsewhere

- paying celebrity CEOs outrageous salaries, like baseball stars

- stealing water from other peoples' aquifers

- trashing the planet[4]

Reich and many other new-paradigm thinkers agree that if voluntary efforts fail to hold corporations accountable, it's unquestionably in the public interest to make certain actions illegal. Yet, we still haven't reached a cultural tipping point; a large sector of the American public is still faithful to a system that has brought home so much bacon. These people view an unfettered free market with something like religious fervor. Since they have done so well in the prevailing economic paradigm, they're frightened by clear guidelines that ensure a level playing field and a more equitable distribution of wealth. They are as shortsighted as they are self-centered; they don't see the many personal benefits of a leaner, healthier society.

Many politicians also give a cold shoulder to regulatory reform, hanging on to sweet memories of American dominance, and to their congressional seats. A growing sector of the population, however, can read the writing on the wall: we need clear, no-nonsense boundaries on corporate behavior as well as CEO salaries to ensure the health and well-being of our families, communities, and natural support systems. Of the hundred largest economies in the world, about half are corporations. They need to be both responsive and responsible, and it's clear that only a massive culture shift can keep corporate power from burning down the house—with us inside.

Fortunately, there's a lot of evidence that such a shift is happening. Local, regional, and national governments all over the planet are stepping away from American hegemony and making publicly endorsed policy changes to avert catastrophe. Many European regulations, for example, offer fundamental choices that Americans lack. With social safety nets like universal health care, support for higher education, and laws that mandate part-time jobs with prorated salaries and benefits in place, Europeans can opt without discrimination for more time and less consumption in their lives. No matter what we call the European paradigm (socialism? social democracy?), there is much that the United States can learn from the European Union's policy initiatives. For example, Europe's carbon taxes and cap-and-trade programs clearly guide and define national directions on climate change. In Sweden and other countries, carbon taxes are counterbalanced by reductions in income taxes—what's not to like? Germany, a long-time coal-producing nation, aspires to ban coal production and use within the next two decades. These are not "government takeovers" but guardianship of the commons on behalf of citizens. How many would still argue that cigarettes are not harmful to our health? Similarly, how many could still argue that power-plant-stack emissions are not harmful?

RESPONSIBILITY

The key word in changing the rules of business is "responsibility." There's no doubt that business can swallow responsibility more easily when public vigilance is strong and front-office leadership is visionary. However, what cannot be logically debated is whether business should be responsible. There's too much at stake now to let real costs like habitat destruction and greenhouse gas emissions be swept into the commons. Americans need to act on our own behalf in all walks of life, beyond the split dogma of partisan politics, creating an economy designed for fairness.

Taking the moral high ground in his groundbreaking book *The Ecology of Commerce,* Paul Hawken asserts, "Businesspeople must either dedicate themselves to transforming commerce to a restorative undertaking, or march society to the undertaker." The ultimate purpose of business, he believes, is not simply to make money, but to increase the general well-being of humankind through service. Hawken's words have not fallen on deaf ears. Many American CEOs thank Paul Hawken for inspiring them to rethink their corporate missions. One of them is Ray Anderson, CEO of Interface Inc., the world's largest manufacturer of modular carpet. Since 1995, Anderson's company has reduced greenhouse gas emissions by 71 percent and water consumption by 74 percent, kept 175 million pounds of old carpet out of the landfill, and invented new carpet-recycling technology. The impetus was Anderson's desire to convert shame into pride. "I realized I was running a company that was plundering the Earth."[5]

As I emphasized in the book *Simple Prosperity,* we need a larger mission for business than money. With that in mind, former New York attorney Robert Hinkley drafted twenty-eight words—a "do-no-harm" clause—that he believes could and should be inserted into all corporate charters. This clause would take away CEOs' broken-record excuse for antisocial, environmentally destructive behavior: "We're legally bound to serve the shareholders." Corporations could continue to make healthy profits, says Hinkley, "but not at the expense of the environment, human rights, the public health or safety, the communities in which the corporation operates, or the dignity of its employees."[6]

Coen Gilbert, former CEO of the athletic shoe company And 1, is on a similar path as founder of a company called B Corporation (the B stands for Benefit). According to legal precedent, when a company is up for sale, owners must sell it to the highest bidder, which Gilbert (and other companies such as Ben & Jerry's ice cream) found out when he sold And 1. But Gilbert and his partners aim to change that. The mission of B Corporation is to help other companies write social and environmental commitments into company bylaws, so future owners and investors will understand that when the company is sold again, it's sold with legally binding agreements. In the past few years, more than two hundred companies with total revenues over $1 billion—including clothing companies, law firms, investment managers, advertising agencies, and restaurants—have adopted the B Corporation "bylaws," a tangible commitment to sustainable ways of operating a business.[7]

Another tangible distinction is to be labeled "socially responsible" by investment firms such as the Calvert Group or Domini Social Investments. According to the Social Investment Forum newsletter (www.socialinvest. org), about one in nine dollars is now invested in financial assets that are screened for social and environmental "purity." The three core strategies of socially responsible investment—screening, shareholder advocacy, and community investing—together account for more than $2 trillion in capital that values a mission wider than profit.[8]

When large pools of money like the California Public Employees' Retirement fund (CalPERS) and Norway's government pension fund begin flowing in a sustainable direction, corporate missions begin to bend. The largest public pension fund in the United States, CalPERS throws its weight around by pushing for legal limits on executive compensation, supporting shareholder resolutions for better company disclosure on environmental impacts, investing in-state; and supporting low-income neighborhoods.

Norway currently has a surplus of capital—more than $300 billion— from oil income that the nation has saved. The Norwegian parliament in 2004 adopted a set of investment guidelines for the surplus, based on environmental and social criteria. The country's ministry of finance scrapped all stocks that didn't meet their criteria, including U.S companies such as Wal-Mart, General Dynamics, Boeing, and Lockheed Martin. (In fact, of twenty-one companies that didn't make the cut, twelve were American firms.)

Being on a bad list of any sort creates great discomfort in corporate boardrooms. In 1990 federal law mandated gathering Toxics Release Inventory data and began listing the dirtiest companies by volume of waste; emissions dropped 40 percent within a few years. One chemical company that found itself on the Top Ten Polluters list reduced its emissions by 90 percent, just to "get off that damn list." Wouldn't any company rather be labeled green than "dirty" in today's world? While many companies are accused of exaggerating how green they are, benefits often spin off from even token efforts at sustainability. For example, while many Wal-Mart practices can never be called sustainable (such as disrupting community economies), when a company of this magnitude demands that each of its sixty thousand suppliers reduce its packaging footprint, those demands ripple through the global economy.

The Environmental Defense Fund pioneered partnerships with megacorporations when it worked with McDonald's in 1990 to reduce packaging waste, including the plastic foam clamshell (300 million pounds of unnecessary packaging were eliminated). Building on that success, the organization convinced McDonald's to require antibiotic-free meat from its suppliers. The Environmental Defense Fund also worked with FedEx to develop a cleaner fleet of delivery trucks. FedEx adopted a diesel-electric hybrid that increased gas mileage by 57 percent, inspiring Frito-Lay and other large-fleet companies to make similar changes.

When citizen activism is methodical and pragmatic, it can move mountains—even corporate mountains. Championed by Rudd Mayer, the Land and Water Fund of the Rockies in Boulder, Colorado, popularized a green energy program, Windsource, that enabled interested utility customers to pay a slight premium to support the development of wind energy. That program eventually stimulated the installation of wind turbine production, more than 250 megawatts of commercial wind energy in Colorado and neighboring states, and was quickly showcased by Xcel Energy Company (whose slogan is "Responsible by Nature") as evidence of the company's commitment to sustainability.

MANY TOOLS IN THE TOOLBOX

Corporate managers want what all individuals want: to meet fundamental human needs like security, adventure, a sense of pride, and status. Many are beginning to meet these needs in new ways, even in the lofty world of business. As congressman Dennis Kucinich has pointed out, humans are programmed to seek status, but why does it need to be based on money and stuff? Why not service in an admirable pursuit? This is the bottom line in the emerging shift in corporate culture: there's far more than money at stake. In addition to profits, corporations exist to provide stimulating jobs, high-quality products, trustworthy links with communities, a sense of purpose and meaning for both producers and consumers, and a respectful alliance with living systems. CEOs that earn five hundred times what a company's average worker earns don't seem to understand these other values.

A recent public interest in local food and products has company managers scurrying to brand themselves as "local," even if their headquarters are thousands of miles away and some of their employees are even more distant. According to Stacy Mitchell of the Institute for Local Self-Reliance, HSBC—one of the biggest banks on the planet—has begun to call itself "the world's local bank." Winn-Dixie, a five-hundred-store supermarket chain, recently launched a new ad campaign under the tagline "Local flavor since 1956."

Still, many business managers finally perceive that corporations are *not* mightier than culture, no matter how much is spent for advertising. To be successful, corporations must take direction from consumer demand, the realities of resource scarcity and climate change, and publicly enacted regulations that protect both people and environment. The day may be coming when—as Paul Hawken has suggested—a corporation that no longer provides overall value can be taken out of service by a vote of citizens. In the end, cooperation is the counterbalance to corporation. American culture in particular must come together around common values, regain its democratic balance, and issue clear directions to an economy that has lost its way.

➤ New Normal Agenda Point #2: New Measures of Success

Old Perspective: Money is the best measure of wealth; economic growth gives society material abundance and lifts people out of poverty. Banks and investment firms should be unregulated so that resources can flow to their most productive uses.

New Perspective: Healthy families, communities, and ecosystems are the best measures of wealth. The best investments over time are the human capital of productive people, the social capital of engaged and caring people, and the natural capital of ecosystems that lie beneath the economic bottom line.

THE HEAVY LIFTING

- When looking at your own life, measure success by things like fewer trips to the doctor rather than by how much you have in the bank.

- When looking at your work, measure success by creating products or providing services that give customers and clients the greatest value but use the fewest resources.

- When thinking about how to vote or what things to advocate at a town meeting, measure the success of a candidate or a law by considering whether or not that person or rule creates the greatest good for the greatest number of people, over the longest period of time.

In the near future we'll be using wider, more qualitative parameters of evaluation than we have in the past. In calculating the gross domestic product, "growth" is simply not a useful measurement. Growth of what? For the benefit of whom? With what sensitivity for preservation of natural and cultural resources?

With monetary growth as the sole criterion, the U.S. economy has been nominally successful in the last several centuries, but a nagging question remains: Successful at what? We may lead the world in GDP, average house size, and ownership of color TVs, but we also lead the industrial nations in debt per capita, child poverty rate, overall poverty rate, number and percentage of people in prison, rate of traffic fatalities, murder rate, carbon dioxide emissions per capita, and per capita consumption of energy, water, pop, and TV reality shows. On the upside, amplified awareness of where we stand can spark a reordering of national and local priorities, resulting in a healthier, less expensive, and more satisfying American lifestyle.

Since energy plays such a key role in the economy and in our personal lives, we'll soon track energy per product or service more precisely. For example, U.S. cement makers spend more energy per ton of cement clinker, and pulp and paper manufacturers on average use more energy per sheet of paper, than companies in Brazil or South Korea. Bringing those efficiencies home to our factories will make the GDP a better reflection of value. Similarly, the average American auto averages five gallons of gas to travel a hundred miles, while the average Italian car uses only three gallons. To more accurately measure performance, in the new metrics, miles per gallon will expand to passenger-miles per gallon (how many *people* traveled how far on a gallon of gas?). Rather than simply totaling bushels of wheat or corn, we'll monitor and value the health of the soil (organic content, microbial life, etc.) and the nutritional value of food.

When a commodity is underpriced, it tends to be overused; so getting the price right will be a priority in each policy decision, whether governmental or commercial. The idea is to set clear guidelines that protect the assets we hold in common, like cultural traditions, clean air, and diverse ecosystems. When legislators decide to tax a gallon of gasoline at a higher rate, they acknowledge that the social costs are higher than previous laws reflected. Writes the Earth Policy Institute's Lester Brown, "The key to building a global economy that can sustain economic progress is the creation of a market that tells the ecological truth."[9] Like a child playing outside in the darkness, the market refuses to hear voices of caretakers calling it back. It doesn't properly assess the value of nature's life-enabling services, and doesn't have the sense to know when a given resource is about to run out.

A study by the International Center for Technology Assessment estimates that the real cost of a gallon of gasoline would be higher than $11 if indirect costs were included, such as oil industry tax breaks, costs of defending oil supply lines, and health care costs of treating respiratory illnesses from pollution. Evaluating the true costs and benefits of choices can yield jackpot decisions that not only result in sustainable outcomes but spin-off dividends such as great neighborhoods, clean energy, well-designed products, and, yes, profit.

REDEFINING SOCIAL PROGRESS

Historian Arnold Toynbee observed that civilizations that ultimately succeed follow a "law of progressive simplification," in which they become culturally richer but materially leaner. Culture shifts that enable a more mindful, moderate way of life have already occurred in many cultures, such as Japan's in the seventeenth and eighteenth centuries. Land was in short supply, forest resources were being depleted, and minerals such as gold, silver, and copper were suddenly scarce as well. Japan's culture adapted by developing a national ethic centering on moderation and efficiency. An attachment to the material things in life was seen as demeaning, while the advancement of crafts and human knowledge was seen as a lofty goal.

Training and education in aesthetics and ritualistic arts flourished, resulting in disciplines like fencing, martial arts, the tea ceremony, flower arranging, literature, art, and skillful use of the abacus. The three largest cities in Japan had 1,500 bookstores among them, and most people had access to basic education, health care, and the necessities of life, further enriching a culture that required very few resources per unit of happiness.[10]

America is poised to make such a transition, and when we do, we'll do it with flair—even as big and clumsy as we are. Meanwhile, smaller countries like Costa Rica, New Zealand, Cuba, and the Scandinavian nations have already headed in a new cultural and political direction, realizing that taking care of the future is intrinsically rewarding. Rather than aping American bad habits like profiting from pollution, prisons, and weapons, these countries use preventive, people-powered approaches like neighborhood health clinics, urban agriculture, hands-on preservation of natural resources, and policies that encourage carbohydrate energy (on a bike or forested trail) rather than fossil-fuel energy (in a noisy, gaudy sports car that goes six miles per gallon).

By reallocating capital and shifting their national focus, Costa Rican citizens transformed their homeland into a global model for small countries, focusing on metrics that matter: a good life with moderate, sufficient income levels; low infant mortality, high life expectancy, and high literacy rates; and access to electricity and clean water. Meanwhile, the gap between rich and poor has declined. Only 3 percent of Costa Rica's government budget goes to police and defense (Costa Rica's constitution forbids the establishment of a military), and 26 percent of the country's land is publicly protected as national parks and forests—real security. Costa Rica is unashamedly competing with countries such as New Zealand, Iceland, and Monaco to become the world's first carbon-neutral nation. (Its goal is to offset carbon emissions from fuels, fertilizers, and other sources by preserving carbon sinks such as forests and loamy farm soil.) Costa Rica is seen as the front-runner in this "carbon-neutral World Cup" because more than 80 percent of its energy already comes from renewable sources such as wind and hydroelectricity. Says the Costa Rican minister of environment and energy Roberto Dobles, "We realize that climate change is probably the major challenge facing humanity today, and it's everyone's responsibility to deal with it."[11]

Sweden's term for "just enough" (*lagom*) is woven through that country's culture and economy. Brands like Ikea, Volvo, and Saab spring from a cultural belief that there is an ideal amount in design and manufacturing; anything more results in dysfunction and diminishing returns. Americans, too, will learn to see that just enough is perfect. An overarching formula for creating an affordable economy is Efficiency + Sufficiency - Deficiency = Affordable Economy. We're reinvesting in sustainable enterprises we can count on, rather than in industries that literally count on us. We're learning at last to harvest the apples while keeping the apple tree healthy.

➤ New Normal Agenda Point #3:
Risky Business or Good Money? Banking on Living Capital

Old Perspective: Money is the best measure of wealth; economic growth gives society material abundance and lifts people out of poverty. Banks and investment firms should be unregulated so that resources can flow to their most productive uses.

New Perspective: Healthy families, communities, and ecosystems are the best measures of wealth, and the best investments over time are the human capital of productive people, the social capital of engaged and caring people, and the natural capital of ecosystems that lie beneath the economic bottom line.

THE HEAVY LIFTING

- For individuals: Put your savings and checking accounts in a local credit union (which offers higher interest rates) and put your investments in a community development fund.

- For banks: Adopt evaluation tools like the Equator Principles, the Carbon Principles, and other specifically sustainable initiatives in emerging industries that are low-risk and high-return.

- For communities: Establish local credit unions and community development funds, encourage employee-owned businesses, and set up revolving loan funds to finance energy efficiency and sustainable transportation.

In 2008 and 2009 there were far more economists scratching their heads than there were bankers writing loan checks. After the housing and credit bubble popped, the flood of easy money that had financed a two-decade economic boom became a dribble, like a plugged-up fountain. Economists such as longtime Federal Reserve Board chief Alan Greenspan couldn't figure out what had happened. As he told an angry congressional committee, "Those of us who have looked to the self-interest of lending institutions to protect shareholders' equity are in a state of shocked disbelief." But even Greenspan and other true believers of unregulated markets see the cracks now.

What happened was this: the middle class couldn't pay the bills or repay loans anymore, even with two-thirds of all adult Americans employed, and personal debt (excluding mortgages) exceeding $16,000 per capita. The economy had shifted in recent decades from solid, tangible assets like manufactured goods and agricultural products to financial sleight of hand, for example, "derivatives"—essentially, devices for making money by buying and selling money. From 1950 to 2005, manufacturing fell from 27 percent of the U.S. economy to 12 percent, while financial services grew from 11 percent to 20 percent. For three decades after World War II, the middle class had enough cash to carry the economy on its shoulders. "The profits from mass production were divided up between the giant corporations and their suppliers, retailers, and employees," explains Robert Reich in the book *Supercapitalism*. "Economic benefits were spread across the nation—to farmers, veterans, smaller towns, and small businesses—through regulation (of railroads, telephones, utilities, and energy supplies) and subsidy (price supports, highways, federal loans). Thus did democracy offset the economic power of large-scale production and widely disperse its politics."[12]

The recycling of financial wealth to all levels of an economy is essential to both democracy and social prosperity, yet current economic practices funnel capital to eager opportunists who need it least and who are most skilled in passing social and environmental costs on to others. The victims are lower- and middle-class people whose goals in life aren't Porsches or vacation homes but simply healthy and happy families. This is the central problem: in its current form, our economic paradigm simply isn't inclusive and democratic. Rather, corporate culture is trained to be aggressive and oblivious; decisions are too often made in boardroom power plays, or by cell phone from the decks of yachts. The typical, coldly pragmatic corporate strategy is to make fewer employees work harder for lower wages while at the same time persuading them to buy more than they can afford. That game is nearly over.

What the U.S. economy urgently needs now is a groundswell of patriotism among union leaders, policy makers, and shareholders, to bring democracy back to center stage. For example, the typical corporation grants each share of stock, rather than each shareholder, a vote in shareholder decisions. This standard practice needs to be changed because it enables speculators to buy a plump portfolio of shares, set policies for risky loans or drugs with unrevealed side effects, take the short-term profits, and get out. Loyalty to places and faces simply isn't part of the script.

Between 1982 and the fall (pun intended) of 2007, the Dow Jones Industrial Average climbed from 803 to 14,165—a 500 percent increase after inflation. Yet only about half of all Americans own stock. In 1982, the average American household saved 11 percent of its income; by 2007, that savings rate was below 1 percent.[13] In fact, by 2007, predatory capitalism had pinned democracy to the ground. The insurance, finance, and real estate industries had locked arms with political leaders; labor unions had been beaten down; and regulations to protect the public from economic gaming had been gutted. (Whatever happened to antitrust laws?) CEOs, who in 1980 were paid 42 times more than the average employee, were by 2005 paid 412 times as much![14] The top 1 percent of the U.S. population now controlled as much wealth as the bottom 95 percent. Investments in the real wealth of healthy children, sustainable communities, and thriving ecological systems were neglected because their profit margins were too low.

REDIRECTING THE FLOW OF MONEY

Capitalism as currently practiced in the United States has just one obsessive goal: to smash the competition and grab a larger slice of the pie. It's all too easy to spot this Monopoly-game mentality in the current housing meltdown. Since the 1980s, banks have been selling bundles of loans to secondary investment markets, as if rundown Baltic Avenue–type properties were really Boardwalk or Park Place. By passing toxic loans on to investors, the banks cleared their own accounts so that they could legally lend more. And lend they did, to millions of naive middle-class Americans who took on more jack-in-the-box debt than they could ever repay.

This malignant episode is just one illustration among many of how economic indicators often mask reality. New-paradigm economist David Korten, no loyalist to business as usual, rips off that mask: "By conventional reckoning, we humans have tripled our wealth and well-being since 1970. Yet indicators of living capital, the aggregate of human, social, and natural capital, tell a very different story." He points out that the Living Planet Index, which tracks the health of the world's freshwater, ocean, and land-based ecosystems, has declined 30 percent since 1970. Also on the decline are indicators of human capital—"skills, knowledge, psychological health, capacity for critical thought and moral responsibility"—and social capital, "the enduring relationships of mutual trust that are the foundation of healthy families, communities and societies." Simply put, Korten believes our economic crisis is about a broken paradigm that consistently places financial values ahead of life values.[15]

The so-called Great Recession has once again trained a spotlight on intrinsic shortcomings in conventional banking and investing. Though we rarely question it, is credit really a healthy or even realistic way to finance an economy? Obviously, we borrow and lend to fuel growth; yet the very existence of interest is a primary reason an economy *needs* to grow. The borrower not only needs to pay back the loan's principal, but his capital has to grow by an increment that exceeds the interest rate. Banks are happy to help, as long as borrowers speak the language of money rather than of human need. Large banks don't have to be accountable to anyone; they exist in cyberspace, with their shareholders and offices scattered around the world. Since their marching orders are simply to create profit, they have remained aloof, and in some cases blatantly aggressive.

Yet multinational banks and insurance companies are not as omnipotent as they like to think, if global citizens remind them who's boss. Like lumbering dinosaurs that will either evolve—quickly—or go extinct, financial institutions that are "too big to fail" are also outrageously unaccountable because they control resources directly related to survival. It's time for the American public to cut these dinosaurs down to size, to make them sensitive to the needs of real people and real places. If this sounds preposterous, remember the Chinese proverb "Those who say something can't be done should get out of the way of those already doing it." There is a vigorous, global, grassroots movement consisting of ethical banking, credit unions, green venture-capital funds, community investment funds, peer lending, microfinancing, social investing, consumer demand, and other purpose-driven pools of capital that is steadily shifting the flow of money in the direction of sustainability. The pioneers of a new economy are inventing mechanisms that slow the velocity of capital so its consequences can be better evaluated; distribute it more evenly and fairly; fund the emerging renewable-energy industry and the redesign of towns and cities; and more accurately reflect and repair "externalized" environmental damages.

Of course, none of this is easy. As change champion Van Jones phrases it, "We are trying to change the status quo, but we all have a stake in it, too. Every day we end up feeding the very monster we are fighting."[16] David Korten has a rational solution: "To get ourselves out of our current mess and create the world we want, we must reboot the economy with a new, values-based operating system designed to support social and environmental balance and the creation of real, living wealth." Korten proposes a paradigm-shifting laundry list of priorities, some of which are summarized in the sidebar below.[17]

· How to Finance the World We Want ·

Use shareholder activism to encourage large banks to endorse and utilize standards like the Equator Principles and the Carbon Principles, which help banks assess and track loans for sustainable projects. This helps them avoid costs related to potential environmental and human health liabilities, and shifts capital to emerging sectors.

Use antitrust legislation to break up huge corporate banks, and put branch offices up for auction to local stakeholders. This will enable local ownership of community banks and businesses, which is eminently democratic. Credit unions, community development funds, and cooperative businesses are more transparent, accessible, and participatory. They can optimize quality of life and environmental quality in each region.

Change the focus of lending policy at all scales in the financial world. Instead of short-term loans for profit, issue more long-term loans for people. When entrepreneurs and small business owners have a stake in the health of their local economies, they work harder and make their communities stronger.

Eliminate subsidies for cheap food, carbon fuels, and autocentric development, making financial investments in unsustainable developments far less attractive.

Remove extremes of wealth and poverty by reimplementing an income tax structure that removes incentives and subsidies to become superrich. This includes taxing estates at a higher rate, because hereditary wealth perpetuates inequality.

Tap philanthropic, nonprofit, and low-profit funds as well as public funds to rebuild local food systems and family farms; retrofit energy efficiency and renewable energy; rebuild national infrastructure according to new-paradigm goals: walkable neighborhoods, public transportation, alternative water and wastewater treatment, greater use of waterways for transportation and naturally existing small-scale hydroelectric potential.

Support the ability of local banks and credit unions to serve as intermediaries between local people who want a secure, modest return on their investments and local people who need funds to buy a home or start a business.

Sources: David Korten, "Let Wall Street Fail," Now, PBS, January 30, 2009, http://www.pbs.org/now/shows/505/new-economy.html; David Korten, "Why This Crisis May Be Our Best Chance to Build a New Economy," Yes!, http://www.yesmagazine.org/issues/the-new-economy/why-this-crisis-may-be-our-best-chance-to-build-a-new-economy; posted June 19, 2009.

CORPORATION VS. COOPERATION: MAKING MONEY A RENEWABLE RESOURCE

One of the main shortcomings of the current big-bank financial system is that it neglects or excludes a large percentage of the population: hardworking, potentially very productive people whose salary, education, or credit history may not reflect their skills and determination. A feature article in Yes! magazine sums up why community banks usually deliver more real value to their depositors and borrowers than the megabanks: "Jerry Moore lost his home, his truck, and his business when Katrina hit," says the article's call-out, "but he didn't lose his connection to Hope—the financial institution that helped him get started and stuck with him when times got tough."[18]

Moore didn't have a credit history when he took a six-week course on local finances and city contracts. But the Hope Community Credit Union, a sponsor of the course, listened carefully to Moore's proposal to start a hauling business, and based on his work record and his idea, the credit union lent him the money to purchase a dependable truck. After that truck was destroyed in the floodwaters of Hurricane Katrina, Moore realized that the market for haulers had just grown exponentially. He again applied, successfully, with Hope for a loan to purchase a few more trucks to increase the scale of his business. Eventually he hired nine employees, most of them also victims of the hurricane.

While many wage earners are forced to use pawnshops, payday lenders, and credit cards with sky-high interest rates, Moore had found a lender whose payback came partially from weaving a stronger community. The Hope Community Credit Union kept in close touch with Jerry, informing him about resources like upcoming contracts, and helping him formulate a business plan. When conventional bankers looked at a man with no credit history, they saw only a potential financial risk and refused to take it. But the credit union saw something else. Comments Hope manager Lynette Colin, "When I looked at Jerry, I saw a resourceful, hardworking man with the drive to make his business succeed." She knew that institutions like Hope have payback rates of over 97 percent, according to a nationwide survey of community development banks, credit unions, and loan funds. When people feel supported and empowered, they find a way to make their jobs and projects work.[19]

For David Griswold, a track record wasn't the limiting financial factor. Rather, it was lower profits than the bank required. Even though his business, Sustainable Harvest Coffee Importers, had in the previous ten years parlayed a small loan into $15 million in annual sales, the bank backed away from the project. (This is a good illustration of Robert Frost's definition of a bank: "a place where they lend you an umbrella in fair weather and ask for it back when it begins to rain.") But the value of Griswold's business was deeper than money—the business was about relationships. He was helping coffee growers learn sustainable farming and connecting them with retailers who paid them fairly. After being pushed out of the mainstream lending market, Griswold found sympathetic ears at a "green bank," ShoreBank Pacific, and a sustainable investment fund, RootCapital. By no means did he receive handouts from these lenders, since each is in business to make a good return. But their returns, like his, were wider than profit alone. From their perspective, if businesses like Griswold's showed steady growth, there would be more sustainable coffee farms, more sustainable fisheries, more jobs, and higher wages. Like Jerry Moore, Griswold found lenders who listened, understood his needs, and knew that nonmonetary returns and slow, steady growth build communities, not just sky-high CEO salaries.[20]

In contrast, in the 1990s and 2000s, the megabanks wooed many homeowners into refinancing, sold their debt to investors, got billions in federal bailout money, and are still on their feet—even though many of the communities they serve were devastated. Does this mean that big banks are incapable of change? No, even the huge banks are going where the future is: restoration of ecosystems, clean energy, and more efficient transportation. Nonprofit organizations like Friends of the Earth have helped turn scores of large banks lighter shades of green. More than sixty banks have voluntarily adopted the Equator Principles and/or the Carbon Principles, which bring holistic evaluation to lending decisions. For example, when a company wanted to borrow money from Citigroup for an offshore oil and gas project, that bank required the borrower to alter its plan so a vulnerable coral reef would be protected. This not only preserved a valuable natural asset but also avoided financially risky cleanup costs and liability down the road.[21]

Though traditionally "in it only for the money," some big banks have experimented with lowering interest rates for green loans while charging higher rates for business-as-usual projects. However, green policies like these are more likely to occur at small banks and credit unions, such as the new E3bank, whose goal is to balance enterprise, environment, and social equity. For example, as a building's design attains higher levels of resource-wise Leadership in Energy and Environmental Design (LEED) certification, the interest rate at E3bank falls. Both the savings from energy efficiency and the lower rates make the lender a better bet to repay the loan. Canada's Citizen Bank gives lower interest on car loans for more efficient cars, and at the UK's Cooperative Bank, a free Home Energy Rating on all house purchases is good for all concerned, since lower utility bills mean lower risk of foreclosure.

One of the smallest banks in the United States, the First National Bank of Orwell, Vermont, weathered the banking crisis as well as or better than the huge banks, lending money to clients that the giants wouldn't touch: people who work at home, burn wood to stay warm, or build their own homes. The Santa Barbara Credit Union in California specializes in loans for solar energy panels, and like other credit unions, can offer low interest rates and fees because it's a member-owned nonprofit.[22] In fact, the nation's credit unions are 90 million members strong, and their trade association estimates that members save $8 billion a year thanks to better interest rates and reduced fees.[23]

There are many sources of money—and nonmonetary wealth—besides banks. According to Federal Reserve estimates, Americans lend more than $89 billion to friends and family every year. For example, entrepreneur Renaud Laplanche got his software company started with $35,000 in loans directly from friends, at 10 percent interest. He paid off his credit cards and laid the groundwork for a business that soon attracted venture capital.[24] There are now many examples of businesses that broker peer-to-peer lending, wherein borrowers with an attractive idea link with lenders; many are online. And companies like Joe Barter LLC broker trades and swaps without any need for banks. Instead of buying office equipment, why not trade a season ticket to hometown football games for it? Itex Corporation, in Bellevue, Washington, is a trade exchange of twenty-four thousand small business members who pay registration and commission fees to connect with products and services they need. For example, a lawyer could provide legal services and earn barter dollars with an accountant who's also in the exchange. Even state governments are taking advantage of bartering in a contracted economy. Minnesota and Wisconsin figure to save $20 million in the next several years by swapping essentials like fingerling fish (used to stock lakes and streams), bullets for the police, menus for prisoners, trucks for bridge inspections, and sign language interpreters.[25]

One of the world's largest alternative monetary systems is the WIR Bank in Switzerland, which enables the exchange of goods and services when conventional currencies are not flowing. Established in 1934 by sixteen businesses, the WIR is now considered a sort of "spare tire" by many of its sixty-two thousand Swiss companies. In Japan, more than fifty alternative currencies are in circulation, including the *fureai kippu* exchange, which circulates credits for elder care. When a person spends time assisting a senior citizen, he or she earns credits that can be given to an aging parent or saved for one's own golden years.[26]

LIVING RETURNS

It seems that only grassroots cooperation can counterbalance the corporatism that dominates and often contaminates our world. America will be more democratic if a larger percentage of U.S. citizens are co-owners and stakeholders in their workplaces and communities. Greenbelt, Maryland, is a model of cooperative ownership at the community level. Built in 1937 as a New Deal initiative, Greenbelt still practices active citizen participation in local commerce, governance, and education. The seven thousand members of the Greenbelt Consumer Cooperative Grocery Store elect board members and get small refunds after expenses have been paid. The Greenbelt Nursery School relies on the skills of parents, staff, and community members to enrich learning at the school, which is considered a shared responsibility. The credit union, the newspaper, and even the local gathering place, the New Deal Café, operate with this shared-benefits, shared-responsibility approach. "When there's a need in the community, you can bet that a team will self-assemble to take care of it," says Mayor Judith Davis.

The Viroqua Food Cooperative in Viroqua, Wisconsin, emphasizes the value of high quality and social connections. A walk through the co-op's aisles is a little like a reception line: you feel like you're actually meeting the growers, whose names, faces, and farms are prominently displayed. "Featured Local Cheese," says a sign in front of a display of apple-smoked cheddar cheese from a local dairy farm. "Hand-rubbed with paprika. Won first place at the American Cheese Society competition." What the co-op is selling is a way of life, and Viroqua residents are buying it. In the past few years, co-op membership has expanded from 890 to about 2,000, and its new store is seven times larger than the old.

When the U.S. economy went off the gold standard, many people felt uneasy, as if the emperor suddenly had no clothes. They realized that money has no inherent value; it's just a set of agreements. Restaurateur Judy Wicks (profiled beginning at page 61) would much rather make those agreements with people she knows. Ten years ago, she sold her stocks and put her life savings into the Reinvestment Fund, a Philadelphia community investment group that loans money to support things like affordable housing, local businesses, and community centers. "I soon discovered that the wind turbines producing renewable energy for our region, including my own home and business, were financed by the Reinvestment Fund," she recalls. "From my local investment, I receive not only a modest financial return (which has recently outperformed the stock market), but also a 'living return'—the benefit of living in a more sustainable community."[27]

➤ New Normal Agenda Point #4: Vibrant Local Economies or Careless, Disconnected Ones?

Old Perspective: The goal of a company is growth. The larger a company is, the greater its economies of scale, and the greater its potential market share.

New Perspective: Growth is much wider and deeper than profits. How can companies remain at human scale and grow in ways that enrich communities, protect natural systems, and create more satisfaction through stronger relationships with employees, suppliers, community residents, and shareholders?

THE HEAVY LIFTING

• Initiate or expand a local business alliance such as the Business Alliance for Local Living Economies (BALLE), American Indepen-

dent Business Alliance (AMIBA), or other producer cooperatives
that collectively purchase, advertise, and lobby for local buying.

In conventional economics, most business efforts move in one direction only:
toward larger profits, more stores, higher volume of goods and services. Business planners and policy makers assume that a business should evolve from a
basement start-up to a global corporation. But there are many flaws in this
way of doing business. As a business gets larger and larger, relationships between the company and its birthplace are lost. Cause-and-effect relationships between the company and its sources of wealth also become fuzzy; it's
(conveniently) difficult to track what environmental and social impacts occur
in which link of the supply chain.

Economist Michael Shuman points out another, less obvious drawback
of the growth-is-always-better model: "There is never one but many economies of scale," he writes. "No one design works for all firms, in all environ-
ments, for all markets." He advocates a worldwide network of local, living
economies in which each business is ingeniously a niche specialist. In *The
Small-Mart Revolution*, Shuman writes, "Create a diversity of locally owned
businesses; design them to use local resources sustainably; and make sure
that together they are fully employing residents and producing at least enough
goods and services to satisfy residents' needs. This is a recipe for local prosperity."[28]

Obviously, no region can supply every product or service, so each local-
ity should export enough to afford the importation of those products the
local economy can't provide—ideally, using fair trade and other standards
of quality. This scenario is not only logical, but also happens to be the way
nature works. In a given ecosystem, each species evolves to take advantage
of locally available resources. Cooperatively, the system makes use of every
scrap, gradually developing skills and channels to elegantly and efficiently
meet needs, giving the system resilience. With a wide diversity of businesses and owners, and perfectly attuned feedback about resource availability, a strong system can withstand threats from the outside, such as
floods, hurricanes, and droughts. Doesn't it make sense to model our economy on natural realities, rather than on abstract monetary theories?

Shuman and many others believe that an economic shift toward flexible, resilient small business networks is inevitable, citing deficiencies in
our current global practices:

Inefficiencies of specialization and customer demands. Consumer tastes vary widely from one country and region to another.

Thus, local banks can better assess the risk of loans and meet borrowers' needs. Regional supermarkets know, for example, that a Hispanic population base demands many varieties of peppers, olives, beans, and salsa.

Inefficiency of distribution. In an era of rising energy costs, distribution expenses can sometimes exceed production expenses. Only eight cents on the dollar goes to farmers, for example, while seventy-three cents goes for packaging, refrigeration, spoilage, advertising, trucking, supermarket fees, and brokers. In local and regional economies, many of these expenses are reduced and eliminated.

A measurable shift to services and experiential purchases. In 1960, Americans spent 40 percent of discretionary income on services, and the rest on goods. In 2003, 59 percent went to services. Says Shuman, "Many services—whether health care, teaching, legal representation, or accounting—demand personal, trusting relationships." We want a real person—not a phone tree—to answer specific questions; after many consumer complaints about remote assistance, Dell brought its tech support services back to Texas.

Shifts in work and place. More than 20 million Americans now do some work at home, and many goods and services no longer require proximity to forests and mines, ports and rivers. But the typical corporate perspective is still global rather than local.

Frustration with low morale and managerial loyalty in corporate jobs. Employees value security from corporate migration; they want integrity in leadership, connection with fellow workers, and participation in creative decisions, all of which are more easily achieved in small business.[29]

Businesses with fewer than five hundred employees account for half of private sector employment in the United States, and these businesses are more likely to have a local base, which benefits from the circulation of capital in the community. Wages and profits earned and spent locally make a community stronger. One study found that $100 spent at a proposed Borders bookstore would circulate $13 in the city's economy, while the same amount spent at two local bookstores would circulate $45. A typical mechanism for that circulation is sales taxes. Buy locally and your city will have more tax revenues to redistribute locally.

The multiplier effect is very similar to the endless cycling of nutrients through an ecosystem. A robin eats a cherry and unintentionally plants a cherry tree nearby. When mature, that tree captures water, builds soil, and provides the perfect branch for a robin's nest. The tree's leaves create a microbial habitat, which enables insects, worms, and baby robins to survive.

"GOOD MORNING, BEAUTIFUL BUSINESS"

For twenty-six years, restaurateur Judy Wicks poured her energies into the White Dog Café in Philadelphia. Though the restaurant started and has remained relatively small, there have been many other ways that Wicks has measured growth. She's never bought into the dominant paradigm that growth is defined solely by increased profits, even though she does believe that economic exchange can be one of the most satisfying and meaningful ways that humans interact. As Wicks sees it, growth is also about increasing knowledge, expanding consciousness, developing creativity, deepening relationships, increasing happiness and well-being—and having fun.

The story of her evolution as a businessperson drew a standing ovation recently at a green expo where I was also a speaker, and I got in touch with her the following week to find out more about how small businesses can heal broken local economies. Many of the thoughts and concepts that follow were outlined in her speech, soon to become a book.

"Money is simply a tool," she emphasizes. "Business should really be about relationships—with everyone we buy from and sell to, everyone we work with, and with the earth itself." Wicks made a conscious decision to stay small, to be one special restaurant rather than a chain. She hung a sign in her closet that she'd see each morning: "Good Morning, Beautiful Business." The sign reminded her of the farmers who were already out in the fields picking fresh organic fruits and vegetables, and of the pigs, cows, and chickens that were out in the pastures, enjoying the morning sun and fresh air. She'd think of Dougie, the goat herder, who claimed that when she kissed her goats' ears it made their cheese taste better! She would think of the restaurant's bakers coming early in the morning to put cakes and pies in the oven, and she'd even remember the growers down in Chiapas, Mexico, handcrafting the organic fair trade coffee beans that made her restaurant so fragrant each morning.

The relationships and beauty she's after have been reflected over the years in various programs, activities, and spin-offs. For example, her decision to pay staff a "living wage" was the result of her realizing that the people she worked with were very important to both her and the business. A living wage is a voluntary commitment by a business owner to pay employees the minimum amount needed to cover the cost of living in a particular location. It's typically far above the federally mandated minimum wage, and at first Wicks refused to consider it.

Then one day three of her kitchen staff all happened to look up at her at the same time as they chopped vegetables and cleaned up. "Looking at their faces, I had an instant realization," she recalls. "Of course I wanted to pay Brian, Tyrone, and James enough to live on—to buy food and clothes, to pay their rent and other expenses. How could I not pay people working at the White Dog enough to cover basic needs? What had I been thinking?" She's very much aware that a small business owner who lives and works in the same community is much more likely to make decisions from the heart, not just from the head. "Without direct relationships, few of us think about the consequences of our economic transactions on other people and communities, on animals and on nature."

Another epiphany came when she drove to a favorite hiking location, a forest north of Philadelphia. "The beautiful ferns that I loved were crumpled to the ground like brown tissue paper because of the drought we were having," she recalls. "And the creek, once rushing waist-deep, had no water at all, only dust-covered rocks. This is what it will be like, I thought, when global warming brings drought and fire to some parts of the world and storms and floods to others." Her personal connection with nature prompted a commitment to purchase 100 percent of the restaurant's electricity from renewable sources.

The White Dog became known for serving healthy food from local sources. It was worth the extra effort to her for several reasons: direct relationships with farmers and growers builds community and provides transparency about quality; local food reduces "food miles" and carbon emissions; and the much fresher food is superior in taste and nutrition. She was especially concerned about the drawbacks of standard factory and feedlot farming of livestock, so she made an effort to find local sources of grass-fed beef and pasture-raised pork. Still another chapter in her business evolution followed an aha realization that she was part of a much wider food system. "There is no such thing as one sustainable business or one sustainable household. Survival of the individual depends on the survival of the whole group." She soon became as much an activist as a business owner, sharing her hard-earned market niche with other restaurants throughout the city. "I had to move from a competitive mentality to one of cooperation in order to build a local economy based on humane and sustainable farming."

The White Dog soon became an education and support center. When the farmer who supplied the restaurant with organic pork needed a refrigerator truck to expand his business and supply other restaurants, Judy Wicks lent him $30,000, which he has since paid back. The Fair Food Project provides free consultation on how to buy local, and is a partner in a local food-distribution business that makes buying local simple. Every year, Wicks staged a Green Dog Day to talk about green business practices and launch new green initiatives, which included a compost project that supplied compost to inner-city school gardens; a solar hot-water system to heat dishwasher water; and a ban on bottled water, which can create water shortages at the point of extraction, carbon dioxide emissions during shipping, and plastic waste at the point of use.

Judy Wicks's overall vision—a sustainable global economy based on a worldwide network of sustainable local economies—has now spread to many other communities. She cofounded the Business Alliance for Local Living Economies in 2001; it now includes eighty or more local networks and more than twenty thousand locally owned businesses. One of the best examples of BALLE's mission is Sustainable Connections in Bellingham, Washington, which now has six hundred independent businesses in its membership. One of that organization's accomplishments is the Food to Bank On program. Recognizing the need for a new generation of farmers to provide locally grown food, that program has offered apprenticeships to thirty or more new organic farmers in the past three years.[30]

Choosing a place and taking responsibility for it are the first steps in building a local living economy, Wicks asserts. Other key principles of the movement include democracy and decentralized ownership—not concentrated wealth; a living return—not the highest return; a fair price—not the lowest price; a life-serving approach—not self-serving; cooperation-based not competition-based; and cultural diversity—not monoculture.

· Creating Local, Living Economies ·

What Consumers Can Do

Eat locally at restaurants that feature regional cuisine.

Frequent local farmers markets; link up with local growers through co-ops, direct delivery services, and community-supported agriculture; rediscover local sources of baked goods, beer and wine, and fresh meat.

Create or promote the use of directories of local business and local products.

Enjoy local recreation and entertainment, supporting local musicians, sports teams, and local traditions such as parades and fairs.

Bank with local financial institutions like credit unions and small commercial banks, especially for home, car, and college loans.

Form buyers clubs to purchase locally produced goods from other regions. For example, forty families in Ann Arbor, Michigan, buy wild Pacific salmon directly from Washington fishers, paying half the supermarket price and putting four times as much money per pound into the hands of suppliers.

What Citizens and Communities Can Do

Make sure city government has its accounts in local banks.

Establish small-business incubators and mentorship programs to train local expertise.

Set up local venture funds, microfunds, and revolving-loan funds that support new-paradigm businesses.

Use zoning regulations to prevent the corporate takeover of Main Street. Encourage mixed-use neighborhoods that combine retail, residential, office, public services, and small-craft operations.

Create a small-business office to help local businesses compete with franchises for contracts, grants, and incentives.

Give a small-percentage bidding advantage to local businesses for government purchasing.

Conduct a series of community visioning forums to steer local initiatives toward a desirable future.

Compile a list of indicators to assess if the community is staying on track with its vision. For example, Whatcom County, Washington, identified a "dashboard of indicators" for tracking the community's health, such as crime rate, civic involvement, and infant mortality.

Identify how local initiatives can replace importation of corporate goods. For example, strong recycling efforts reduce dependence on global textile, paper, and metal industries; locally produced biofuels reduce consumption of international oil; and local reuse and repair businesses reduce importation of computers and appliances.

Source: Michael Shuman, *The Small-Mart Revolution* (San Francisco: Berrett-Koehler, 2006), 116–17 186–87, 209.

> ## New Normal Agenda Point #5:
> ## Beyond the Assumption of Consumption: Policy
> ## for the People

Old Perspective: Policies should be universal, sweeping society toward goals such as economic progress and national uniformity.

New Perspective: Policies should match specific conditions such as geographical and cultural uniqueness. They should guide human behavior toward desired outcomes such as fairness, equal opportunity, avoidance of waste, and preservation of natural and cultural assets. In general, policies should provide the greatest good for the greatest number of people.

THE HEAVY LIFTING

- Discuss, propose, and support policies that confer health, equity, time affluence, efficiency, cultural enrichment, and the preservation and restoration of nature.

Thomas Jefferson warned more than two centuries ago that change is inevitable: "As new discoveries are made, and manners and opinions change, institutions must advance also to keep pace with the times."[31]

Policy analyst Charles Siegel of the Preservation Institute is doing his best to oblige. Siegel researches and writes about the "compulsory consumption" that's built into government and corporate policies regarding choices about work and free time, housing and parking, medical care, child care, and many other everyday concerns. "We should focus on policies that let middle-class Americans choose whether they want to consume more or have more time for their families, communities, and personal interests," says Siegel.[32] He points out that most Americans work full-time because they must. Part-time jobs typically have lower hourly pay and no benefits. Instead of using higher productivity at the national level to increase consumption, why not use it to reduce work hours?

In 1933, when jobs were scarce, Americans almost had a thirty-hour workweek, which would have shared the work and nurtured a more productive, healthier workforce. This might have resulted in extra time for all Americans, as Kellogg employees enjoyed with a six-hour workday that lasted from 1930 to 1985. With two hours added to each weekday, there were more "room mothers" in classrooms. City parks, community centers, skating rinks, churches, libraries, and YMCAs became centers of activity. Kellogg workers recall that the balance of their lives shifted from working to living. What to do with their time became more important than what to buy with their money.

The nationally mandated thirty-hour workweek was a near miss: the Black-Connery bill passed in the Senate but was vigorously opposed by business leaders. Instead of promoting shorter hours to fight unemployment and keep employees healthier, business leaders pitched "a new gospel of consumption," and the bill was defeated in the House by just a few votes. The Fair Labor Standards Act of 1938 set the forty-hour workweek in stone, and the work-and-spend culture went into high gear, propelled by World War II, which geared up production to levels history had never seen before. In 1950, marketing analyst Victor Lebow wrote, "Our enormously productive economy demands that we make consumption a way of life, that we convert the buying and use of goods into rituals, that we seek spiritual satisfaction, ego satisfaction, in consumption. We need things consumed, burned up, worn out, replaced, and discarded at an ever-increasing rate."[33] Did Americans choose this consumptive way of life, or were we corralled into it with drumbeats of patriotism, social engineering, and economic fundamentalism?

Siegel believes that by law, part-time employees who do the same work should get the same hourly pay as full-time employees. They should also have the same seniority (based on the number of hours worked), the same chance of promotion, and the same benefits (prorated) as full-time workers. Does this sound impossible to implement? Not really: the entire European Union has already adopted agreements like these to end discrimination against part-time workers. As a result, employee-chosen part-time work is becoming quite normal in the EU, with Holland leading the charge. In 2005, for example, nearly half of all Dutch employees worked fewer than thirty-five hours a week, including 75 percent of all women and 23 percent of all men.[34]

A similar logic applies to autocentric policies that dictate what American towns and cities look like. Sprawl is essentially a government program that began right after World War II, when the federal government subsidized mortgage deductions, highways, and cheap gasoline to encourage suburban growth. Those subsidies are still in place, forcing Americans to pay for a car-centered transportation system whether or not they drive. Since streets and traffic signals are paid for out of cities' general funds, residents pay for them through sales taxes and property taxes—even if they bicycle or take public transit and use only one-tenth as much street space. It's the same theme with "free" parking. Even if we don't drive because we are too young, too old, too poor, or disabled, we get charged for parking by employers, property sellers, and businesses, who build the costs of parking into wages, mortgages, and price tags. Now, parking policies are being rethought. In Washington, D.C., planners have rewritten fifty-year-old codes to require fewer parking spaces for commercial and residential buildings. (Earlier mandates required four spaces per 1,000 square feet; the new law requires only one.)

Child care is a third example of compulsory consumption. The average American child now spends ten hours less per week with parents than in 1970. "Fifty years ago, one parent working 40 hours a week supported the typical family," says Siegel. "Today, the typical family is supported by two parents working 80 hours a week."[35] The economy takes up too much of our time.

Flaws in the day-care system are in plain sight yet are disregarded because we assume—or want to believe—that our present lifestyle is working. The current tax credit for day care gives parents an incentive to work longer hours and spend less time with their children, because it pays for day care. However, parents and caretakers who work less and care for their own children get nothing. Siegel suggests that nondiscriminatory tax credits could be given to low- and middle-income families—he estimates about $7,000 a year per child. Households that need day care, such as those with single parents, would be covered, and other families could also choose whether the tax credit should cover day care or help them work shorter hours to have more time with their kids.

Obviously, policy and design modifications can help give Americans a wider range of choices. The most sweeping—and critical—choice of all might be the choice between "your money or your life." When the culture's policy makers unlocked the door marked "Money," they in effect barricaded the door marked "Life."

· Policies That Reward Sensible Lifestyles ·

1. U.S. income tax policy discourages saving and investing by taking a bite out of income. Solution: Lower income taxes and instead tax carbon-heavy fuels and technologies, as more than twenty EU countries already have.

2. Mandatory forty-hour workweeks don't offer workers the choice of trading less income for more time. Solution: Enact laws that guarantee equal pay for part-time workers, as many EU countries already have.

3. The lack of a national health-care policy (already in place in most industrial countries) necessitates work that is sometimes unwanted, to retain health benefits. Solution: Implement national health care, decouple it from employment, and shift the United States from a treatment to a preventive-health-care mentality.

4. Free parking at workplaces rewards driving but offers no incentives for alternatives such as walking, bicycling, and carpooling. Solution: Give a stipend to all employees, rewarding nondrivers and letting drivers pay for parking.

5. Day-care tax credits assume that employees would rather pay for day care than work less and care for their own children. Solution: Credit a fixed amount per U.S. child; let parents choose how to spend it.

6. Flat-rate trash policies discourage recycling. Solution: Implement "pay as you throw" policies that charge by the volume of unrecycled trash, while pickup of recycled goods is free.

7. Current beverage-container policies don't reward recycling. Solution: Enact a federal "bottle bill" law, as eleven states already have.

8. Suburban sprawl wastes time, money, land, and energy. Solution: Enact local, state, and federal policies that encourage public transit, compact development, and mixed-use zoning.

Source: Charles Siegel, *The Politics of Simple Living: A New Direction for Liberalism;* David Wann, *Simple Prosperity.* St Martin's Griffin, NY, 2007. p. 138.

Linguist and author George Lakoff has studied the "framing" and values of political leaders, arguing that policy should be based on universal values such as freedom, fairness, and equality—not just total quantity of jobs or housing starts. He identifies empathy, responsibility, and an ethic of excellence as the scaffold for value-based policy. Sustainable, equitable outcomes begin with empathy: "Empathy is not mere sympathy. Putting oneself in the shoes of others brings with it the responsibility to act on that empathy. Empathy-based values are opposed to the pure self-interest of a laissez-faire free market, which assumes that greed is good and that seeking self-interest will magically maximize everyone's interests."[36] His thoughts are directly relevant to this book's discussion because they envision outcomes far more comprehensive and socially desirable than "faster" and "more."

THE BIRTH OF A BRIGHT NEW ETHIC

Companies and other organizations should also take direction from values, observes Dov Seidman in the book *How.* "Laws tell you what you can do. Values inspire in you what you should do. It's a leader's job to inspire those values in us." He believes that a company can be sustainable when its employees believe in the mission and doing the right thing (such as making a high-quality product) out of principle.[37]

Devin T. Stewart also assigns a lofty position to values and ethics as a compass for cultural transformation. An expert on global policy innovations, Stewart believes that sustainability will provide the information flows and feedback loops to help us transition from an industrial civilization toward an ecological one. That transition begins, says Stewart, with the articulation and application of an ecological ethic he calls the Green Rule: "Do unto the Earth as you would have it do unto you" or "Do unto future generations as you would have them do unto you." He sees evidence of the Green Rule already in use: "Consumers increasingly demand products that coincide with their moral awareness, and politicians are under pressure to implement policies that mitigate the stresses of globalization. These forces can come together to produce products that are recycled, carbon neutral, or fair trade, and policies that battle climate change, poverty, and global diseases."

The Golden Rule ("Do unto others as you would have them do unto you") is expressed in more than a hundred religious texts, notes Stewart, including those in the Christian, Hindu, and Islamic traditions. Many Eastern faiths extend the Golden Rule beyond one fellow human to encompass all living beings: "As a key concept in Chinese, Greek, and Indian philosophy, the Golden Mean emphasizes tolerance, moderation, and pluralism. Aristotle's maxim 'nothing in excess' and Confucius's idea of equilibrium speak to modern concepts of sustainable living."[38]

➤ New Normal Agenda Point #6:
Reevaluating the Household Budget

Old Perspective: Convenience, effortlessness, and magazine-cover appearance are the most important goals in a household, enabled by processed and precooked foods, appliances that make life automatic, chemicals that kill all potential invaders, and a lifestyle support system of pipes, wires, and lines of credit. We don't need skills for cooking because processed food is just as filling, and cheaper. We don't need repair skills, either, since most manufactured goods these days are not repairable anyway. Health is not our responsibility, so let's stock up on snacks and rent a few movies from Netflix.

New Perspective: Passive, automatic lives are not satisfying after all. They often prevent us from maintaining good health and strong relationships—and feeling physically and mentally healthy. We want to be active and engaged in activities that use our abilities and make sense socially and environmentally. It's time to redistribute our household income to things like more nutritious food, continuing education, and experiences that deliver real value.

THE HEAVY LIFTING

- Instead of just turning up the air-conditioning or the heat, actively participate in the operation of your house. For instance, set a schedule to close and open the window blinds or shades in order to control heat in both summer and winter.

- Instead of buying everything prepackaged at the local supermarket, plant a garden; learn how to make wine, salad dressing, yogurt, bread, and house cleaners.

What a relief that American core values are quickly being rediscovered—in direct proportion to the rising costs of energy, food, insurance, higher education, drinking water, and other necessities. Whether we relish the prospect or not, our daily routines will change dramatically in the next ten years. What if an average household's annual expenditures of roughly $45,000 went to different priorities? What if its purchases (and decisions not to purchase) brought more durability, greater vitality, more satisfying entertainment, greater intellectual growth, and more laughter into the home? These choices might result in major attitude adjustments—psychological makeovers—that would make discretionary time seem far more valuable and a huge income seem less necessary.

What would happen if we spent more for food, less for housing; more for exercise and preventive health care and less for prescription drugs; more for meaningful experiences like classes and passion-filled hobbies and less for stuff? My belief is that we'd be happier and need to work less because we'd need less money; we'd be healthier and less anxious. The truth is, a leaner lifestyle is often healthier. If we adapt our household budgets to more closely match changes in the real world (like steadily rising energy costs), we will have less of a bad impact on living systems, and begin to be and feel more self-reliant. Many of the changes in store for us are not so bad if we ride the horse in the direction it's going: away from production and consumption as defining characteristics of our society, and toward preservation, time affluence, and expression as qualities of a new era.

In 1900, the typical American household spent more than a third of its budget on food, which was higher quality for several reasons: it was more likely to be fresh, it came from richer soil with more minerals in it, and it wasn't stripped of nutrients by processing. We are relearning that what we eat affects the way we feel; by spending more for good food and less for Target trinkets, we can have more overall value.

Changing the structure of our daily lives so that we are participants in life rather than just observers helps provide twice the satisfaction for half the resources. By deemphasizing objects and reemphasizing good information, art, experience, health, and connection, and by choosing quality over quantity—which may seem at first like we are spending more, since quality carries a higher price tag—we are actually getting more overall value.

Some federal agencies refer to U.S. households as "consumer units," an insult that should incite acts of consumer disobedience rather than bargain-day stampedes. Sadly, however, the term is all too appropriate. Most American homes are codependent with a lifestyle-support-system of roads, wires, pipes, lines of credit, satellites, and a collective identity determined by the supply side. Yet, just about any household budget offers continuing opportunities for creating a healthier, less expensive lifestyle that's also easier on the environment. Because changing circumstances will demand it, we have to rethink the values that shape our decisions and rearrange our priorities to match those values. In other words, we must reach a new agreement about what constitutes a life well lived. We can imagine a symbolic flag flying over millions of homes, signifying that people are assertively changing the *patterns* of their lives, not just the pieces.

Rather than consumer units, our homes can be units of creativity and productivity that provide a higher percentage of what we need. We can produce rather than consume entertainment, with house concerts or poker games in our own living rooms and backyards. We can be as bold as the current first family, replacing a chunk of lawn with miniature fruit trees and rows of vegetables. The food we eat can make us feel more vital, and save us money by helping us avoid needing drugs and expensive medical treatments. (Forty percent of the most prevalent diseases are related to diet, including heart disease, cancer, diabetes, allergies, and depression.) Some of our transportation needs can be fueled by carbohydrates from the garden rather than by hydrocarbons from Middle Eastern oil wells. By making a few well-researched choices about energy and water efficiency, we can cut our utility bills by a third. With this new, more sensible way of thinking, we can easily imagine avoiding $1 million of expenses per household over the course of a lifetime, and enjoying many more hours of leisure.

• How a Sustainable Lifestyle Generates More Than • $1 Million of Value

You save thousands of dollars a year by avoiding purchases, maintenance costs, and loan interest payments for new cars, gadgets, and clothes you no longer covet, because you've found other values to be passionate about.

You save thousands in interest payments because you have very little debt.

You cut energy, water, and resource bills in half because your car is more efficient; you live in a more compact, resource-efficient house; and the things you need are close by.

You don't need expensive resort-style vacations, because you've learned it's cheaper to create your own culturally rich vacations, and also because you're more content being home than you were before you changed your life.

You reduce food costs by cutting restaurant dining in half, since the food is usually precooked and served in huge portions that make you feel bloated; and by preparing food at home that is higher in nutritional value (and flavor), so less food is needed.

You reduce lawn care, day care, and wrinkle care because you convert your lawn to a vegetable garden, you and your spouse alternate staying home with the kids, and a less stressful lifestyle results in fewer wrinkles (and less concern about them).

You save on entertainment costs for spectator sports and home movie theaters because active entertainment (playing sports, talking with neighbors, practicing a craft, playing an instrument) is really far more engaging and stimulating.

You don't need diet programs, equipment, books, tapes, classes, psychiatrists, hypnotists, and over-the-counter drugs, because you're not overweight.

You don't have dental problems from chronic soda, candy, and cigarette consumption. Foods like yogurt and frequent exercise have been proven to prevent gum disease that can cost $5,000 to $10,000 to treat.

You have lower mortgage payments and less consumer spending after selling a house larger than you need. All remaining debt is erased with the profit from selling the house.

Though $1 million in savings might seem far-fetched to some readers, blogger and self-made millionaire Jen Smith can easily substantiate that estimate with transportation savings alone. She writes a blog called *Millionaire Mommy Next Door* and speaks on national TV about financial independence. In a recent post she asked her readers, "Would You Ditch a Car for $1,000,000?" She begins by telling her own story. "22 years ago, my husband and I sold one of our cars to pay for our wedding and honeymoon. We intended to replace the sold vehicle eventually—after we built up our credit score so we could get a car loan—but as time went by, we discovered that sharing one car between the two of us was no big deal. We learned to carpool, drop one another off, take turns, group errands, walk, bike, take the bus, work from an in-home office, go places together. Surprisingly, 22 years later, we still share just one car."

Then Jen does the math: the average American spends $9,369, excluding loan payments, to drive fifteen thousand miles, according to the American Automobile Association. (This sum includes fuel, routine maintenance, tires, insurance, license and registration, loan finance charges, and depreciation costs.) Jen asserts that by choosing alternatives to the standard 2.28 vehicles per household, her family has already saved a small fortune. And if the family continue to share one car instead of owning two for the next twenty-nine years, and invest their compounded annual savings at 8 percent return per year, they'll save an *additional* $1 million. The point is not to "give up" the good life to save money, but rather to *redefine* the meaning of the good life, in terms of overall value rather than just symbolic stuff.

If you are unwilling to be without personal wheels, what about eating out less, thus avoiding the MSG, salt, fat, corn syrup, and supersized portions many big chain restaurants serve? Not only will you know exactly what's in your food; you'll also save another $1 million, Jen concludes:

- Replace your $9.50 restaurant lunches (sandwich, fries, soft drink, sales tax, tip, and mileage) with a nutritious $3.00 lunch brought from home.

- Deposit your $143 monthly savings ($6.50 daily, twenty-two working days a month) into a Roth IRA retirement account.

- Invest in equities (stocks, mutual funds) at a 10 percent annual long-term average rate of return.

- Let your lunch account simmer for forty-one years, after which it will be worth $1,000,837.

Jen suggests combining the brown-bag lunch club with a twenty-minute walk to the park. This walk-and-talk would burn more than a million calories over the course of a career—the rough equivalent of 365 pounds that don't have to be cussed at and battled back. With or without a continuous chain of brown-bag lunches, by making exercise part of our daily routine, we avoid many expenses related to weight-loss programs. (The weight-loss industry takes in a bulging $30 billion a year.) How much would you expect to pay (in 2009 dollars) to lose thirty pounds for a better relationship with your spouse, or to attend a close friend's wedding or a high school reunion? At Jenny Craig, it might be $400, not including food, while if you go with the Zone Diet, which includes exclusive home delivery of Chef Selected meals and snacks, you'll shell out $4,000.[39]

The list goes on and on. By giving up bottled water (who wants to drink plastic particles anyway?), we might save a few hundred dollars a year. Getting more mileage from each haircut by having a few different hairstyles; changing the car's oil ourselves; buying supermarket brand-name foods— collectively, these habit changes can add up to hundreds or thousands of dollars a year. But the real payoffs come in better health, time affluence, closer friendships, more stimulating work, and a sense of purpose. These rewards are concrete and tangible, yet may require a shift in values to perceive, pursue, and collect.

SEEING WITH DIFFERENT LENSES

According to U.S. Bureau of Labor Statistics (BLS), data, the average American household divides about $50,000 among fourteen major categories, including:

Product or Service	Percentage of Annual Expenditures*
Housing (shelter, utilities, household operations, housekeeping supplies, furnishings, equipment)	34.1
Food	12.4
Food at home	7.0
Food away from home	5.4
Personal insurance and pensions (including Social Security)	10.8
Entertainment	5.4
Apparel and services	3.8

Product or Service	Percentage of Annual Expenditures*
Cash contributions	3.7
Education	1.9
Reading	1.2
Alcoholic beverages	0.9
Tobacco and Smoking products	0.7
Miscellaneous	1.6

*Based on 2007 data available at www.BLS.com

Certainly, there are many opportunities to save money in these typical categories; for example, giving up smoking will cut expenses for medical and dental products and services. The real cost of a pack of cigarettes is far higher than its counter price. Journalist Hilary Smith estimates that a forty-year-old who quits smoking and invests the money could accumulate $250,000 by age seventy. "Smokers pay more for insurance and lose money on the resale value of their cars and homes. They spend extra on dry cleaning and teeth cleaning. Long term, they earn less and receive less in pension and Social Security benefits." (Which is another way of saying if they die or work fewer years because of illness, they can't collect Social Security.) They also face the prospect of not a getting a job to begin with, since some employers like Weyco, a medical benefits administrator, and Alaska Airlines require breath tests to hire and retain non-smoking employees."[40]

STRETCHING THE BUDGET, SHRINKING THE FOOTPRINT

If our typical household buys food wisely and wastes less than the national average—14 percent—it will save money, there's no doubt about that. Our typical household could also save money by contributing less to charities and campaigns, but the larger issue is, what changes in the budget would not only save money but deliver greater *real value*? To answer this question, we need to reflect on what we truly need.

We may think it's the iPod we want when really we're after the social recognition that comes with it. But there are other ways of connecting socially. Chilean economist Manfred Max-Neef identifies nine categories of essential needs: subsistence, protection, participation, affection, identity, understanding, creativity, leisure, and freedom. Though it's a bit painful to think about, Americans work and commute up to 100,000 hours per lifetime in an attempt to meet these needs. The decisions we make in a household should acknowledge that throughout history and across all cultures, people have sought security, safety, meaning, and ways of expressing themselves.

In household spending, identity is near the top of the list. The way we decorate, the way we use space, and the activities we do in our houses all reflect how we want the world to see us. Identity can be a key leverage point in shifting the culture in a more sensible direction. What if we intentionally alter our identities to reflect changing realities in the world? All of a sudden, solar panels—which we once considered ugly—might begin to look beautiful. They signify a new way of meeting essential needs like freedom (from mainstream rules of aesthetics), protection (from insecure sources of energy), and participation (in a cultural revolution). Installing solar panels is like hoisting your new identity up a flagpole.

Now that you are expressing different values, the household budget begins to change. There are no bigger-screen TVs on your wish list. Having a new outfit every month seems much less important, so trips to the mall become less frequent. Much of your free time is devoted to remodeling the basement so that you can set up a loom, a Ping-Pong table, and a cool space (literally) to make wine and store produce from the garden. All these activities bring down your expenses for entertainment. You're watching life less and living it more. You invite neighbors over more, which reduces transportation expenses, because you used to travel across town to see friends. Maybe you form a food co-op with some of your neighbors, buying produce directly from a local farmer, who soon becomes a friend himself. You arrange to work a few days a week from home, and convert one end of the living room to a home office, further reducing your transportation expenses without sacrifice or deprivation.

The radius of your life seems to be getting shorter. Instead of identifying with the whole metropolitan area, you now think of yourself as a local citizen. In *The Small-Mart Revolution*, Michael Shuman offers his top-ten list of actions that strengthen the bond between household and local economy:

1. **Localize your home.** By moving your mortgage to a local bank or credit union, you help build a local network of trust, and finance community improvements.

2. **Cut auto use in half.** Decreased driving contributes to community prosperity by reducing both air pollution and the paving-over of natural landscapes (thus preventing water pollution and landslides, and retaining CO_2-absorbing trees).

3. **Eat out locally.** Eating at locally owned restaurants keeps money in the local economy, improves health, and often provides a taste of the region you live in.

4. **Find local entertainment.** "The more a community can unglue residents from their TV sets and involve them in local music, dance-halls, film festivals, fairs, and street parties, the more likely that community can succeed," writes Shuman.

5. **Use local health care.** Shift from a treatment mind-set to a prevention mind-set. Good nutrition, regular exercise, and healthy community life—all inherently local activities—reduce the need for nonlocal emergency medical equipment and prescriptions

6. **Buy fresh food.** By definition, fresh food is local. It's usually healthier, requires less packaging, is not processed, and supports a person you may know.

7. **Localize household energy use.** Hire a local energy consultant to make your house as efficient as possible, sometimes without up-front costs. (You make payments to energy service companies that are financed out of savings.)

8. **Give to local charities.** Contribute to nonprofit organizations whose work you can see and feel, such as local food banks, hospitals, and churches.

9. **Localize car services.** Use local businesses to wash, wax, detail, and repair your vehicle. They're usually more pleasant to work with, and they know your car better than the chain-store employees do.

10. **Drink locally and stop smoking.** Microbreweries and niche vineyards provide an increasing share of the nation's alcohol, often made from local ingredients. Learn to appreciate their craft. And why mess with tobacco? The $323 a year Americans spend per capita for this degrading habit (which many of us have indulged in) is just the tip of the iceberg.[41]

When we look at the household budget through these clear lenses, we begin to see how value-driven household spending can deliver a higher quality of life. By slowing down to the speed of life, the average household can become much more than just a "consumer unit"—it can be a place where people come to life.

➤ New Normal Agenda Point #7: Redirecting the National Budget

Old Perspective: Since we have so many resources, we don't need to worry about waste, and since there are more applicants than jobs, we can force employees to work long hours. Although half of our national economy is debt, we always seem to land on our feet. Our story is a happy one.

New Perspective: With better policies and designs, and a new ethic, the American economy can deliberately rearrange its priorities to achieve greater efficiency and decrease the debt at the same time.

THE HEAVY LIFTING

- Certain technical procedures are demonstrably more effective—for example, world leaders produce more cement or paper per unit of energy than U.S. industries do. Support incentives for—and buy products from—companies that use energy efficiently and whose products are durable and reliable.

Money flows through a nation's economy the same way it flows through a household economy. In each case, we try to meet fundamental needs like security, health, identity, and fairness by allocating resources wisely. However, we often make decisions based not on need per se, but on fuzzier, catchall concepts like price and profit. For example, a household budget often includes cheap junk food or useless lottery tickets even though we can't realistically expect them to meet basic needs like nutrition or financial security.

In the U.S. economy, money too often marches—like the broomsticks in *The Sorceror's Apprentice*—to misguided military missions, dysfunctional design of communities, and industries that don't protect natural assets (which are worth far more if left intact than the products themselves). We let our cultural wealth and infrastructure degrade too because there is less profit in preservation than in speculative investments in real estate or high-tech start-ups. Clearly, our priorities need to be rearranged, which may involve valuing money less and life more.

GIVE ME LIBERTY OR GIVE ME DEBT

On both the household scale and the national scale, we count on deficit spending to keep our lifestyle humming. (The average American carried

$17,000 of personal debt in 2009, excluding mortgages, according to Experian; and national debt is now more than half of GDP. In 2008, the United States paid $451 billion in interest on that debt.) It's fine to be hopeful, but let's face it: sometimes our financial decisions are based on nothing *but* hope, as in the recent, hyperactive housing bubble that popped onto our faces like bubble gum. We need a more qualitative way of evaluating financial decisions of all sorts. Imagine looking out your back window as you mentally assess your household's net worth. "We're not making progress," you might say, shaking your head. "Our backyard isn't getting any bigger." Obviously, you'd be beating yourself up for nothing; the yard doesn't need to become bigger to improve your quality of life; it needs to become *better*. It needs your creativity and care to become more productive, safer, securer, and more beautiful. But it surely won't get any bigger, because adjacent land is already being used.

So it is in the national economy—bigger isn't necessarily better, and it's also not a sure thing. We're borrowing more each year than either financial or natural systems can generate on a continuing basis. However, the United States obliviously continues to borrow from other countries to build more roads and suburbs, finance more wars, and buy more gadgets. Meanwhile, other nations place a higher priority on meeting real needs. John de Graaf, coordinator of the nonprofit organization Take Back Your Time, told this author "A 30-year trend of income tax cuts for the rich has decreased quality of life overall in the U.S. In contrast, Western European countries invested in their social contracts. Strategic investments in health care, education, transportation, and common space reduced the need [and desire] of individuals to maximize their own incomes." Which strategy meets human needs such as security, meaning, and social connection better?

Rather than avoiding expenditures by designing better products, using preventive approaches in health care, or mandating more efficient transportation technologies, we're stuck in the same old paradigm: add fertilizer (capital) and watch it grow. This approach includes a very dysfunctional corollary: waste, do-overs, and detours are okay as long as they feed the GDP—basically a bulging box of growth.

It takes a while for top-dog empires like ours to perceive cracks in fundamental assumptions, and diminishing returns on investments. "If it ain't broke, don't fix it" goes the old saw, but here's the truth: it *is* "broke," and so are millions of Americans. With luck, our perceptions will quickly become sharp enough to cut through the arrogant, broken habits and assumptions that now hold us hostage.

CREATING A PREVENTIVE, NONPROFIT ECONOMY

As we did in the discussion of household budgets, let's look at how money is earned and spent in America, and identify key leverage points. Where is capital being wasted? Where are we spinning our wheels? Where are we substituting technology for nature when nature can do a more precise and less expensive job? By shifting our assets in a sustainable direction, we can create a more affordable culture that requires less capital to deliver comparable value. An overall goal should be to reduce the volume of transactions because, as climate change expert and physicist Joe Romm phrases it, "We have been getting rich by depleting all our natural stocks, but in the process we are destroying a livable climate." The economy that will serve us best preserves and generates more natural and social capital and requires less manufactured capital—an appropriate trade in a world where resources per capita (land, water, minerals, oil) are quickly shrinking.

To get there, we'll need to think holistically about industries and systems, replacing deficiency with efficiency. Some of the changes taking place are so huge that we can't get them into focus. For example, since 1970, the relative importance of finances and manufacturing have flipflopped in the U.S. economy. Insurance, finance, and real estate lending have become roughly a fifth of America's GDP, while manufacturing of durable and nondurable goods has dropped to about one-tenth of the economy.

The insurance industry has changed the direction of health care; it's now more appropriate to call it disease care. The system is designed to charge whatever desperate patients will pay; as a result, Americans now spend the most per capita for health care of any industrial country—about $8,000. Yet, we spend the least per capita for food, as a percentage of income. Food systems expert Michael Pollan sees huge opportunities for national savings. "We're spending $147 billion to treat obesity, $116 billion to treat diabetes, and hundreds of billions more to treat cardiovascular disease and the many types of cancer that have been linked to the so-called Western diet," he writes.[42]

Comments *New York Times* columnist David Brooks, "The voracious health care system (now 18 percent of the U.S. economy and rising) soaks up money that could go to education, the environment, economic development, and a thousand other priorities." Sidestepping the ongoing debate over who should coordinate health care—the private sector, government, or nonprofits—Brooks observes that the real problem is "insane incentives."[43] He refers to the current industry practice of paying doctors based on the *quantity* of patients they see and the number of treatments they prescribe (such as drugs, scans, and surgeries) rather than focusing sharply on wellness. Yet, recent policy innovations in Ohio and Minnesota demonstrate a more effective, preventive way of providing health care. At the Cleveland Clinic—that city's largest employer—doctors and other professionals know full well that at least half of U.S. health-care costs come from preventable illnesses like heart disease, diabetes, cancer, depression, asthma, and allergies. They've concluded that it would be more effective—and less expensive—to encourage wellness rather than treat illness. As a first step, the hospital stopped hiring smokers, a policy that had a cascading effect: smoking rates fell throughout the county. The clinic also offers employees and the general public a six-week program emphasizing the benefits of healthy food, regular exercise, and stress reduction. (And the clinic has upgraded the nutritional content of its own meals, realizing that good food saves money because it heals.) When employees reach their fitness goals in the program, they earn a bonus of $100, paid out of savings from lower insurance claims. In other words, prevention more than pays its own way—in a company or a nation.

Medica, a large insurance provider in Minnesota, is challenging the disease-care paradigm too, subsidizing a new payment system for doctors. Instead of being paid for each procedure performed (which gives them an incentive to perform more), doctors at Fairview Health Services (a hospital and clinic) will receive fixed salaries, and will be encouraged to increase the number of *preventive* actions their patients take, such as mammograms, exercise, and colonoscopies.

Michael Pollan predicts that the entire insurance industry will soon catch on to the huge benefits of preventive approaches: "A patient with Type 2 diabetes incurs additional health care costs of more than $6,600 a year; over a lifetime, that can come to more than $400,000.[44] Insurers will quickly figure out that every case of Type 2 diabetes they can prevent adds $400,000 to their bottom line. Suddenly, every can of soda or Happy Meal or chicken nugget on a school lunch menu will look like a threat to future profits."

Recent studies suggest that the huge gap between rich and poor is another major contributor to poor health in the United States. In other words, the economy itself is making us sick by creating stress and insecurity. In *The Impact of Inequality,* epidemiologist Richard Wilkinson writes that employee ownership may be as effective in preventing disease as vaccines or body scans.

The public debate on health care has highlighted another new-paradigm principle concerning the economy in general: Certain procedures are demonstrably more effective than others. Rather than choosing the most exotic and profitable technologies, the supply side of the economy needs to be given incentives and market share for choosing procedures that use the least energy, provide the greatest access, and perform the most reliably.

There are abundant opportunities in the U.S. economy to shift from a fix-it-up paradigm to a preventive one, making our life more affordable at both the household and the national level. By realigning our priorities with our values, understanding the way systems work, and being clear about what outcome we are trying to achieve, we can in effect become a "nonprofit" society that prevents and avoids the need for continuous, often destructive economic growth.

Military expenditures provide more disturbing data. When all expenses for the Department of Defense (including social and medical support for veterans and active participants in the "War on Terrorism") and the Department of Energy's nuclear weapons program are totaled, they equal 54 percent of the federal budget—about $1 trillion a year! This staggering sum is equal to the spending of the next fifteen countries combined, or 47 percent of the entire global military budget. Environmentalist Lester Brown proposes using one-sixth of the annual global military budget—roughly $160 billion a year in 2008—to supply human needs like security and freedom peacefully rather than aggressively. Brown calculates that with this cooperative annual investment by the world's nations, everyone in the world could have primary education, adult literacy, family planning, and universal health care. Less than $100 billion a year would reforest the earth, restore the planet's rangelands and fisheries; stabilize water tables, and protect biological diversity and cropland topsoil.[45]

Nobel Prize–winning economist Joseph Stiglitz and Linda J. Blimes observe in the book *The Three Trillion Dollar War* that for a fraction of the cost of the second war in Iraq "we could have put Social Security and Medicare on a sound footing for the next half-century or more." The money spent every day on the war could enroll an additional fifty-eight thousand children in Head Start for a year; make a year of college affordable for 160,000 low-income students; or pay the annual salaries of four thousand more police officers. What kind of security do we want to finance?[46]

REARRANGING THE AMERICAN ECONOMY

The way our civilization now looks and functions is largely the result of how we allocated capital during the past century. We spent tens of trillions of dollars centralizing, incorporating, and consolidating production systems, taking advantage of economies of scale and expectations of high returns on investment. Yet our legacy is precarious and unsustainable: a suburban sea on a lifestyle support system; an interstate highway system that costs $50 billion a year to maintain; an agricultural "green revolution" that is codependent with cheap oil; a petrochemical industry the by-products of which have contaminated the entire biosphere. The insurance industry, health-care industry, waste-management industry, banking industry, and real estate industry   all are built on a naive belief that their scaffolding will remain secure, that there will not be significant changes in resource availability, climatic conditions, human population, or availability of capital.

We've recently rediscovered that financial or paper wealth is also frequently based on the belief that a hungry market will continue to buy anything novel or sought-after. But value is not a function of optimism. Ask insurance managers what a New Orleans house is worth now that premiums have doubled, tripled, or even quadrupled after Katrina. Of the fifty-eight most expensive insurance payouts in history, fifty-five are weather-related, and as the world's climate continues to change, the frequency of budget-bending floods, droughts, wildfires, and hurricanes will increase exponentially. In fact, Andrew Dlugolecki—director of one of the world's six biggest insurance groups (CGNU)—has warned EU policy makers that unless unprecedented action is taken to curb global warming, the resulting damage could exceed the dollar value of all the world's resources by 2065. "Insurance clients are not well prepared for climate change," says Dlugolecki. "They're not adapting, not reacting to the possibilities of damage and government policies on emissions. That means insurers have a big job to do to prepare their clients for dealing with climate change."

Dlugolecki, an expert at assessing future risk, points out how severely the risks of climate change could impact the supply chains of multinational corporations. "Every sector and activity is affected in some way by climate change, either by the weather or by the various regulations that governments are going to bring in to control emissions," he says.[47] Agriculture is affected the most directly, potentially threatening the health of billions; however, the construction, energy, and tourism industries are also especially vulnerable.

Ask any forward-looking banker what a huge, poorly insulated house without access to public transportation will be worth when demand for oil exceeds supply. The stability of the global economy depends on how well humanity can substitute preventive approaches for wasteful and poorly designed ones. The relatively successful response to another planetary challenge—depletion of the earth's ozone layer—demonstrated that the market could find solutions quickly. When scientists discovered that halogen compounds including chlorofluorocarbons (CFCs) were tearing apart ozone molecules in the earth's atmosphere (putting plant and animal life at risk from ultraviolet radiation), policy makers quickly set a ceiling on CFC production, and chemical corporations found alternative chemicals and spray cans that slowed the rate of ozone depletion, just in time.

This international response triggered a U.S.-led initiative called Pollution Prevention (P2), which, by design, avoids both health effects and costly cleanups of toxic chemicals. Since 1990, when Pollution Prevention guidelines were enacted, more than 200 billion pounds of air, water, and solid pollution have been avoided, according to EPA data. Between 2004 and 2006, about two thousand companies, municipalities, and agencies documented savings of $6.5 billion after focusing on better procedures, products, and technologies. A classic example is the 3M Company, which over the past three decades has completed more than 5,600 P2 projects that saved more than $1 billion.

Similarly, the energy revolution will be funded largely by avoided costs. Rather than generating more energy than we need—and then wasting it— why not make each device and technology as efficient as possible, so that less money will be necessary? In an economy so bloated by overproduction and overconsumption, potential savings are almost limitless. To reduce transportation, design better towns and cities that people like to walk in. To reduce mining impacts and costs, gradually phase out the use of coal-fired power plants, one of the largest emitters of greenhouse gases (Germany is already doing it). Enact mandatory recycling of metals like tin, copper, iron, lead, and bauxite to reduce the economic and ecological costs of extraction. Regulations like European "take-back" laws could encourage better design and far more effective recycling, as they have in Europe, and in a handful of American states that require companies to take back and recycle electronic products. When manufacturers are required to take back their products at the end of their life, designers and engineers work harder to create quality products that are durable, lightweight, nontoxic, and easily recycled—not just for altruistic reasons but for pragmatic ones: the products are coming back and need to be dealt with.

In the agricultural sector, new-paradigm farmers rely on techniques and inputs that originate on the farm. They reduce fertilizer use by growing cover crops they incorporate into the soil; they avoid pesticides by using natural controls; and they avoid antibiotics by grazing their livestock rather than raising the animals in feedlots, where they eat costly grains that (in the case of cattle) they can't properly digest. By rotating crops and incorporating organic material into their soil, these farmers create a spongelike humus that conserves water. If these techniques were used throughout the country, billions of dollars could be saved every year. The industry just needs incentives to make a huge U-turn in the way agriculture is practiced.

Since government constitutes 13 percent of the U.S. economy (roughly 9 percent state and local, 4 percent federal), this sector is rich with opportunities for bringing cost-saving, green innovations into the economy. New-paradigm procurement policies increasingly include specs for recycled content, energy and water efficiency, minimal packaging, and other culture-shifting qualities. The U.S. military is one of the world's largest consumers of energy. In 2007, the 340,000 barrels it consumed every day made it the largest single purchaser of oil. Yet, over the last decade, all branches of the armed forces have committed to significant energy-saving initiatives and increased their use of alternative energy and fuels, reports energy expert Joe Romm. For example, a 14.2-megawatt solar photovoltaic array at Nellis Air Force Base in Las Vegas, Nevada, saves $1 million in energy costs annually. There will be many more such projects, since the Department of Defense received $3.6 billion to implement energy-efficiency measures and facility upgrades.[48]

By far the greatest opportunities to avoid spending at the national and international levels are inherent in nature itself—not generally thought of as an economic sector. Nature provides clean air and water, pest control, pollination, and many other services worth more than all the products of the global economy put together. As we move into an era of restoration, undisturbed nature will once again be perceived as the primary source of wealth.

3

Overfed but Undernourished

The food industry is humanity's largest single system, and arguably, its most important. But there are many signs that this system needs repair and reinvention. As scholar and farmer Wendell Berry observes, "Industrial agriculture has proven to be immensely productive, but at the cost of destroying the means of production." In the United States, the growth, distribution, preparation, and consumption of food uses more energy than all the country's automobiles, planes, trains, and buses combined—about one-fifth of the nation's overall energy use.

Including the global livestock industry—which now numbers about 20 billion animals—the international food industry contributes more than a fourth of total greenhouse gas emissions. It has the single greatest impact on water quality and directly exposes the greatest number of people to toxic chemicals. "It is enormously destructive of farmland, farm communities, and farmers," summarizes Berry. "It wastes soil, water, energy and life. It is highly centralized, genetically impoverished and dependent on cheap fossil fuels, on long-distance hauling, and on consumer ignorance. This is an agriculture with a short future."[1]

With a steady increase in international trade, and a market-driven focus on processed and packaged food, we pay far less attention to the quality of our food than we used to; we've become separated from its origins and its cultural significance, both geographically and psychologically. What key choices and decisions can we make to reconnect? This chapter explores high-leverage changes that can shift the direction of the food production and delivery system, making it stronger and more responsive to the needs of both people and nature.

When humans first learned how to cultivate crops about ten thousand years ago, a whole new way of life emerged, because a single tilled acre could now produce one hundred times the calories that a hunting and gathering lifestyle could. These efficiencies freed up time so that humans could build communities, create masterpieces of art, and explore the mysteries of science. Millennia later, efficiency is still the predominant goal, but largely in search of profit. Our current policies, research expenditures, farming methods, and technologies all reflect an obsession with "fast, cheap, and easy" quantities of food. It's all about bushels per acre and per hour, and resulting profits. But the key questions is, What is our food system doing to the land, water, climatic stability, and our health, the base of any economy?

Just fifty years ago, world population was a mere 3 billion; partly because of agricultural productivity, another billion people have been added every twelve or thirteen years, at the pace of 70 million more humans every year— the equivalent of adding the eight largest American metropolitan populations (New York City, Los Angeles, Chicago, Dallas, Philadelphia, Houston, Miami, and Washington, D.C.) *every year*. Every single day, another 200,000 people are added to the planet. In a world where farmland is becoming extremely scarce, where will thirty-four thousand new farmable acres come from, each day? So far, from tropical rain forests and savannas, which, if left intact, are key ecological assets in the prevention of global warming.

The stark reality of human population necessitates a new way of thinking about food. The assumptions and goals that guided agriculture in a world of 1 billion (1800) or 2 billion people (1930) are no longer valid in a world that is suddenly pushing 7 billion. Our primary goals now need to center on preserving the functionality of our farms, or else the system will collapse, as agricultural systems already have in empires of the past. Yield and profit are important, but so are preservation of soil and water, restoration of biological diversity, safety and healthiness of food, reduction of fossil-fuel energy and greenhouse emissions, and fit with an increasingly urban population.

Fortunately, the global food system can adapt relatively easily (though it won't be a snap), for several key reasons: agriculture has until recently been solar-powered, and it can be again, when oil becomes too expensive to prop up the industry. The supply-and-demand economics of the food system are accessible to consumers, who are becoming more aware of the overall *value* of food purchases. Because food affects the most important issues of our times—energy, health, security, biological habitat, and climate change— agriculture will come under increasing cultural and political scrutiny. The trend toward organic produce and alternative artisan products, grown in market gardens and on small farms, will continue, not just because it can be financially lucrative, but also because the work is satisfying to a certain green-thumbed sector of the population.

Increasingly, refugees from the global industrialized food system are hungry for alternatives, remembering that food connects. Food activists like Alice Waters are leading the charge toward "slow food" and mindful eating based on what humans actually need. "When we eat fast-food meals alone in our cars," she writes, "we swallow the values and assumptions of the corporations that manufacture them. According to those values, eating is no more important than fueling up, and should be done quickly and anonymously."[2] Yet, food is far more than that, she believes; throughout human history, it was a way to come together, to express our identity, and be rooted in the earth. Food delivers not just physical health, but also social health. "At the table, we learn moderation, conversation, tolerance, generosity and conviviality; these are civic virtues," says Waters. "The pleasures of the table also beget responsibilities—to one another, to the animals we eat, to the land and to the people who work it."[3]

Food is an issue that gets people's attention and mobilizes activism. When food prices shot up in 2008 because of rising energy costs, there were food riots in dozens of countries. The demand side of the food market has incredible influence on the producers, processors, and distributors. When new research created markets for low-fat foods, organic options, less sugar, less salt, whole-grain carbohydrates, free-range meat, and so on, the food industry had no choice but to respond. Boycotts of certain brands of food and certain companies help keep corporate producers focused on quality. For example, because of public concern, McDonald's requested that its meat suppliers cut their use of antibiotics.

A recent story on *60 Minutes* reported that Masai farmers in Kenya were using the pesticide Furadan to poison lions, to reduce risk on their farms. That story resulted in manufacturers stopping shipments of the pesticide to Kenya. Concern about diseases like type 2 diabetes led to the banning of trans fats in New York City and California restaurants. When consumers demand certified organic fruits and vegetables, pasture-raised beef, sustainably harvested fish, and bird-friendly coffee and cocoa, even Wal-Mart, Costco, and Target begin to restock their shelves.

The overall direction of agriculture has been "bigger is better," both in the size of farms and the produce grown on them. Tomatoes and apples are bigger now, but are they better? Several recent studies have documented that as produce gets larger and more flawless in appearance, vitamins and minerals decrease, on average, along with taste and aroma. In the last half century, plant scientists and crop breeders have doubled and tripled the yield per acre of most major fruits, vegetables, and grains, but the "almost single-minded focus on increasing yields created a blind spot" in nutritional content, says Brian Halweil, author of the Organic Center's report "Still No Free Lunch." The report documented examples like these:

- The more a tomato weighs, the lower its concentrations of vitamin C, vitamin A, and lycopene, a natural cancer-fighting chemical that makes tomatoes red.

- Sweet corn, potatoes, and whole-wheat bread show double-digit declines in iron, zinc, and calcium. http://www.organic-center/ reportfiled/yield-Nutrient-Density-Final.pdf executive summary pp. 5–10 September 2007

- Milk from high-production dairy cows has lower concentrations of fat, protein, and other nutrition-enhancing components than the milk from dairy operations of twenty years ago or more.[4]

Other studies concur: somehow nutrition and flavor have taken second fiddle and even third fiddle to size and appearance in breeding. By examining United States Department of Agriculture (USDA) data on nutrient content spanning more than half a century, Donald Davis at the University of Texas discovered declines of up to 40 percent in minerals, vitamins, and proteins. The focus on yield per acre and marketability has also resulted in decreases of anticancer and antitoxin compounds known as phytonutrients.[5]

The good news? Sometimes we consumers reap quality improvements by accident, as when breeding research accidentally results in *healthier* produce. When researchers bred for sexier-looking, bright orange carrots, their work yielded unexpected increases in vitamin A. Breeders seeking to make watermelons sweeter accidentally increased levels of vitamin C, according to participants at a recent meeting of the American Society for Horticultural Science. But for the most part, nutritional decline continues. Washington State University researchers Stephen Jones and Kevin Murphy conclude, "You would have to eat twice as many slices of modern bread as you would of the older variety to get the same nutritional value." How did this happen? "The breeders and growers never looked at whether the nutritional content stayed the same as the yield increased," says Jones. He explains that food producers often call the shots, demanding traits other than nutrition, such as wheat that makes a good cookie, a fluffy loaf of bread, or pizza dough that's easy to work with.[6]

The following key choices can help us change the entire direction of the food system—bringing health, wisdom, and natural balance back to agriculture and the food system. By choosing well-grown, healthy food, we are also choosing the kind of society we want. Do we favor an inclusive, community-minded, ecologically informed food system, or a system driven by profit alone?

➤ New Normal Agenda Point #8: Elevating Food to a Higher Priority

Old Perspective: Food should be fast, easy, fun, and so cheap that it's okay to waste it. Cooking does not fit these criteria because it requires concentration, "extra" time, and engagement, so processed food is superior. The origins and quality of my food are not as important as their standardized, predictable consistency.

New Perspective: Food connects the grower, distributor and eater with the living system that it came from, in a chain of value that begins and ends in health and well being of both land and people.

THE HEAVY LIFTING

- Understand that what you're eating is not just enjoyable (or not) but part of a bigger system that affects you and the planet.

- Observe how the food you eat affects your digestive system, endurance, and sense of well being. Good food equals good mood.

- Decrease your reliance on prepared dinners and fast food. Learn one new recipe a month. Learn to can vegetables and fruit. Learn how to freeze homemade dishes such as soups, casseroles, and sauces.

Food is the most universal symbol of America's age of excess. The average American's dinner comes from five different countries, with combined airfreight and ocean freight distance often exceeding ten thousand miles. At least three-fourths of that meal is processed and packaged, its nutrients stripped away and replaced by texturizers, sweeteners, and flavor "enhancers."

Let's visit Homer Simpson for a few minutes as our "average American" proxy watches TV and snacks. From the research of people like Dr. Brian Wansink, author of *Mindless Eating,* we know that Homer is thinking—in his colorfully primitive way—that if he has the chips 'n' dip, he'll also have the friends, the laughter, the adrenaline rushes, the companionship, that he sees in the commercials and sitcoms. We know that unlike many Europeans and Asians—whose body wisdom directs them to stop eating when they're full—Homer's cue to stop will be when his beer is gone, the big bowl is empty, or the TV show is over. Homer will eat more M&M's if they are different colors rather than just one color; more chips if they come in transparent packages so he can preview and crave them; and more fruit if it's presliced, even if it was sliced weeks ago and preserved in space-age packaging. In an age of excess, Homer forms a perception of how much food is "normal" to eat, then eats a little more because he feels he deserves it.

Unbeknownst to Homer, product wizards throughout the food industry strive for ultimate "snackability" that induces what one marketer, Barb Stuckey, calls "mindless munching," in which the hand moves hypnotically back and forth between bag and mouth. These maestros of munch deliver an endless stream of products that don't imply a portion size the way a whole apple or slice of homemade pie does, so there's no obvious signal, or need, to stop.[7]

Is "fun food" what we really want? Though it may seem overwhelming to change eating habits that have developed over lifetimes, complete with recipes, symbols of identity, and memories, change we must, because our mainstream diet is sapping our personal energy and health, and stripping resilience from the biological systems we evolved with and the culture we built. When we remember that the human diet has evolved over millions of years, we begin to think of "normal" in a more appropriate way. So is Homer Simpson, a caricature of the average American, crazy? In a word, yes. Many of us are living in a candy-shop psychosis in which we consider it a sensible trade to let the ice caps melt and the tumors take root if the Whoppers and Pop-Tarts just keep coming. That illusion, however, is fading in a society that is beginning to see diet as a moral decision, related to essential human needs like vitality, social connections, fairness, security, kindness, and even sanity. In a world of changing values, people of the near future may not respect us if we are mindless, self-centered eaters.

If these ideas make our food choices seem like an overwhelming responsibility (and an intrusion on our personal freedom), we can keep it simple, as food system expert Michael Pollan suggests: Eat food (real food). Not too much. Mostly plants. Following are a few guidelines that would lead to profound social changes:

- Eat less meat to take a huge bite out of global warming and improve your health. A single meat-free meal a week times 300 million Americans is not a deprivation, but a social movement!

- Eat food that comes from your region—it is fresher and healthier, and requires less packaging and much less transportation.

- Rediscover the pleasure of sitting down with family and friends and eating a meal together.

- Avoid foods that contain or require the use of chemicals your grandparents never heard of. Let's keep chemicals out of the living systems that preserve and maintain wilderness, clean the world's air and water, and recycle wastes.

- Get informed about food policies that affect your family, your community, and the country. You'll find lots of important information on the Web and in local newspapers.[8]

Mindful eaters avoid the empty calories of junk food in favor of high-value, high-energy food that makes each day go more smoothly. Why not bring our brains to the table and devise a few personal food strategies, such as:

- Don't bring junk food into your house. Save healthier versions of chips, ice cream, and cookies for special occasions, and store them only as near as the supermarket. When you have a snack attack, have some fruit or a handful of nuts, or pop some organic popcorn in olive oil (sturdy cast-iron or stainless-steel pots work great because the popcorn doesn't burn).

- If you have thirty years left to live, that's roughly thirty thousand meals! Why not make most of them satisfying, one week at a time? Identify a dozen or so healthy recipes and structure weekly menus. If it makes life easier, rotate your menus through the same days of the week, so you'll know when to buy what.

- Forget about soft drinks, even diet ones. Picture Homer Simpson's belly every time you crave one. Since Concord grape juice provides many of the benefits of red wine and tastes great, keep a few bottles in the fridge. Combine with cranberry juice and dilute with tap water for an inexpensive, healthy drink.

- Give a higher priority to fresh potatoes and lower priority to French fries, often cooked in saturated fat and drip-dried. Fresh potatoes have only about 100 calories per medium-sized spud and provide lots of vitamins C and B, niacin, iron, and copper—and 6 percent of the daily recommended amount of protein. They are great in breakfast burritos with "cage-free, natural" eggs, to get a good start. (Organic eggs are even better.)

- Mass-produce healthy soups, sauces, salad dressings, and cooked, whole-grain cereals in your own kitchen. Can or freeze them to save time, energy, and money as well as reduce packaging and greenhouse-gas emissions.

- Allow yourself one luxury "treat" per shopping trip to avoid throwing in three or four.

- Create a "car pack" if you spend a significant amount of time in your car—a lunchbox with raw nuts, fruit, and high-end, healthy snack bars. Even more convenient than the drive-in, your customized car pack can save money and energy, and eliminate all that packaging.[9]

➤ New Normal Agenda Point #9: Shopping for Change, or Just More of the Same?

Old Perspective: A consumer's best grocery-store strategy is to spend the least amount of money to get the largest amount of food. Shop in the center aisles of a conventional supermarket, where the processed foods with the cheapest calories are displayed.

New Perspective: It's important to save money on groceries, but good food has more value per pound, so it may be worth slightly more money in trade for better flavor, lower health-related expenses, lower dental bills, and fewer over-the-counter drugs and dieting programs. With healthy food as part of our routine, we perform better at work, at school, or on the sports field.

THE HEAVY LIFTING

- Be a consumer activist: request healthy, regionally grown food at your local supermarket.

- Read labels when choosing brands, understand what's in the food you're buying, and, when you're satisfied, stick with the brand you like.

- Send e-mails in support of your favorite products and, when appropriate, make suggestions: Ask the manufacturer if it will consider less packaging for one of your favorite items. Suggest an organic version of the cereal or frozen vegetable you use.

"Spend $10 on organic, shade-grown coffee and you help protect songbirds like the Baltimore oriole, which migrates to Central America in the winter," writes one advocate for rethinking our food system. Is this kind of message likely to change your choice of coffee? Do you care about the songbirds? Sure you do, especially when you find out that this particular bird eats insects in your backyard; but when you're standing in the supermarket aisle, price wins out, especially in lean times. Now, if there were a crowd of people (like a golf tournament gallery) watching every shopping choice you made, you'd drink nothing but shade-grown, and you'd probably discover it has better flavor, too. Food choices are beginning to change; we can see that when the mainstream supermarket chains debut their own store-brand organic breads, soups, and cereals, and when cities large and small organize weekly farmers markets (there are now close to 5,000 in the United States)

In the book *Buyology: Truth and Lies About Why We Buy,* marketing expert Martin Lindstrom re-creates the convoluted, interconnected thoughts that percolate in our brains as we make choices. Standing in front of the peanut butter display, Lindstrom's shopper thinks,

> *I associate Skippy with childhood . . . it's been around forever, so I feel it's trustworthy . . . but isn't it laden with sugar and other preservatives I shouldn't be eating. . . . Same goes for Peter Pan, plus the name is so childish. And I'm not buying that generic brand. It costs 30 cents less, which makes me suspicious. In my experience, you get what you pay for. . . . The organic stuff? Tasteless, the few times I had it . . . always needs salt, too. . . . Plus, didn't I read somewhere that "organic" doesn't necessarily mean anything, plus it's almost double the price. . . . Jif . . . what's that old advertising slogan of theirs: "Choosy Mothers Choose Jif." . . . Well I am a fairly discriminating person.*[10]

This stream of consciousness illustrates that we make choices based not just on price, but on relationships, associations, emotions, memories, identity, and values. Using multifocus lenses, we fill our shopping carts with choices we hope are trustworthy, safe, comfortable, unique, healthy, green, and cheap—but not too cheap. (Wouldn't hunting and gathering be easier?) We make many of these decisions quickly as we nervously consult our watches, and unfortunately, the food Americans bring home often results in obesity and diet-related diseases such as diabetes and heart failure. The processed foods that now fill supermarket shelves are low in water and fiber (making them easier to ship) but packed with added fat and sugar, making them less filling, more fattening. Author and activist Bill McKibben observes, "The supermarket crammed with its thousands of brightly pack-aged offerings is a mirage: if you could wave a magic wand and break every-thing down into its constituent ingredients, a pool of high-fructose corn syrup would fill half the store."[11]

How can we escape? The only thing that will really work is a cultural movement that demands changes in what the food industry provides and how it provides it. Processed food is artificially cheap right now because energy has been cheap, and because our tax dollars subsidize the growing of crops like wheat, corn, and soybeans—primary ingredients in industrial food. As a society, we don't charge ourselves for the many environmental and health side effects of food. We allocate less of our household budget to food than we ever have before, and we don't, as a nation, allocate enough capital to mentor new farmers. We need to spend more, not less, for food as a percentage of total expenditures. By rearranging both our household and our national budgets, we should give a higher priority to fresh, healthy food and a lower priority to electronic gadgets, mall booty, cars, lawns, and vaca-tions. Our overall expenses don't have to go up; they just need to be re-aligned with our changing values. By choosing higher-quality food and better ways of growing it, we also begin to reshape the American culture.

In the meantime, here we are in the supermarket aisles, making the best choices we can. Though brightly colored promises on the boxes and packages ("all natural!" "low-fat!" "high in Omega 3!") seem a little overwhelming, with patience and peer support, we can learn what these slogans really mean, step by step. For example, "free-range" egg-laying hens are typically out of cages but inside barns or warehouses. They have some outdoor access, but how much is not specified, and there is no third-party quality control. A higher level of quality assurance for eggs is "USDA Certified Organic," which guar-antees not only outdoor access, but also an organic, all-vegetarian diet free of antibiotics and pesticides.

The fact is, food labels like these are an agreement, an understanding, between producer and consumer for a certain level of quality, a certain set of core values. The labels not only help the buyer but also guide the grower, holding production standards higher. Rather than remaining Lone Rangers for truth, justice, and quality in food, many Americans are now opting to let Whole Foods, Trader Joe's, or the local food co-op prescreen food prod-ucts for key traits like fair trade, and organic, local, and ecological sensitivity. After learning what brands they prefer, they also learn which conventional supermarkets carry those products, often at slightly lower prices. (And they learn to request those products from conventional store managers.) Step by step, they are changing not only the household diet, but also America's diet.

"You shouldn't need a Ph.D. in nutritional biochemistry to go supermarket shopping," says David Katz of the Yale Prevention Research Center, who wants to bring a "traffic light" labeling system to the United States. "The index, with green, yellow, or red labels, should take into account the quantity of calories, beneficial nutrients, and potentially harmful nutrients such as trans fat, in a serving of any given food. Why shouldn't even dummies wind up with a shopping cart filled with the good stuff?"

The eatingwell.com Web site concurs with Katz that label reading should be easier, but maintains that a lot of important nutritional information is already on the labels, if you know how to scan them. Here are the Web site's shopping suggestions:

Limit Products With

Saturated fat: As low as possible; less than five grams per serving.

Trans fat: Should be zero ("hydrogenated" or "partially hydrogenated" oils means trans fats).

Sodium: As low as possible. The FDA allows a "healthy" label on foods with less than 480 mg per serving for entrees, less than 360 mg for all other foods.

High fructose corn syrup: A cheap form of highly concentrated sugar (words ending in "ose" denote sugar).

"Enriched" or "wheat" flour (aliases for "white"). Choose whole-wheat flour instead.

Choose Products With

The shortest possible ingredient list.

Fiber: Three or more grams per serving.

Whole grains: Preferably first or second in the ingredients list.

"Liquid" or "high-oleic" vegetable oils: heart-healthy unsaturated fats.

Fruits and vegetables: Dried or fresh, in whole form.

➤ New Normal Agenda Point #10:
Organic or Conventional Food?

Old Perspective: Organic food is appealing because it's more natural, but the price is too high, and isn't it really just an elitist, New Age fad?

New Perspective: We can't afford *not* to eat organic food, since the health and environmental costs of industrial farming are too high. Humans have eaten organic food for 99.9999 percent of our history. The price of organic food will come down as farming practices change and market demand grows. Until then, buying organic food supports the regeneration of the industry.

THE HEAVY LIFTING

- Spend more of your budget on food and less on gas or gadgets.

- When considering organic brands, think about more than the price. Consider the health of your kids, the health of the world's wildlife, and the quality of the soil we all rely on.

- Encourage community foundations, chambers of commerce, and local governments to train new organic farmers to meet the rising demand.

Americans undervalue organic food both on the table and on the farm, for similar reasons. As a culture, we don't yet recognize the difference in quality between organic and conventional food, between organic and conventional growing. For example, we don't recognize collectively that it's more accurate to define the word "organic" by what it is rather than by what it isn't. True, certified organic means that toxic chemicals and fossil-fuel-based fertilizers are not used, but the only way farmers can make that kind of agriculture work is by operating their farms as living systems: building the soil with organic, once-living material—which provides fertility, water retention, disease resistance, and good drainage all at the same time.

Rotation of crops prevents disease and maintains fertility; using cover crops like alfalfa pulls free nitrogen right out of the air; recycling "wastes" like manure, crop residues, and by-products of regional industries such as coffee roasters or fruit canneries makes full use of existing resources. This information-rich way of farming provides habitat for wildlife (which reciprocates with natural pest control), conserves water, and helps preserve family farms in rural and metro-edge communities.

The fact that average levels of nearly a dozen nutrients are 25 percent higher in organic produce translates to greater calmness, endurance, mobility, and allergy resistance, sharper senses, and a better sex life—a higher quality of life, not just prevention of heart disease or cancer. Those who associate organic food with tightwads or hippies may not be aware that the White House chef has routinely served organic food to the Clintons, the Bushes, and now the Obamas. In fact, the world's finest chefs prefer organic produce because it tastes better. The use of powdered fertilizers causes crops to take up more water, diluting the taste. In addition, conventional produce has fewer of the enzymes and minerals that enhance flavor.

Since only 2 percent of the country's population now lives on a farm, we don't think of ourselves as having a direct role in farming, yet each of us eats an average of a ton of food every year. Farms and ranches still cover more than half our land, and consume three-fourths of our water and 70 percent percent of our antibiotics. "If you eat, drink, or pay taxes; or care about the economy, the environment, or our global reputation, what happens on farms is a central if unseen part of your life," says journalist Michael Grunwald. If this is so, what kind of farm do *you* want?[12]

· Benefits of Organic Growing and Eating ·

Protects the health of children. University of Washington researchers analyzed urine samples of 110 preschoolers, only one of whom had no measurable level of pesticides. That one child's parents ate exclusively organic food and didn't use pesticides in their home or on their lawn. EPA-documented effects in children of exposure to certain pesticides include poorer growth and impact on neurodevelopment.[13]

Protects the health and productivity of farmers. A recent Mayo Clinic study of about 1,200 Iowa farmers revealed those older than seventy were twice as likely to develop prostate cancer as men the same age who were not farmers. Researchers concluded that the difference was because of exposure to toxic chemicals.[14]

Prevents soil erosion. The Soil Conservation Service estimates that more than 3 billion tons of topsoil are eroded from United States croplands each year, eroding seven times faster than nature creates soil. In organic farming, cover crops, terracing, and high organic content prevent erosion.

Conserves energy used on farms. Organic farming produces the same yields of corn and soybeans as does conventional farming, but uses 30 percent less energy, a twenty-two-year farming trial study concludes.[15]

Prevents exposure to pesticides in the home. Pesticides are poisons designed to kill living organisms. In addition to raising the risk of cancer, pesticides are implicated in birth defects, nerve damage, and genetic mutations. Why bring these chemicals into our homes from our farms and gardens?

Promotes biodiversity on and around farms. Organic farming preserves natural habitat and biodiversity, while conventional farming typically uses methods (monocropping and pesticides) that destroy natural habitat and reduce biodiversity. Beneficial insects such as bees flourish on organic farms but often suffer from "colony collapse" on conventional farms.

Supports an emerging industry with a smaller footprint. Organic methods of growing crops generate fewer greenhouse emissions, largely because energy-intensive fertilizers and pesticides are not used.

Better flavor, more healthy nutrients per pound. Many studies give strong evidence that produce grown organically promotes nonaggressive behavior in schools and prisons and increases performance on academic exams—largely because of increased nutrient density.

"I get it," you say. "Organic is healthier and better for the environment. But that doesn't change the fact that it's more expensive." However, in real terms, organic is *less expensive* because it delivers more nutrition. It uses fewer resources to produce similar, and sometimes superior, yields, and is more resilient: organic farming is less affected by the frequency of rain or the volatility of oil prices. Organic methods perform much better in droughts because rich soil holds water far more effectively; and as oil supplies continue to dwindle, the price of organic produce will begin to seem like a bargain.

What if you had a way of prioritizing which organic products to buy? It seems logical to choose organic for the foods you eat the most and for the produce that is sprayed most heavily. Based on extensive analysis of federal pesticide test results, the Environmental Working Group recommends opting for organic with these foods:

  Dairy products: Milk, yogurt, and cheese are considered healthy bone strengtheners, especially for children, but adding hormones and antibiotics undermines the simple goodness of commercial dairy products.

Meat (including poultry and eggs): Animal products can contain antibiotics, hormones, and even heavy metals like arsenic, which is used to make animals grow fast.

Ketchup: Even besides the pesticide issue, research has shown that organic ketchup has nearly double the good-for-you antioxidants of conventional ketchup.

Coffee: Conventional coffee farming relies heavily on pesticide use and contributes to deforestation around the globe.

· The Dirty Dozen (Most Heavily Sprayed) ·

Fruits	Vegetables
• apples	• bell peppers
• cherries	• celery
• grapes, imported	• potatoes
• nectarines	• spinach
• peaches	
• pears	
• raspberries	
• strawberries	

Source: Environmental Working Group, http://www.ewg.org/node/27777.

Why not eat what our bodies are designed to eat? Humans haven't evolved fast enough to deal with processed, precooked scrambled eggs and Hot Pockets. (Hopefully our genes won't stray to accommodate these short-term fads.) Though our ancestors hunted and ate far leaner animals than we do—species closer to modern deer and elk than the typical cow—it's fashionable these days for meat to be fatty and tender, as if the goal of eating was heart disease.

➤ New Normal Agenda Point #11: Making Regional Food Webs Work

Old Perspective: Large companies like Kraft, Tyson, ConAgra, Cargill, and Nestlé have given us so much variety, so many convenient choices in all seasons of the year. Their huge scales of operation have enabled prices to remain affordable. This is the good life!

New Perspective: The food-industrial complex has made a mess of the American diet, which in turn has spread around the world. Corporate control of the growing and marketing of food has resulted in the loss of health, crop and animal diversity, family farms, cultural traditions, soil, and trust. The best way to counterbalance corporate dominance is for communities, counties, and states to strengthen their regional food webs.

THE HEAVY LIFTING

- Form a neighborhood food co-op for better food and social connection.
- Support farm-to-school programs.
- Watch for locally produced food in the supermarket.
- Support local farms in a different way: advocate the development of a municipal composting program to pick up and distribute organic food and yard wastes.

The mantra we hear time and again is that consumers vote with their dollars. True, but to express civic convictions in dollars alone is to underestimate our power to create a sustainable food system. We're far more than consumers. We're also school board members and concerned parents; farmers and scientists; shareholders and employees in food companies; and voters who influence political decisions. While some might insist that corporate farming is the only efficient way to grow food, they may not be aware that industrial food is so cheap largely because it receives heavy subsidies from taxpayers for commodity crops like corn and wheat, while fruit and vegetable growers using sustainable practices get nothing.

Consolidation in the food industry has reached freakish proportions, in the United States and globally. Corporations have bought out more than 600,000 U.S. farms since the 1960s, and now just four huge companies pack 84 percent of beef and crush 80 percent of soybeans. Corporations produce

98 percent of poultry; 2 percent of farms produce 50 percent of all agricultural products in the country. As corporate control of the food industry has increased, dietary and crop diversity has decreased: iceberg lettuce, frozen and fried potatoes, potato chips, and canned tomatoes now make up almost half of the vegetable consumption in the United States, and a mere four crops account for two-thirds of what we eat.[16]

COOPERATION

When the size and marketing clout of corporate farms threatened Wisconsin's small family farms, growers banded together to create a market niche for organic food. From its original membership of seven farmers, the Organic Valley cooperative has grown to more than 1,200 family farms across the nation, making it the largest organic farmer-owned cooperative in North America.[17] Recognizing the need for a new generation of farmers to provide locally grown food, some cities sponsor farmer training programs like Bellingham, Washington's "Food to Bank On" project, which connects beginning sustainable farms with training, mentors, and market support. Area food banks have received $50,000 in fresh produce from these farmers since the program's inception in 2003.

Civic response to the corporate dominance of agriculture has been ineffective, but it has now found its center of gravity: relocalization. Like the organic-food movement, local food has quickly come into America's mainstream, promoted in great detail by the likes of Barbara Kingsolver (*Animal, Vegetable, Miracle*), Michael Pollan (*In Defense of Food*), and Gary Nabhan (*Coming Home to Eat*). A survey of more than 1,200 chefs, many employed by chain restaurants or large food companies, identified locally grown food to be one of the hottest food trends in the country. Entrepreneurs such as Three Stone Hearth in Berkeley, California, are stepping into the niche, providing customers with home delivery of gourmet meals crafted with local produce.[18] A company called Edible Communities recently launched a network of thirty-three region-specific "Edible" magazines (e.g., *Edible Atlanta*) to promote local foods and flavors. Clearly, many Americans want flavorful food with a face.

The challenge is finding mechanisms to connect farms directly with markets and people. A small employee- and farmer-owned company in Portland, Oregon, brokers food from local farms to supermarkets. This is typically a difficult sell, since supermarkets prefer year-round deliveries of uniform, flawless produce, in large and reliable quantities. The Organically Grown Company became a persuasive agent, convincing farmers to stagger crops, purchasing backup supplies from warmer locations in Oregon and California, and ensuring that all deliveries are attractively presented. So successful have its efforts been that the company now has a staff of 160. Similarly, the geographical diversity of the Rainbow Farming Cooperative— about three hundred family farms in Wisconsin, Michigan, northern Illinois, and the South—makes produce available year-round.[19]

Cleveland, Ohio's revitalization vision is based in part on urban agriculture. The city's Food Policy Council (FPC), spearheaded by citizen activists, teamed up with city councillor Joe Cimperman, a strong supporter of urban farming because it's "good for the economy, nutrition, health, and public safety." Together, the city council and the FPC are pushing for zoning changes that will permit garden plots of one acre or more and also allow chicken raising and beekeeping.[20]

Farmers markets and farm-to-school programs are two of the most visible examples of how regional food webs can be woven. In just three decades, close to five thousand farmers markets have become local traditions in America's towns and cities. The Greenmarket system in New York City has the country's largest network, with a centerpiece market in Union Square and about sixty others in the city, including Harlem, the South Bronx, and Bedford-Stuyvesant, where blight has often left residents in urban food deserts that have no supermarkets and shops. A pilot project gives food stamp users greater access to healthy food because they can use food stamps at farmers markets.

Several variables have converged to bring farm-to-school projects into the mainstream: new federal and state regulations with nutritional requirements for schools, an epidemic of obesity among students, generous grants from various foundations, and pioneering efforts in cities like Berkeley, California. Berkeley's Unified School District approved a school lunch program that delivers "farm to fork" education about planting, growing, and biology—in addition to instilling healthy eating habits that can last a lifetime.[21] Students in more than two thousand school districts in forty states are eating farm-fresh food for school breakfast or lunch. Overall, schools report that from 3 percent to 16 percent more students eat school meals when farm-fresh food is served.[22] Many benefits besides better health for the students result from programs like these: teachers learn to incorporate food and agriculture into their curricula; parents change their shopping and cooking patterns; and food-service staff gain knowledge and interest in local food preparation.

A local food web is more resilient than a monolithic, global food web, and able to prevent large-scale catastrophe. "When a single factory is grinding 20 million hamburger patties in a week or washing 25 million servings of salad, a single terrorist armed with a canister of toxins can, at a stroke, poison millions," writes Michael Pollan. "Such a system is even more susceptible to accidental contamination: the bigger and more global the trade in food, the more vulnerable the system is. The best way to protect our food system against such threats is to decentralize it."[23]

⋄ Benefits of a Regional Food Web ⋄

- Helps reduce greenhouse gas emissions and energy use. (A typical food item travels up to 2,500 miles from farm to plate—25 percent farther than most food traveled in 1980.)

- Reduces the need for packaging and processing.

- Provides healthy produce that can be picked at its peak, providing much better flavor.

- Reconnects people with their communities and the land their food comes from.

- Eating local keeps 90 percent to 100 percent of the money you spend in your town.

- Provides accountability—the closer you are to where your food comes from, the more control you have over how it is grown.

How can individuals help weave a local food web?

- Shop at local farmers markets.

- Support farm-to-school programs, crop gleaning programs, and municipal composting to reuse local nutrients.

- Reduce food waste in households, restaurants, and supermarkets.

- Organize or participate in a Food Policy Council, in which citizens help direct local food decisions.

- Join a Community-Supported Agriculture (CSA) program, in which participants "subscribe" to produce grown by a local farmer.

- Start a community garden, or grow a garden in your yard.

➤ New Normal Agenda Point #12:
Which Direction for Food Policy, Oil or Soil?

Old Perspective: Food policy is beyond individual control, best handled by agribusiness and food-industry lobbyists and farm-state politicians. Agricultural policy should stress yield per acre and dollars per unit of food produced—in other words, quantity over quality. Food policy should be based on "what the market wants" rather than on health or environmental stability.

New Perspective: Food and farming policies are directly related to national as well as personal security, and need to assume a higher priority at all levels of decision making. In agricultural policy, we need to protect the source of our food, get more hands and minds into growing, and stress quality over quantity, since the quality of our food is a key determinant of whether our society is thriving or simply surviving. How can we make good decisions unless we're healthy and clear-headed? In food policy, nutritional science should safeguard public health, especially the health of young children, who are incapable of separating food fantasy from truth.

THE HEAVY LIFTING

- Support and advocate for sustainable food policies at all levels, from the federal farm bill to local ordinances that mandate high-quality food.

- Advocate for full disclosure of calorie contents in your favorite restaurants.

- Increase the number of courses that teach children about sustainable farming techniques.

- Support and promote a national ban or limit on the amount of junk-food advertising directed at kids.

Food policies are formulated at all levels and in all sectors of the economy. Individuals have personal policies such as "no red meat" or "five fresh fruits and vegetables, every day." They share their policies with friends and colleagues, rebuilding a dysfunctional food culture one conversation at a time. When asked their opinion by a polltaker or asked to sign an Internet petition, they are aware of the issues. Communities and cities create policies that range from sponsoring community garden networks to banning trans fats in more than twenty-five thousand restaurants, as New York City did. State and federal agencies manage the bigger picture, setting the direction for subsidies, agricultural research, and agricultural practices such as which pesticides can be used, or criteria for USDA-certified organic produce. A recent federal regulation on what can be served in school cafeterias spawned more stringent policies in states such as Kentucky, which now forbids serving any beverage that has more than 10 grams of sugar. Food-related policy and direction are also created internationally, as in the United Nations' Billion Tree Campaign, which has thus far encouraged the planting of more than 3 billion trees in 150 countries. (The goal is 7 billion, one for each human.) These protect farmland from wind erosion, hold the soil in place, and help prevent weather disasters related to global warming.

Positive changes in food policy also occur in corporations, often instigated by public pressure. For example, Tyson Foods, one of the world's largest meat producers, announced in 2007 that its poultry would no longer be treated with antibiotics, a reaction to popular demand for safer meat. Yum! Brands, the world's largest operator of fast-food chains, announced in 2008 that it would add another item to its various menus: information about the calories in each food item at KFC, Pizza Hut, Taco Bell, Long John Silver's, and A&W Restaurants. Again, public sentiment and the activism of nonprofit organizations such as the Center for Science in the Public Interest instigated this nutritional coup.

As a society, we're moving (with baby steps) beyond "fast, cheap, and easy" to a more mindful way of growing and eating food, based on values that we've held dear for millennia. In an anthropological sense, we seem to perceive, at last, that industrial food is a threat from "outside the community" that requires us to mobilize to protect ourselves. Certainly, we are on strong moral ground: Western scriptures, including the Bible, the Talmud, and the Koran, are in absolute agreement that food is a moral, even sacred, substance; that it should be grown and eaten with humility and gratitude; with empathy for and stewardship of animals and plants, and generosity toward fellow humans. In our times, the ethics of food have become straightforward: use water, energy, and land more efficiently and mindfully, or watch the civilization unravel. "We need to quickly wean the American food system off its heavy 20th-century diet of fossil fuel and put it back on a diet of contemporary sunshine," insists food expert Michael Pollan. In a *New York Times* essay, "Farmer in Chief," he suggests radical changes in U.S. farm and food policy to incoming President Obama (some are included in the table at page

108). Pollan is especially troubled about the current farm bill, which is revised and amended about every four or five years:

> For the last several decades U.S. agricultural policy has promoted the overproduction of five commodities, especially corn and soy. . . . The result? A food system awash in added sugars (derived from corn) and added fats (derived mainly from soy), as well as dirt-cheap meat and milk (derived from both). The real price of fruits and vegetables between 1985 and 2000 increased by nearly 40 percent while the real price of soft drinks (aka liquid corn) declined by 23 percent.[24]

Pollan documents the inverse relationship between cheap food and expensive health care: "It is no coincidence that in the years national spending on health care went from 5 percent to 16 percent of national income, spending on food has fallen by a comparable amount—from 18 percent of household income to less than 10 percent."[25] The money saved on cheap food is more than wasted later, in the form of taxes (for crop subsidies), health insurance premiums, doctor bills, community dysfunction, reduced worker productivity, environmental cleanup, and habitat destruction.

In large part because of federal policy, family farms are withering while corporate farms are getting plump. President Jimmy Carter, who grew up on a peanut and cotton farm, explains why: "From 1995 to 2005, the richest 10 percent of cotton growers received more than 80 percent of total subsidies, while more than half of America's cotton farmers received no subsidies at all. American producers of cotton received more than $18 billion in subsidies between 1999 and 2005, while market value of the cotton was $23 billion. That's a subsidy of 86 percent!"[26] Between 1982 and 2007, farms with incomes less than $250,000 a year declined by 32 percent, while monster farms with revenues larger than $5 million increased by 220 percent.[27]

Food is much more than a political or an economic issue, much more than a collection of trends and styles. Arguably, the reliability of food supplies in a climate- and water-challenged world is the largest security challenge humanity has ever faced. "We are in a race between tipping points in natural and political systems," says Lester Brown of the Earth Policy Institute. From farm to plate, our industrial food system depends on cheap supplies of oil (for fertilizer, farm machinery, transportation, processing, refrigeration, and preparation), and as the ever-expanding world population eats more processed food and meat from distant sources, the energy consumed by the food sector continues to rise. This may result in many global warming impacts directly related to agriculture. "Rising temperatures, falling water tables," summarizes Brown in his data-rich book, *Plan B 4.0*.[28] To give just one example cited in the book, if the Himalayan and Tibetan glaciers that feed China's and India's largest rivers continue to melt, grain production in the world's largest grain-producing countries—China and India—will plummet right off the graph. And in a supply-and-demand-driven economy, the prices of grain, meat, milk, and many processed foods will skyrocket.

◆ Selected Policies to Help American Agriculture ◆ Become More Sustainable

Food Policy	Desired Result	Who Does It
Guidelines to limit junk food advertising to kids.	Reduce the $10 billion spent annually on ads directed at kids, to reduce health-related Impacts.	Norway, Sweden, and Quebec have banned all advertising on children's TV programs; the UK has set nutrition standards for food advertising.
Support requirements that fast-food and chain restaurants must display calorie content on menus.	More than 75 percent of Americans want to know what they are eating so they can eat healthier.	Citizen and nonprofit activism have already driven company policy, and several states will soon pass laws.
Form Food Policy Councils (FPCs) at the local level, with active involvement of local citizens	FPCs empower citizens to help create food and agricultural policy.	100 FPCs in the U.S. help establish farmers markets, use vacant lots as gardens, and conduct other actions that strengthen the local food web.
Implement municipal composting to utilize food waste from homes, restaurants, and processors.	Free access to food and yard waste can help small farmers stay in business and can reduce the environmental impacts of fertilizer overuse.	San Francisco has a city-scale composting program for food, food-soiled paper, and plant waste with a goal of 75 percent participation by 2010.
Shift subsidies from quantity to quality of food, rewarding farmers who preserve soil and water and grow healthy food.	When U.S. food policy changes direction, American health care costs will fall, and biological habitat will increase.	The U.S. Conservation Reserve Program paid farmers to retire cropland for 1–15 years. Build on that success.

Food Policy	Desired Result	Who Does It
Offer incentives for farming practices that sequester carbon dioxide, such as increases in organic soil content, cover crops, and private forests	Agriculture can play a major role in climate change policy, however conventional agriculture will not be as effective.	New Zealand will incorporate agriculture in its emission trading scheme; NZ is also spending millions to reduce livestock emissions through breeding and feed upgrades.
Increase the number and quality of degrees in sustainable agriculture and ecological farming systems.	Increasing the opportunities in farming can create millions of "green jobs" and boost regional economies, helping create a post-petroleum, sustainable economy.	Notable eco-farming curricula are offered at UC Davis, Cal Polytechnic, U. of Washington, Iowa State U., U. of Hawaii, and Evergreen State College.
Preserve and restore farmland in metropolitan areas.	Reconnects residents with the source of their food; reduces transportation, processing, and packaging.	Fairview Gardens in Goleta, CA. is completely surrounded by suburbia. Inner-city farms in Detroit and Cleveland are models.

➤ New Normal Agenda Point #13: Urban Agriculture: Produce for People or for Profit?

Old Perspective: Farming is "undesirable work" that does not pay well unless the farm is huge with millions of dollars of high-tech machinery. Modern agriculture is so efficient that only 2 percent of the U.S. population needs to farm, compared with 90 percent in Thomas Jefferson's era, and 30 percent when Teddy Roosevelt took office.

New Perspective: Many studies indicate that large gardens and small farms are more productive per acre than large farms, but require more highly skilled labor, done by people with more knowledge about the ecology of a farm or garden system. Growing fruits, vegetables, and grains is once again seen as a desirable way of life that delivers many values at one time: a meaningful and useful way to spend time; health that comes from stimulation, exercise, and fresh food; relationships with people to grow and market the food. Urban agriculture takes advantage of good underlying soil, which was typically one reason why people settled where the city now is.

THE HEAVY LIFTING

- Support zoning changes and city council representation that encourage urban agriculture.

- Help administer tool-sharing and knowledge-sharing cooperatives to encourage urban gardening and farming.

Up to 30 percent of America's food is now grown in metropolitan areas where 93 percent of Americans live. Rural farmland continues to vanish because of erosion, water scarcity, industrial and retail development, and urban sprawl. (Sprawl alone causes annual cropland losses equal to a swath of land half a mile wide, stretching from New York to San Francisco.)[29]

Fairview Gardens Farm in Goleta, California, is a classic example of a metro farm that literally held its ground. Now completely surrounded by cul-de-sacs, shopping malls, and picket fences, the 12.5-acre farm stayed in business by becoming a nonprofit organization in 1997. The mission of the Center for Urban Agriculture is to preserve the region's agricultural heritage and demonstrate that sustainable agriculture can coexist with suburban development—an unfamiliar yet very valuable partnership. The center offers five hundred families a cornucopia of a hundred different fruits and vegetables, also nourishing the community with cooking and gardening classes, workshops, farm festivals, tours, lectures, apprenticeships, and hands-on school programs. "We incorporate experiential learning opportunities like digging up a carrot and tasting its sweetness, or studying the strawberry with all five senses," explains the center's Web site. "Students investigate soil, complete farm chores and even collect warm eggs."

But it wasn't always a beautiful day in the neighborhood, as founder-farmer Michael Ableman details in his book *On Good Land*. At first the surrounding suburbanites hated the sound of the roosters and tractor, and the earthy smell of organic soil. But Ableman and his crew gradually won the neighbors over with chemical-free fruits and vegetables, from arugula to heirloom zucchini. It became the well-loved farm in the center—a model for how a neighborhood might feed itself in the challenging years ahead, when oil is no longer cheap.

The citizens of Cuba have already experienced a post-oil scenario and adapted, out of desperation. When the Soviet Union fell apart, Cuba was left to fend for itself, since the island nation depended on Soviet imports for oil, food, fertilizer, and pesticides. From 1989 to 1993, the Cuban economy contracted by 35 percent, and foreign trade fell by three-fourths. Writes journalist Jason Mark, "The average per-capita calorie intake fell from 2,900 a day in 1989 to 1,800 calories in 1995. Protein consumption plummeted 40 percent. As Cubans lost weight, cats disappeared from the streets of Havana, destined for family soup pots."[30]

Havana resident Vilda Figueroa was one of the first urban gardeners in a grassroots culture shift in which gardens spontaneously sprouted in urban nooks and crannies all over the city: in vacant lots, in strips next to parking lots, at the edges of garbage dumps, and even on rooftops. Even the lawns of municipal and office buildings morphed into carefully tended garden plots. Figueroa and her husband began to train other city residents to grow fruits and vegetables, and the knowledge spread quickly. Seeing the energy and potential of this movement, city government established an urban agriculture department that made food production legal on unused land.

The city provided agricultural expertise, seed banks, compost, biological controls, and tools. Astoundingly, thirty-five thousand acres of urban gardens soon produced 3.4 million tons of food. In 2009, about 90 percent of Havana's fresh produce was grown by more than thirty thousand people on eight thousand plots that ranged from the size of a bedsheet to a city block. Now, not only is daily caloric intake back to 1989 levels, but, according to some reports, Havana residents are beginning to worry about obesity.

Could a change like this, from industrial to small-scale agriculture, happen in the United States, countering the land-hungry expansion of the last fifty years? Certainly not at the same pace as in Cuba; however, in cities like Detroit, Cleveland, and others—victims of the vanishing-factory syndrome—urban agriculture is already happening on a large scale. Detroit's population began to fall in the 1960s after civil unrest, and the city spiraled downward because of chronic unemployment. Today, a city built for a population of 2 million has less than 1 million residents. The exodus hollowed out one-third of the city's area, leaving more than forty thousand vacant lots—an estimated 40 square miles of empty space. What's emerging is sprawl in reverse: a suburban ring around a rerualized core. Like Havana, Detroit faced challenges that required a new identity, which some residents refer to as "from Motor City to Garden City."

More than eighty acres have been converted to agriculture through the Detroit Garden Resource Program Collaborative. This umbrella consortium's member groups train a cross-section of Detroit residents in soil building, composting, crop cultivation, beekeeping, and fruit-tree planting. In various neighborhoods, "toolbanks" provide tools, compost, mulch, tomato stakes, seeds, and transplants inexpensively, and offer gardening classes and workdays. When the housing meltdown of 2008 cut still deeper into Detroit's damaged real estate, county officials allowed nonprofits to grow produce on twenty tax-foreclosed vacant properties. Much of that produce is distributed to low-income residents through soup kitchens and Youth Farm Stands.

Building on the momentum, local businessman John Hantz recently proposed establishing the world's largest urban farm on Detroit's lower east side. He hopes that city, county, and state governments will sell cheaply or donate 70 acres of land for Phase 1 of his project, with payback coming in increased tax revenues.[31]

So far, Milwaukee, Wisconsin, has zoned as "agricultural" only one parcel of land within its city limits. But given the unqualified success of Growing Power, there may soon be other urban agriculture projects in the city. Since 1993, Will Allen, a recipient of a MacArthur Foundation "genius" fellowship, has nurtured the Growing Power project, providing 159 varieties of food from many sources (including vegetables and fruit from its fourteen greenhouses, goats, ducks, bees, turkeys, and two kinds of fish in aquaponic tanks). Growing Power composts more than 6 million pounds of local food waste a year from sources including the farm's own waste, discarded food from local food distributors, spent grain from a local brewery, and coffee grounds from a local café.[32]

The two-acre parcel of land is right in the middle of what Allen calls a food desert. There are no grocery stores in the neighborhood, but lots of fast-food joints, liquor stores, and convenience stores that don't offer much in the way of nutrition. But Growing Power is an oasis, offering fresh produce, free-range eggs, grass-fed beef, and homegrown honey, even in winter. The company also markets "Farm-to-City Market Baskets": weekly deliveries of twelve to fifteen varieties of produce for $16. Each week, Growing Power distributes 275 to 350 such baskets to more than twenty agencies, community centers, and senior citizens.[33]

· Benefits of Urban Agriculture ·

- Reclaims marginal and abandoned land, also providing tax revenues.

- Reduces transportation-related energy consumption.

- Makes healthy food accessible to local residents, including low-income, underserved populations.

- Educates students and lifelong learners about how to grow fruits and vegetables.

- Provides pleasant green spaces for recreation such as "horticultural therapy."

- Reduces the impacts of industrial farming on natural habitats and biological diversity.

- Provides jobs for urban residents—part-time and full-time.

- Makes use of urban resources that would otherwise be waste, such as storm water runoff and food waste from restaurants, workplaces, processing companies, and households.

- Can be a community center, as the Cheyenne Botanic Garden in Cheyenne, Wyoming, is—providing rehabilitation for at-risk youth and recreation for the elderly.

➤ New Normal Agenda Point #14: Taking the Lawn into Our Own Hands: Grass Clippings or Juicy Strawberries?

Old Perspective: Gardening is a hobby for the elderly—"little old ladies with blue sneakers." It's too slow to be exciting, and what you harvest isn't worth the headache of fighting bugs, pulling weeds, and making sure the crops get water. It's impossible to fit into my schedule, and I can get all the produce I need at the supermarket. Besides, it's not "cool" to be a gardener.

New Perspective: It *is* cool to be a gardener in today's changing culture. Gardening provides a way to express yourself; a way to be engaged, challenged, focused, and caregiving, all basic human needs. For those whose personalities and aptitudes are a good match with growing food, gardening is not an "extra" activity, but can become a central activity—even a way of life. Time spent in the garden is not an expense but a form of income and personal growth.

THE HEAVY LIFTING

- Create edible landscapes where you live, work, and go to church. Start small, but think big: plant your favorite vegetable or fruit, in either a container or a special little bed filled with loamy compost you made yourself. When you find you can't stop thinking about your tomatoes or strawberries, expand beyond where you live. A strawberry patch behind the church rectory? A tomato patch outside an office that's surrounded by more than blacktop? Who knows? Backyard chickens and a bin of composting worms at the town hall just might be in your future.

When we take the risk of planting a seed or a tree, we step right into the flow of nature. We become part of a daring experiment in which the seed is hope and the tomato is joy—juicy, flavorful joy. Ironically, life's mysteries become more manageable as the garden presents greater challenges. Between 2008 and 2009, the percentage of Americans who risked time and energy to grow fruits, herbs, and vegetables increased by 19 percent, according to a survey conducted by Harris Interactive. (And the previous year was also up, by 10 percent.) Picture 43 million households putting off mowing the lawn to instead hoe rows of bell peppers and strawberries. Why the increased interest? Fifty-eight percent of U.S. gardeners say they want better-tasting food, and about half want to make sure it's healthier and safer. In today's economy, 54 percent also want to save money on their grocery bills. One gardening family tallied up the value of the previous year's yield, and subtracted expenses. "If we consider that our out-of-pocket costs were $282 and the total value generated was $2,431, that means we had a return on investment of 862 percent," says Maine resident Roger Doiron.[34]

It's clear that Americans are paying more attention to the quality of our food. We are much more interested in where it comes from and how it's grown. After thirty years of gardening in Colorado, I know the agonies and ecstasies of growing. We gardeners of the Rocky Mountains and high plains face daily trials by fire—drought, hail, fluke frosts, and watering restrictions among them. We develop thick, redneck skins, and when hailstones the size of river rock shred the lettuce a few hours before a dinner party, our first inclination may be to throw childish tantrums and vow never to garden again. Instead, many of us lace up our boots and get out the seeds. Why? Because gardening meets a wide range of human needs.

I looked at economist Manfred Max-Neef's list of human needs the other day, which reminded me that the "food-miles" of a given backyard vegetable can better be measured in feet; that the best way to know if your food is safe is to grow it yourself; and that gardening is a challenging sport you can eat. If what we truly value in life are subsistence, protection, affection, understanding, participation, leisure, creation, identity, and freedom, gardening delivers about 100 percent. So when we take the lawn into our own hands, we don't have to feel like we're in a hurry, since just about everything we genuinely need is already provided, if we slow down and harvest both the food and the satisfaction. Gardening is not an add-on activity, but a possible replacement for trips to the mall, staying late at the office, watching one more TV crime show, or aimlessly surfing the Web.

Gardening allows us to be active producers rather than passive consumers, and it gives us a sense of control over what's in our food. With stickers from all over the world, conventional food is impossible to hold accountable. (E.g., pesticides that were banned years ago in the United States are still used in other countries.) Gardening also provides stress reduction, exercise, healthy food, and connection with nature.

So it shouldn't be surprising when we meet or read about people like Kipp Nash and Debbie Dalrymple, whose enthusiasm for gardening runs so deep that they garden their own lawns and their neighbors' too. Nash is a thirty-two-year-old green-thumbed bus driver who came to Boulder, Colorado, looking for a way to learn about farming. But farmland near Boulder is by no means cheap, and after he had fully planted his own yard, the only land available was the back and front yards of neighbors. He began asking them to let his start-up company design and dig gardens in their yards in exchange for produce from the garden. Doing his gardening between the morning and afternoon school bus runs, Nash keeps some produce and sells the rest to Neighborhood Supported Agriculture customers and local restaurants. He now has thirteen yards in his minifarm system, totaling close to half an acre, and still likes to watch the faces of passersby as he works in clients' front-yard gardens. "Wow, they're growing food in their front yard," Nash hears them say. "That makes so much sense; why aren't we all doing that?"

When Debbie Dalrymple came back from a year of travel, the weeds in her yard were four and five feet tall. "I decided to turn most of my lawn into a garden," she recalls. "It made more sense than replanting grass. I started having so much fun that I wondered if other people would want to do it too." When she heard Kipp Nash speak at a Go Local conference, she knew her idea of gardening the neighbors' yards could work, and she began to piece together what is now a fifteen-yard farm. She asks for a three-year commitment from participants, who are each automatically enrolled as subscribers in her Community Supported Agriculture (CSA) venture. They harvest produce from their own yards and also receive weekly baskets from Debbie's other harvests. She plants high-maintenance crops like carrots and tomatoes in yards that are closest to her house, and low-maintenance crops like winter squash in more remote yards, creating computer-generated designs of each yard to optimize solar, soil, and sidewalk conditions. When a crop is about ready to be harvested, she e-mails recipes to her patron-clients, suggesting a melt-in-your-mouth eggplant parmesan dish to use the ripe eggplants at the end of the row. "I have never loved anything this much," she says, with a tone of grateful disbelief.

From my own perspective, there are many benefits and few disadvantages in converting lawns—at least partially—into edible landscapes. For the past ten years, my front lawn has been a lush, fragrant ground cover of strawberry plants; I really haven't noticed a downside to this variation on an American theme. Probably the greatest benefit is watching through my kitchen window as neighborhood kids sneak into my yard and steal strawberries, an adventure they may remember years from now. Whatever berries the kids overlook, the birds get, but there's another boxed-in strawberry patch out in the garden, so who cares? I feel great knowing I've taken one small square out of the 23-million-acre green quilt that blankets America. Americans pay $30 billion a year to maintain that quilt, an average per-lawn expense of about $500. As America's largest single crop, the lawn consumes about 270 billion gallons of water each week, enough to instead water 81 million acres of organic vegetables.[35]

Lawns use ten times as many chemicals per acre as industrial farmland, and more than half of those herbicides and fertilizers are wasted, washing into our rivers, lakes, and streams. The luxurious power mowers that now dominate our neighborhoods emit more air pollution in an hour than a 1990s-vintage car emits in eight hours or 350 miles—and as much noise as a jackhammer. As with many other choices in this book, deciding which lawn mower or herbicide to choose becomes irrelevant and unnecessary if you decide to unplant your lawn and plant a garden instead.

What if you don't have a lawn to convert? Join a community garden, or even start one. In my hometown (Golden, Colorado) a group of residents approached the city's sustainability coordinator about starting a garden, and quickly found out that city staff had been brainstorming where a community garden could go. After assessing five or six likely sites, the group has found a home. According to the American Community Gardening Association's Web site, the steps to starting a community garden are fairly straightforward: convene a group of neighbors, community organizations, and church members; form a planning committee; assess the skills of group members; find a sponsor; find a site; provide a solid communication network; put rules and expectations in writing; publicize the garden; and harvest your first salad greens.

What kind of gardening techniques should you use? There are many variations on organic growing, but one of the most methodical and successful is biointensive, a system developed by Californian John Jeavons, author of the bestselling garden bible *How to Grow More Vegetables*. These techniques are essentials in the biointensive system of growing.

· Biointensive Gardening Techniques ·

Double-dug, raised beds	Soil is loosened to a depth of 24 inches, aerating the soil, facilitating root growth, and improving water retention.
Composting	Maintains the health and vigor of the soil, providing micronutrients and billions of busy microbes.
Intensive planting	Encourages soil microbes, reduces water loss, and maximizes yields.
Carbon farming and calorie farming	A focus on the production of calories for the farmer and carbon for the soil ensures that both the farmer and the soil will be adequately fed.
Use of open-pollinated seeds	Open-pollinated (nonhybridized) seeds help preserve genetic diversity and produce cultivars specific to a garden's conditions.

Source: http://www.growbiointensive.org/.

Says Jeavons, "Our research has rediscovered the scientific principles that underlie millennia-old traditional farming systems, which make it possible to grow food with 67 percent to 88 percent less water, 50 percent to 100 percent less fertilizer, and 99 percent less energy than commercial agriculture, producing two to six times more food per unit of land."[36]

➤ New Normal Agenda Point #15: Changing the Climate, or Changing the Way We Farm?

Old Perspective: Conventional agriculture is a stewardship profession, working with natural systems to produce what humans need at affordable prices. Environmental impacts are justified by the need to feed hungry people.

New Perspective: Agriculture as an industry is not as "natural" as it was seventy-five years ago. The process of growing food emits more greenhouse gases than the transportation sector, and more than manufacturing and residential emissions combined. It is the most unregulated sector in the global economy. For example, while wastewater treatment plants are required for *humans* in all industrial countries, no such treatment is required for the planet's 20 billion livestock, whose wastes generate huge volumes of methane and nitrous oxide. Agriculture offers huge opportunities to reduce the threat of global warming if we make fundamental changes in the way we farm.

THE HEAVY LIFTING

- Encourage a cultural transition back to organic agriculture that will store more carbon in the soil, provide more jobs, and consume less energy.

- Produce and consume less meat, which will have multiple benefits: fewer greenhouse emissions, better overall health, greater energy efficiency, and less chance of spreading diseases via antibiotic-resistant microbes.

When we think about the causes of global warming, we're more likely to point a finger at coal-fired power plants and buildings with poorly insulated roofs than at farm fields. Yet, recent data indicate that the food system as a sector is the largest emitter of greenhouse gases. Livestock production alone contributes 18 percent, and other agricultural practices such as fertilizer production and use, irrigation, and the operation of farm machinery contribute at least another 5 percent. The impacts of our industrialized food system don't stop there, however. In fact, the *growing* of food accounts for only a fifth of the energy used to bring food to our tables. The other four-fifths is used to move, process, package, sell, store, preserve, and prepare food. The refrigerator emits far more carbon dioxide than the tractor.

Agriculture produces greenhouse gases in several basic ways: direct use of fossil fuels to power machinery; application of both manufactured fertilizers (which are energy-intensive) and manure (which emits methane) to fields, and decomposition of wastes; radical indigestion in cattle, which can digest grass perfectly but not grain; deforestation to clear land for crops and grazing; and soil tillage that releases gases from the soil.

The Worldwatch Institute's 2009 report on the state of the world, *Into a Warming Planet,* identifies five strategies to help reduce greenhouse-gas emissions:

- Put more carbon and compost into the soil (fundamentals of organic farming).

- Grow a higher percentage of carbon-storing crops (including cover crops) on farmland.

- Raise livestock with more climate-friendly methods (including a higher percentage of range-fed meat).

- Protect existing forests and grasslands to absorb greenhouse gases.

- Restore vegetation in degraded areas to absorb gases.

Though these strategies may seem inaccessible to a largely nonfarming population, there are several key ways that citizen-consumers can help change the way food is produced (no small challenge, since agriculture is a ten-millennia-long habit). By helping to reverse two key dietary trends of the past half century—fossil-fueled food and relentless increases in meat consumption—each of us can play a leading role in preventing climatic catastrophe. An increase in the consumption of organic food will help store more carbon in the soil, and a decrease in per capita consumption of meat can reduce all three major greenhouse gases: carbon dioxide, from fertilizer manufacture and deforestation to raise livestock; nitrous oxide emissions from manufactured fertilizers (used to grow the grains and soybeans that fatten livestock before slaughter); and methane, which is emitted from livestock and their manure. Methane and nitrous oxide are many times more potent greenhouse gases than carbon dioxide, a primary reason why livestock production is a global-warming nightmare.

If we think about food and agriculture systems not just logically (profit, price, and yield) but *bio*logically, fundamental flaws are right in our faces. First, our reliance on nonrenewable resources like fossil fuels creates a sense that stewardship of soil and water are less necessary. Yet, agriculture is quintessentially solar-powered and can lead the way to a future powered by renewable energy. Second, we're doing very strange things with food: cattle are designed to eat grass, but we force-feed them grain in crowded feedlots, which requires massive doses of antibiotics. (Seventy percent of the antibiotics produced in the United States are fed to livestock.) We are grain-eating omnivores who can't digest grass and require only 30 to 50 grams of protein a day, yet we eat more like 110 grams a day including a half a pound of meat, which in turn causes health effects like heart disease, cancer, and diabetes. Isn't it time to rethink both the way we eat and the way we farm?

Yes, personal as well as cultural changes will be necessary, but once the overall direction is set, the changes can be incremental and relatively painless. We can get a lot of mileage out of a few simple dietary changes. For example, eating no meat on a given day is like driving about twenty-five fewer miles in a car with average fuel efficiency. If every American took on this meat-free-day challenge, it would be like taking 8 million cars off American roads.

Maybe, in addition to starting a garden on the White house lawn, the first family should challenge each household to learn a few gourmet meatless recipes every few months. Instead of bacon and eggs for breakfast, try hunger-busting ten-grain cereal and fresh fruit. Instead of burgers for lunch, prepare pita sandwiches filled with fresh vegetables and hummus. Instead of steak for dinner, serve pasta topped with fresh tomatoes and pesto. According to a group of Swedish researchers, producing a pound of beef creates eleven times as much greenhouse-gas emission as a pound of chicken and one hundred times more than a pound of carrots, so it appears we will be far more sustainable if we find a few good recipes for chicken curry and carrot cake.[37]

As our personal and national dietary habits change, we help level an upward trend in developing countries like India and China, since meat eating is largely about keeping up with the Joneses in other industrialized countries. We also send a clear signal to the world's farmers: that we value the preservation of a stable climate, one of our most precious, commonly shared assets.

4

Getting Carbon Out of Our Systems

Because technological innovation and social consensus can move so fast, predictions about seismic shifts in the economy often lag behind reality. For example, there were whispers in the early 1990s about an "information superhighway"; but before any of us fully grasped what this might mean, dozens of computer wizards had already become billionaires, a digital infrastructure had self-assembled, and millions of employees and Web surfers suddenly materialized in front of humming machines that retrieved data faster than a speedy base runner can steal second. And the electronic beat pulses on.

So it was with the sleight-of-hand creation of the suburbs in the 1950s, a convergence of affordable land, a national infatuation with automobiles, and incentives from the federal government that instantly reshaped the entire culture. Fourteen million heroic military personnel with sudden-family syndrome starred in a made-for-TV drama about GI families who now occupied *American* territory. Economists, politicians, and investors were giddy about what this mass movement did for the GDP, although in a sense we had declared war on our own soil, deploying bulldozers in place of tanks.

Then there was oil, a surprise inheritance that quickly became an addictive, intravenous way of life. When oil was first pumped out of the Pennsylvania ground in the 1850s, it was considered a nuisance by drillers looking for water; but in the blink of a historical eye there were more than half a billion cars on the world's roads and highways (whose drivers often texted, shaved, and wolfed fast food as they dodged oncoming traffic). The design of cities was radically altered in the age of petroleum—along with the way we use land, the logistics of the food system, the manufacture and distribution of products, the nature of tourism and business travel, and especially, the pulse of finance.

In each major social shift, the time was right and the new way of life spread exponentially. The equation Change = Economic Growth was common to all these shifts, and it also applies to the global energy rush that is now revving up. "The powerful interaction of advancing technology, private investment, and policy reform have led to a pace of change unseen since Thomas Edison and Henry Ford created the last great energy revolution a century ago," writes Christopher Flavin, director of the prestigious Worldwatch Institute.[1] Suddenly, energy efficiency and renewable technologies have become one of history's brightest hopes, maybe just in time to avert climatic upheaval, looming resource wars, and soaring oil and food prices. Even those who are terrified of change realize they'd better get on board or be left at the station. The Earth Policy Institute's Lester Brown is noticeably relieved, after decades of tireless green advocacy: "This energy transition is being driven by the intensely exciting realization that we are now tapping energy sources that can last as long as the earth itself."[2]

Once again, reality is dancing circles around prediction. Although the carbon industry spends millions to portray the renewable-energy revolution as immature and impotent, a coalition among governments, industry, and nonprofit organizations thinks otherwise. They are innovating, investing in, and installing new energy technologies at a clip reminiscent of the 1990s computer and cell phone booms. From out of nowhere, clean energy is suddenly in the race, outperforming old energy in venture capital investments and plant start-ups. Beginning in 2006, renewable energy (including large hydropower) generated more electricity than the world's roughly four hundred nuclear power plants. Between 2000 and 2005, global wind energy capacity more than tripled, and in the United States alone, the wind industry grew tenfold in the last decade, recently lapping Germany as the world's largest generator of wind power.

With 31 gigawatts of installed wind capacity in 2009, the United States suddenly produced enough juice to power 8 million American homes. In 2008 and 2009, more than two hundred wind farms came online, and thousands more are queued up, waiting to tie into an expanding grid. At current growth rates, the wind industry is on a trajectory to generate one-fifth of the nation's electricity by 2030, especially if federal tax credits and utility commission incentives remain in place. Installed U.S. wind power already avoids CO_2 emissions equivalent to those of 9 million cars, and the benefits range far beyond the green part of the spectrum. At the end of 2008, about eighty-five thousand Americans were employed in the wind industry, including operators, "prospectors," manufacturers, and marketers.[3] In addition, wind projects boost many local tax bases, and support rural economies by providing steady income—wind royalties—to farmers and ranchers who then spend money in the local economy.

The solar cell industry is also growing, at 40 percent a year in the United States, led by California, where more than fifty thousand home-owners have already installed solar panels on their roofs. On a larger scale, fifteen solar *thermal* power plants are planned in California, Arizona, and Nevada. These "power towers" use large sun-tracking mirrors to concentrate sunlight and generate electricity with steam-powered turbines. New heat-storing technologies enable solar thermal plants to extend their hours of power generation for up to six hours past sunset, enabling the plants to take advantage of premium peak-hour profits.

Similarly, breakthroughs in geothermal technology enable power generation from lower-temperature underground sources than in the past. About a hundred geothermal plants are now under construction, and research estimates from various government and academic sources indicate that geothermal energy in the United States could supply the equivalent of one hundred large coal-fired power plants by 2030. Biomass and biofuels are also expanding exponentially, as researchers continue to investigate the potentials of various plant species as fuel and chemical feedstock, since corn-based ethanol (now the primary biofuel in the United States) has a low net energy ratio and displaces land needed for food and feed crops. However, there is no doubt that biofuels from more efficient sources (such as algae) will play a role in fueling next-generation cars and machinery, and that plants will be a major source of industrial molecules in the not-too-distant future.

From a wide array of data, Christopher Flavin estimates that solar hot-water heaters could provide half the world's residential and industrial hot water; solar cells could easily supply 10 percent of grid electricity in the United States by 2030; solar thermal plants in the U.S. Southwest could at some point meet all American electricity demand; and wind power generated in Great Plains states like Wyoming, Texas, Kansas, and the Dakotas could also provide as much electricity as America currently consumes.[4]

So what are we waiting for? Answer: finally, we are *not* waiting, though there are still some obstacles to be removed—like a lack of strategically located and integrated transmission lines—before the energy revolution can proceed at full speed.

➤ Following the Money

The potentials for energy efficiency, strongly supported by federal stimulus spending in 2009, are almost as impressive as the prospects for renewable energy.[5]

With opportunities like these, a Niagara Falls of capital is starting to flow into "clean technology," even in a troubled economy. Says John Doerr, one of the early investors in Google, "Green technologies could be the largest economic opportunity of the 21st century."[6] According to a 2009 study published by the Pew Charitable Trusts, the clean-energy economy grew 9.1 percent between 1998 and 2007, providing 777,000 jobs in an emerging economic sector. However, 2008 was the year that energy investments caught Wall Street's attention, as investments in alternative fuels, electricity, storage technology, and efficiency (mostly in buildings and various industrial processes) rose 83 percent in one year, outperforming telecommunications, media, and other hot sectors. One hundred fifteen "clean-tech" mergers or acquisitions occurred in the first half of 2008, which began to remind investors of the computer bonanza.

Although the financial meltdown of late 2008 slowed the flow of all capital, alternative fuels, electricity generation, energy efficiency, and smart grid technologies rebounded by mid-2009. President Obama's immediate attention to regulatory opportunities such as increased appliance and automobile efficiency standards sent a clear signal that the energy paradigm was indeed changing. The American Recovery and Reinvestment Act put nearly $85 billion worth of financial muscle behind the new president's campaign promises: direct spending and tax incentives for energy and transportation projects, much of which took effect in 2010.

In addition, Clean Energy Funds in thirteen or more states now support renewable energy development through grants, subsidies, and loans worth more than $3.5 billion, and many cities are using bond financing and revolving-loan funds to support the energy revolution as well. Though still hypersensitive to high-risk loans, megabanks such as Wells Fargo further extended the credibility of energy financing by issuing $2 billion in loans for green building projects and $700 million for solar and wind projects.

Though Florida calls itself "the Sunshine State," and Texas—once the oil capital of the world—is presently the wind capital, it is clearly California that offers the most evidence that the energy revolution is real. Writes *Time* magazine journalist Michael Grunwald, "California is not just ahead of the game; it's playing a different game."[7] After the energy crises of the 1970s, California policy makers shifted gears. A key legislative decision decoupled

California utility profits from energy usage, enabling companies like Pacific Gas & Electric and Southern California Edison to make money by promoting energy efficiency and renewable energy. At the same time, the state enacted groundbreaking efficiency standards for buildings and appliances, including, most recently, flat-screen TVs. The results speak for themselves: per capita consumption of natural gas in California has dropped by about 50 percent since 1970, and energy use has remained stable in the Golden State while soaring 50 percent in the rest of the country. Californians have avoided $56 billion in energy bills as well as the need for twenty-four new gas-fired power plants.

California has long been a trendsetter and trailblazer. From the roof of the NASDAQ-indexed SunPower Corporation in Richmond, California, you can look into the past: across the bay are the hulking silhouettes of Chevron oil storage tanks, but the five thousand employees at SunPower have shifted to a different era, assembling and marketing some of the world's most efficient solar panels. The company builds solar farms for utilities, such as a 25-megawatt facility for Florida Power & Light (currently America's largest solar-panel plant); roof panels for big-box stores and subdivisions; and also lots of panels for homeowners in the Bay Area, where 40 percent of the nation's solar roofs collect free energy.

The California energy nexus—which has attracted about 60 percent of U.S. clean-energy investments since 2006—demonstrates a crossover from fields as diverse as semiconductor technology, computer engineering, physics, biotechnology, and aerodynamics. For example, many companies that made their name in the 1990s computer boom are now venturing into green energy. Cisco, which assembled the inner workings of the Internet, will now help assemble the "smart" transmission grid. Soladigm is using semiconductor-industry expertise to make energy-efficient windows. Down the coast, San Diego has recently become the epicenter of research on converting algae to energy, recently scoring a $600 million joint venture between ExxonMobil and Synthetic Genomics.

Globally, some of the world's largest corporations are vying for a piece of the action, including giants like Dow Chemical, Duke Energy, Ford, and General Motors. Applied Materials is focusing on solar photovoltaic energy; (PV), GE, on wind; DuPont, on biofuels; Goldman Sachs, on wind and utility-scale solar; and Royal Dutch Shell, on wind, hydrogen, and solar PV. It's way too late to lampoon or downplay renewable energy; the race is on.

• High-Leverage Examples of the Energy Revolution •

Project or Program	Results
Germany achieved world leadership in renewable energy by passing binding legislation that specified national targets from renewable energy for electricity.	In 2007, clean energy generated 250,000 green jobs and $38.8 billion in associated economic activity in Germany. The original target of 12.5% of total electrical production by 2010 was met three years early, and upgraded to 45% by 2030.
Japan sets industrywide efficiency targets, based on the most efficient industry example.	Partly by making industries like cement and steel increasingly efficient nationwide, Japan consumes one-half as much energy per dollar of economic activity as the United States.
Adobe Systems in San Jose, California, performed extensive upgrades on its headquarters building in energy, water, waste, and materials.	Electricity use was cut by 35%, natural gas use by 41%. The initial investment of $1.4 million was paid back in about a year, and annual energy savings at the huge facility are $1.2 million.
Whole Foods became the only Fortune 500 company in 2006 to offset 100% of its electricity use, by purchasing renewable energy credits (sold by energy generators through brokers) that subsidize the growth of wind and other clean energy.	More than 700 million pounds of carbon dioxide pollution is avoided annually, according to the EPA—the rough equivalent of taking 60,000 cars off the road.
California utility Pacific Gas & Electric has signed a multibillion-dollar agreement with BrightSource Energy for seven solar thermal projects to be built in the Mojave Desert.	The 1,300 megawatts of solar thermal capacity will provide enough electricity for about 400,000 homes and prevent the emission of 1.5 million tons of CO_2.
Denver billionaire investor Philip Anschutz is developing a 2,000-megawatt wind farm in south-central Wyoming, along with a 900-mile transmission line through Las Vegas and Phoenix to southern California.	The development of transmission capacity from wind-rich Great Plains states to power-hungry western cities will open up new opportunities for wind and other renewable sources.
Plug-in hybrid vehicles, powered by renewable sources of electricity and biofuels, are far more efficient than gasoline- or natural-gas-powered vehicles. The technology is ready and tax credits are in place.	Converting to an electric fleet of cars and mass transit will eliminate U.S. dependence on foreign oil, reduce green-houses gases and air pollution, and be less expensive to operate.

Project or Program	Results
ExxonMobil signed a $600 million contract with Synthetic Genomics to develop bioengineered algae organisms that secrete oil through their cell walls, enabling large-scale, cost-effective industrial production.	Producing biofuels industrially eliminates competition between food and fuel on farmland. Algae is energy-rich and could be used synergistically to clean power-plant emissions. Water can be recycled in an industrial system.
U.S. universities such as Arizona State, the College of the Atlantic, Harvard, Middlebury, and Tufts are vying to be the greenest campus. In a *Princeton Review* survey of 10,000 college applicants, 63 percent said that a college's commitment to the environment could affect their decision to go there.	After pledging to reduce its greenhouse gases by 75 percent by 2050, Tufts has already reduced its emissions to 1990 levels by switching from oil to gas in some facilities, installing photovoltaic and solar hot-water systems on the roof of a new residence hall; and installing superefficient LED lights in a parking garage.
California's Million Solar Roofs legislation, passed in 2006, gives incentives for the residential and business installation of rooftop solar equipment: utilities must buy excess energy at competitive prices, and developers must offer solar energy as an option on new houses.	If the target of 1 million solar roofs by 2018 is met, the initiative will provide 3,000 megawatts of clean energy and reduce the output of greenhouse gasses by 3 million tons—equivalent to taking 1 million cars off the road. It will help give "power to the people" by making decentralized energy normal and even patriotic.

➤ What Happened . . . ?

After decades of hitting the snooze button, the energy revolution is jumping out of bed. After the BP oil spill and many freakish weather events related to climate change, it has finally become clear to the general public that fossil fuels are an environmental time bomb, and that we do have options. There's a growing awareness that demand for oil and natural gas will soon exceed supply—no matter how fast we "drill, baby, drill"—which will drive prices ever upward. And a tipping point has finally been reached regarding conventional energy's role in climate change. A 2009 Pew poll found that 58 percent say that climate change is happening now, while another 7 percent believe it will happen in the future unless we take action. After looking at the financial risks associated with building new coal-fired power plants (such as inevitable regulations and fuel-cost volatility), the utility industry has postponed or canceled more than one hundred proposed coal plants in the past 6 years. Michigan's governor placed five new coal plants on hold, calling for alternatives that would produce more much-needed jobs per invested dollar, and the governor of Kansas (a wind-rich state) has likewise vetoed the state legislature's attempts to approve a new coal plant.

President Obama's rhetoric at a 2009 Earth Day speech in Iowa lit up the NASDAQ index the next day (where several new energy stocks now are tracked): "The choice we face is not between saving our environment and saving our economy," he said. "It's a choice between prosperity and decline. The nation that leads the world in creating new sources of clean energy will be the nation that leads the 21st-century global economy."[8] In fact, in a rapidly expanding market for renewable energy, the United States is currently losing ground. Even though U.S. green industries are growing, in many other countries, such as Germany, China, Japan, Italy, they are growing even faster. In solar-cell technology, for example, America's share of the global market fell from 44 percent in 1996 to below 5 percent in 2005.[9]

➤ New Normal Agenda Point #16: Energy from Flows Rather Than from Stocks

Old Perspective: Energy is limitless and automatic; it makes our lives convenient and pleasant, providing abundance. Shouldn't life be effortless? If we constantly increase the supply of energy, "Reddy Kilowatt" can deliver electrons whenever and wherever we want them, and Dino can bring each of us twenty-five barrels of oil every year for our own private use. Energy supply should be centralized and aggressively defended. Health effects from burning fossil fuels and even climate change are a small price to pay for such affordable convenience.

New Perspective: In the process of burning our fossil-fuel inheritance, we have demolished critical biological habitats, imperiled public health, and now risk clobbering the planet's climate, under the pretext that there are no viable alternatives. Global dependence on carbon-rich fossil fuels is a security threat for both suppliers and consumers; it concentrates wealth and power, and enables a way of life that is careless and out of scale with human needs. We should reduce demand—with efficiency, systems redesign, and a shift in cultural values—rather than increase supply. The energy we generate should be clean, affordable, and based on natural flows rather than geological stocks of energy.

THE HEAVY LIFTING

- Phase out the coal industry, as Germany has already begun to do, incrementally replacing it with clean energy.

- Rebuild a "smart" national electricity grid and electrify a large part of the mass transportation system.

- Make energy efficiency a criterion for every decision you make, from the light bulbs you buy to urban design you can influence with your vote.

- Invest in and install renewable sources of energy like wind, solar, geothermal, and biofuels.

The inevitable yet remarkable turnaround in the energy industry is vindication for longtime energy guru Amory Lovins, who for more than three decades patiently pointed out the opportunities of a "soft path" for energy. First as an advocate with Friends of the Earth, then as director of the Colorado-based Rocky Mountain Institute, Lovins called for an "undiscovery of fire" in our overall energy system, and the pursuit of "negawatts" (via energy efficiency) rather than megawatts (primarily via fossil fuel generation). "At least half your electricity bill is fixed distribution costs to pay the overheads of a sprawling energy system: transmission lines, transformers, cables. Meters and people to read them, planners, headquarters, billing computers, interoffice memos, advertising agencies," he explained back in the 1970s.[10]

Lovins realized early in his career that many American engineers, planners, designers, and elected officials were not familiar with whole-systems approaches, or didn't have time or authorization to use them. Still, such approaches make thermodynamic sense and need to be given priority. "Where we want only to create temperature differences of tens of degrees, we should meet the need with sources whose potential is tens or hundreds of degrees, not with a flame temperature of thousands or a nuclear temperature equivalent to trillions—like cutting butter with a chainsaw," he wrote. By the laws of physics, he explained, generating electricity by burning fossil fuel is inherently wasteful, since only a third of the fuel value becomes electricity—the rest escapes as heat, unless it's captured and used in factories and buildings. Energy consumers in all walks of life are paying for that waste.

Although renewable energy has more sex appeal than efficiency, Lovins recognized that the world wasn't ready for a solar economy in the 1970s, and that renewable sources weren't quite ready for the world either. He focused his analytical skills and those of his staff on efficiency and engineering excellence in buildings, motors, furnaces, pipes, vehicles, appliances—just about everything that requires energy. Whole-systems analysis told him that, for example, when a building's components are all optimum, expensive furnaces and air conditioners can be much smaller, or even unnecessary.

Refuting the claim that preventing climate change will force a trade-off between the environment and the economy, Lovins maintains, "Using energy more efficiently offers an economic bonanza, because saving fossil fuel is a lot cheaper than buying it." He points to chemical manufacturer DuPont (and many other major corporations) as evidence: "DuPont boosted production nearly 30 percent but cut energy use 7 percent and greenhouse gases 72 percent in the past decade, saving more than $2 billion in the process," he writes.[11]

In contrast to the energy system that currently dominates our way of life, Lovins outlined the many advantages of a soft-energy path based on infinitely renewable sources of energy. The soft path he envisioned is diverse, running on mini power plants in many locations. It is more flexible, more accessible, and easier to understand than brittle, centralized sources of energy. It is matched in scale and geographic distribution to end uses—things like toasters, cars, and motors—taking advantage of free distribution of most natural energy flows.

• Intrinsic Benefits of Renewable Energy •

Reduces or eliminates distribution losses, waste heat, and infrastructure costs.

Provides greater security, since it is less likely to be a terrorist target (including the documented threat of computer terrorism) and not as likely to cause resource wars.

Provides a boost to rural communities, where much of our renewable energy flows, and grows.

Allows operations to begin more quickly after blackouts, reducing financial, health, and security risks.

Shorter construction times (two to five years rather than five to fifteen years) reduces financial risk.

Provides far more jobs per dollar invested.

Enables a more illustrious place in history for our generation.

Reduces trade deficits as oil imports decline.

Uses far less water than fossil-fuel-powered and nuclear plants, which require huge amounts for cooling. Solar and wind power use almost no water, except during product manufacture.

By examining the economic, social, and environmental benefits of renewable flows of energy, it is easy to conclude that a softer energy path can actually make us better humans. Certainly, social equity and democracy could be more easily achieved; aggression and insecurity at the national level would undoubtedly decline as well. Futurist Paul Hawken imagines how affordable, mass-produced solar energy could increase the self-reliance of citizens in less industrialized countries: "With innovations in solar technology, if you were to run all the news presses of the world for five and half days, printing solar film on to panels—you could meet all the world's energy needs." Hawken believes that this new type of solar energy can be made in Africa, by Africans with African materials, instead of being manufactured and marketed overseas by corporations with large profit margins.[12]

The ability to sell solar energy back to the grid at a fair return is also a very democratic innovation that literally confers "power to the people." By generating solar, wind, microhydro, or geothermal (heat pump) energy right at the point of use, householders and small business owners can break their dependence on volatile energy prices, giving them wider choices and greater security and freedom. Renewable energy has already passed various security checkpoints in crises like the flooding in New Orleans after Hurricane Katrina. Solar-powered lighting allowed New Orleans to respond faster than surrounding Louisiana towns. The U.S. military recognizes intrinsic benefits like flexibility, reliability, and security too; renewable energy provides more than 8 percent of the electricity for U.S. military installations.[13]

THE ENERGY KALEIDOSCOPE: PATTERNS OF CHANGE

The energy revolution will more than pay its own way but may require even greater flexibility in human behavior than computer, car, and suburban revolutions because cheap fossil fuel was a once-in-an-epoch bonanza. (Imagine if you were living on an inheritance, and the money began to run out.) Fossil fuels are millions of years of stored solar energy—"ancient sunlight" in Thom Hartmann's words. They are packed with energy-rich, concentrated molecules, and to replace them, we'll need to deploy not only renewable energy but the Siamese twins, efficiency and sufficiency, in moderation. The Japanese concept known as *mottainai*, which loosely translates as "Don't waste resources; be grateful and respectful," incorporates both efficiency and sufficiency. Do the job well with the right amount of the right materials. Meeting energy needs well might be thought of as:

$$SS = EMR$$

where SS is sustainable supply, E is efficiency, M is moderation or "just the right amount," and R is renewable sources of energy. The hybrid vehicle, powered by several different forms of energy, is a perfect metaphor for the hybrid energy system that lies directly ahead. To replace carbon as our primary energy source will take a coordinated array of other sources and strategies. (When considering the concept of sufficiency, it's important to remember that happiness and fulfillment do not spring from energy per se, but from meeting needs like comfort, security, nutrition, and support as precisely as possible.) As technologies like wind and solar begin to supply a larger percentage of our electricity, the appliances and vehicles at the other end of the power line need to be efficiently engineered, and the energy sources themselves need to interrelate to reach optimum performance. For example, wind and solar are a dynamic duo because conditions that are bad for wind (calm, sunny days) are often great for solar, and vice versa.

There will be major shifts in how we meet our needs as we adapt. For example, 95 percent of the energy used in transportation and agriculture now comes from oil. If the United States prudently follows Europe's lead, more passengers will ride in every vehicle (more trains, buses, and vans), and smaller vehicles will be powered by diverse, clean sources of energy. New neighborhoods will be designed to be more self-reliant and walkable, and even existing neighborhoods will change in shape and function. Local governments will increasingly change zoning laws to allow stores and restaurants right on the block—which will reduce overall vehicle miles traveled. Within the next decade, about 55 percent of the world's population will live in urban areas, where mass transit is not only more efficient but in many cases more pleasant.

Agriculture will change radically as well, substituting natural pest control for energy-intensive pesticides, and biological assets like cover crops and compost for fossil-fuel-based fertilizers. There's a resurgence of interest in small-scale farming and market gardening based on skill and attentive, engaged human labor; in the future, there will be more shovels and fewer computerized tractors at the source of our food. When the price of oil shoots up, the entire pattern of growing, distributing, processing and packaging of food will change.

In a more localized economy, the throwaway mind-set will finally be seen as absurdly dysfunctional. It is one thing when we can afford to have our wastes whisked away—no muss, no fuss—but when transportation costs skyrocket, we'll make greater use of products that last. Disposable packaging will seem frivolous when a higher percentage of food is bought from regional sources and petroleum-based plastic begins to rise in price. The patterns of work may change as well. With eightfold increases in productivity in the last century, we can meet our needs quite well by working fewer than forty hours a week, if the essentials of our lives are high quality; mindless waste is against the law; and our social direction is less materialistic. Full employment of a part-time workforce will enable a different paradigm of moderate consumption and unlimited human potential. Many will choose time affluence rather than monetary affluence if the electorate insists that part-time workers receive prorated benefits. With more time available for exercise and healthy diets, a groundswell of preventive health care will come into the mainstream. Americans will have both time and human energy to become politically informed and socially engaged. This isn't a fairy tale but a pragmatic way out. Corporations will bring jobs back from overseas when rising shipping costs outweigh lower labor costs. Interrelated industries will take greater advantage of synergies to optimize the use of resources. For example, biorefineries will spring up that produce fuel, livestock feed, chemicals, and even nutritional products, all in one location. If algae plays a central role in the biofuel industry (as major investments forecast), existing power plants and biorefineries might become components of an "industrial ecology." CO_2 emissions from a steam-venting, monster power plant could boost algae growth and, more important, reduce the threat of climate change. Since power plants currently utilize 39 percent of the nation's fresh water for cooling, why not capture the heat from that power plant to first heat nearby buildings, then use return-loop warm water to optimize algae growth for biofuel? Another partner in this industrial park might be a cement-manufacturing factory that also captures CO_2 from the power plant, converts it to carbonate, then incorporates the carbonate into concrete, as California-based Calera Corporation's process does. The point is, many aspects of the energy revolution are taking placing within a shifting matrix of technologies, social norms, and resource availability.

Yet, some of the greatest opportunities are embedded in social habits—our way of life. For example, the production of meat is very energy intensive because so much fertilizer is used to grow feed crops like corn and soybeans—and because of the refrigeration required to store meat. However, to take advantage of this energy-saving measure, we'll have to change our deep-seated habit of meat consumption. Similarly, mass transit, which makes so much more sense from an energy standpoint than millions of cars, is relatively unfamiliar to Americans, so guarded are we about personal space. And the ever-expanding presence of electronic gadgets poses a fundamental anthropological question: What do our genes make of our passive lifestyle? To use less energy in the cyber universe, it seems, we need to use more human energy in the real world—a major paradigm shift. Yet, as the mayor of London recently phrased it, "To tackle climate change we don't have to reduce our quality of life, but we do have to change the way we live."[14]

➤ New Normal Agenda Point #17: Prospecting for Energy and Efficiency Opportunities

Old Perspective: Energy is cheap, so why conserve? It's more fun to invest in cars, sports equipment, and vacations than in furnaces, high-efficiency windows, and programmable thermostats. We don't need to pay attention to turning off lights and computers—we have good salaries. We'd never consider putting solar panels on our roof because our Homeowners Association (HOA) would never approve them.

New Perspective: Energy is expensive, and the more we use, the more bizarre global weather patterns will become. (Ironically, the more we use air-conditioning, the hotter it will get.) "Fun" is not really the overall goal. Investing in energy efficiency and renewable energy offers things we need: security, in case energy continues to climb; comfort without all the noise from furnaces, fans, and air conditioners; participation in social change; and the respect of neighbors and friends. And HOA perspectives are changing too: there's more to life than appearances.

THE HEAVY LIFTING

- Pay attention to your house's energy and water flows.
- Purchase energy-efficient appliances.
- In your workplace, support the acquisition and/or development of energy-efficiency opportunities.

Let's look at the way energy is used in the United States and how it could be used more productively. Broadly speaking, energy used in America can be classified into four general categories: industrial, transportation, residential, and commercial.

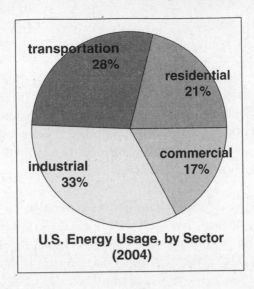

U.S. Energy Usage, by Sector
(2004)

Roughly 39 percent of the nation's total energy now comes from oil, 22 percent from coal, 23 percent from natural gas, 8 percent from nuclear, and 8 percent from renewable energy, including large-scale hydropower. However, these percentages are destined to change as state targets for renewable electricity are met, as the price of oil escalates, and as the costs of building new coal and nuclear plants are recalculated to consider environmental risks and potential regulations. In addition, a slow but steady switch to superefficient cars like plug-in hybrids will reduce the 61 percent of oil now used in vehicles. So the die is cast in terms of reducing carbon emissions; but will this reduction happen quickly enough to prevent climatic crisis? The following sector-related comments anticipate further shifts, and target game-changing opportunities in energy generation and use. (Percentages are author estimates, based on data from the U.S. Bureau of Labor Statistics, the Earth Policy Institute, and other sources.[15]

WHERE ENERGY IS SPENT, AND HOW TO SPEND LESS OF IT

Industry (Production and Processing of Goods—author estimates)

40 percent petroleum refining and chemical manufacture

19 percent steel

8 percent other metals

9 percent paper

7 percent cement

5 percent food processing

With leadership from forward-looking companies, and incentives from federal stimulus capital, there are now many programs in industry for process innovations, lighting upgrades, fleet fuel-efficiency improvements, digital control solutions, and water management; and there are still many opportunities to generate much less industrial energy per unit of product—a third to a half less.

Heat generated in industry and power generation often goes up the stack or into the nearest river. Yet, energy expert Tom Casten estimates that the waste heat could provide up to 20 percent of U.S. electricity needs (up from its current 7 percent) if it was used to turn turbines.[16] The concept is simple: when you have waste heat, generate electricity; when you generate electricity, use all the waste heat. Called "cogeneration," this technology is already widely used in manufacturing metals, glass, and silicon. Waste heat can also be used to heat or cool (with absorption chillers) buildings. Denmark and the Netherlands generate 40 percent of their electricity with cogeneration, and also widely employ "district heating" in buildings.

The petrochemical industry uses more energy than any other manufacturing sector, yet certain trends may begin to significantly reduce energy consumed. For example, research is expanding in the field of green chemistry, using chemicals that come from living organisms (such as microbial enzymes or soybeans) rather than once-living organisms (such as fossil fuels). Green chemistry pathways typically use less energy per unit of product because they take place at room temperature and have fewer intermediate steps. (However, this transition will be gradual because some chemical pathways and reactions are centuries old.) If organic agriculture takes a larger share of the market, less energy-intensive nitrogen fertilizer will be necessary to produce the same yields. Trends that may reduce energy consumed in the manufacture of plastics include a backlash against plastic containers because of health and environmental effects; a trend toward localization, reducing the need for plastics in shipping; and a gradual transition to plastics made with green chemistry.

By using recycled rather than virgin steel, paper, aluminum, plastics, and other materials, the world's most energy-intensive manufacturing industries can radically reduce energy use. For example, the recycling of steel cans in the United States is currently only 60 percent, but as that percentage increases, more efficient equipment that utilizes recycled materials can be used. According to the Environmental Policy Institute, if three-fourths of steel production were to switch to electric arc furnaces using scrap, energy use in the steel industry could be cut by almost 40 percent. Similarly, if all cement producers worldwide used the most efficient dry kiln process in use today, energy use in the cement industry could drop 42 percent.

It's a similar story throughout the industrial sector: recycling and changing the processes in energy-hungry industries like paper, cement, aluminum, transportation equipment, and fabricated metal products can reduce overall energy consumption in manufacturing by 50 percent or more. However, in some cases, cultural change may produce larger reductions than efficiency improvements. For example, more than one-sixth of the energy used in the food-processing industry is used in animal slaughtering and processing. Only a reduction in meat eating will significantly reduce energy use in this case. About half of the paper manufactured is used for packaging and wrapping paper; about 30 percent is used for printing and writing paper; and 20 percent is for newsprint and household uses. With the failure of many newspapers and magazines, the possible reduction of paper use from cost-conscious·changes in office policy, and increased use of electronic products like Kindle, only toilet paper is likely to remain at current levels of production. (And even there, a transition to a narrower width and less "fluffy" paper will reduce materials and energy use.)

The innovative European experiment with "extended producer responsibility" (also known as the take-back law) may well lay the groundwork for a radically different flow of materials through the global economy. This law requires manufacturers to take their products back at the end of their useful lives. Rather than ending up in a landfill, packaging, electronic products, and other goods are collected at central locations and sent back to manufacturers. This brilliant political innovation encourages designing for durability, modularity, and nontoxicity in products, and increases recycling by closing the loop in the flow of "nutrients," just as nature does. EU countries have also adopted industry-altering efficiency standards for twenty-three different appliances and electrical end uses, from battery chargers to street lighting. Even more ambitious is Japan's Top Runner program, which sets appliance standards based on the most efficient products already on the market. Though voluntary, this program successfully relies on Japanese pride in quality products to set new performance levels.

Transportation (Ground, Air, and Water—author estimates.)

61 percent gasoline fuel

21 percent diesel fuel

12 percent aviation

When it comes to efficient transportation, the United States is bringing up the rear. While Americans continue to insist that we "see the USA in our Chevrolets" (or Hondas), Europeans and Asians long ago questioned the dominance of the automobile, due to traffic congestion and quality of life as well as the rising costs of doing business. In the United States, 88 percent of 133 million commuters travel to work by car, and fully one-sixth of all global oil goes into miserably inefficient American cars and trucks. (In 2009, the average gas mileage for American vehicles remains less than 22 miles per gallon, compared with the 25 miles per gallon for the Model T Ford a century ago.)

Meanwhile, in more than one hundred cities worldwide—from Stockholm to Singapore—car-free zones have been carved out of the urban fabric to discourage car travel at strategic times of the day and week. After London started charging a fee (about $10) to drive into the center of the city between 7:00 a.m. and 6:30 p.m., bus travel increased by 38 percent and traffic congestion and delays decreased by 36 percent. Hasselt, Belgium, is a great example of how avoided costs can pay for systemic changes. To avoid building a hugely expensive highway to accommodate increasing traffic, the Hasselt city council opted in the mid-1990s to make bus travel free. Bus ridership increased tenfold, and the city center blossomed.

In Holland and Denmark, bicycles provide up to a third of all transportation. In Japan, world-class bullet trains have been operating for close to half a century, making travel between major cities a breeze. The line from Tokyo to Osaka carries 117,000 passengers a day who travel three times faster by train than by car. Japan's high-speed rail system is a model of precision engineering: trains are on average no more than six seconds late, and there has never been a fatality.[17]

There *will* be high-speed rail in the United States, despite decades of delay. More than three hundred preliminary proposals were submitted in response to an $8 billion line item for high-speed rail in the 2009 stimulus package, and thirteen projects shared the funding: High Speed Rail: California's ambitious master plan to connect San Diego, Los Angeles, San

Francisco, and Sacramento with high-speed rail received a $2.3 billion boost. The state's voters have already approved $10 billion in bonds, and according to high-speed rail proponents, if California's population continues to swell, the costs of building additional freeway and airport capacity would be comparable.[18]

Other projects funded by the American Recovery and Reinvestment Act of 2009 include Tampa-Orlando; Chicago-St. Louis-Kansas City; Chicago-Milwaukee-Madison-Twin Cities; Charlotte-Raleigh-Richmond-Washington; and Seattle-Portland.

Freight-carrying trucks consume about a fifth of all transportation energy in the United States, another high-leverage point for rail. According to rail transport expert Alan S. Drake, if freight trains were converted from diesel-powered to electricity-powered and 85 percent of long-haul trucking was done by rail, the United States could reduce oil use by 12 percent. Shippers would still need to use trucks to move goods to and from freight yards, but that's not a huge challenge with today's container designs. In Drake's proposal, an additional benefit would be that railroad rights-of-way could be used for transmission lines, an asset that would be partially funded by utilities and energy investors. "Rail spur lines could also serve as sites for long rows of wind turbines," writes Drake. He argues that cranes for installing the huge turbines could be delivered by rail, eliminating the typical challenge of getting cranes to remote areas.[19]

Air travel is a pollution problem because its exhaust fumes are deposited in the stratosphere, contributing about 3 percent of global greenhouse gases. Boeing estimates that biofuels could reduce flight-related greenhouse-gas emissions by 60 to 80 percent, by blending algae fuels with existing jet fuel.[20] However, if high-speed rail expands globally, it will probably replace a sizable percentage of air travel, because carbon dioxide emissions per passenger mile on high-speed trains are about one-fourth those of jetliners.

When the average energy costs of manufacturing as well as operating various forms of transportation are figured, it's no surprise that the SUV category leads the pack. But it is a surprise that bus transit comes in a close second:

• Fuel Consumed per Passenger • Mile (in Btus)

Light truck (SUV)	4,329
Bus transit	4,318
Airplane	4,000
Private car	3,500
Amtrak train	2,800
Rail commuter	2,600
Vanpool	1,300

Source: U.S. Department of Energy Transportation Energy Data Book.

Pat Murphy, director of the nonprofit organization Community Solutions, envisions a "Smart Jitney" mass transit system that can be far more quickly implemented than rail or bus lines because it optimizes the existing vehicle fleet as well as drivers. The system would use GPS-equipped cell phones and the Internet for ride reservations and coordination. "Each person who wants to take a trip would use his or her cell phone or web browser to request a ride from the system. The system will locate the appropriate vehicle and driver to pick up and deliver the riders making the request," says Murphy. The technology involved is already in use by UPS and FedEx to optimize package delivery, he adds. "Jitneys are flexible in terms of schedule and route, providing any time, any place pick up and drop off service."

A Smart Jitney system could enroll you and me as drivers whose driving performance would be evaluated by in-vehicle instrumentation. Passenger satisfaction would go into the database as well, using a rating system similar to that on Amazon.com and consumerreports.com. The overall goal of this electronic carpooling and vanpooling system would be to increase passengers by a factor of three, thereby reducing the number of vehicles on the road and the congestion and pollution they create. Though this type of system would demand a great deal of social flexibility, variations of it are quite likely to occur.[21]

Of course, there has been a flood of discussion about hybrid cars and next-generation plug-in hybrids. Their potential for revolutionizing the energy system is huge, since electric motors are three times more efficient than gasoline engines. Powering a fleet of vehicles largely with electricity will enable cars to run on wind energy at a gasoline-equivalent cost of 75¢ a gallon. As promising as this conversion is, it will take at least fifteen years for a substantial turnover to hybrids and electric vehicles. The good news is that the conversion is already under way.[22]

The most efficient way to get to a certain destination is to be there already. Yes, we need reliable supplies of alternative fuels and various forms of multipassenger transit, but the most pressing challenge of all is to provide *access by proximity*. We will inevitably create a more sensible American landscape by radically "remodeling" the suburbs and metro area neighborhoods where more than half of America now lives. Instead of burning miles, fuel, and time, why not design and redesign diverse neighborhoods that can provide what we need, right where we need it? With strong citizen support, innovative policies will provide light-rail networks and jitney-type systems that interconnect metro areas, but with luck, remodeled suburbs will have large market gardens, locally owned businesses, and silent, pollution-free neighborhood power systems, right on Daisy Lane.

Residential (Households—author estimates)

31 percent space heating

12 percent water heating

11 percent lighting

11 percent electronics, including computers

11 percent air-conditioning

8 percent refrigeration

5 percent cooking

5 percent cleaning

Energy consumption in homes is dominated by the heating and cooling of living space and water. Much of this demand can be met in the future by solar energy, space-age windows, thicker insulation, and heat pumps, which transfer heat (or coolness) from the ground into a house. In fact, at the highest level of heating and cooling performance, the German Passive House is so well insulated and leakproof that little or no mechanical heating and/or cooling is needed. However, of the more than 100 million homes that are already built in the United States, 65 percent are underinsulated, with 40 percent of total air leakage occurring in the attic. This reality makes the installation of solar energy and high-performance windows less cost-effective. Although it has very little show-and-tell value, insulation is the first line of defense in America's homes, and is especially critical in reducing the risks of climate change because many of these homes will still be around for at least another fifty years.

While many houses have been oriented to favor views or simply to face the street, the potential for passive solar is still quite large. Enlarging windows on the south sides of buildings, optimizing their glass, and providing heat-retaining curtains can let a home's furnace snooze for much of a winter day, and add to a household's quality of life. Active solar energy to supply hot water and electricity is becoming increasingly affordable with economies of scale expanding and utility, state, and federal incentives in place. In sunny Spain, all new buildings must incorporate solar water heating, and 40 million Chinese homes have already installed it.

With the imminent banning of the standard incandescent bulb (beginning in 2012, with 100-watt bulbs in 2012 and ending with 40-watt bulbs in 2014) come huge opportunities for shaving's America's collective utility bill. A swift turnover of bulbs to the emerging LED bulbs, combined with motion sensors to turn lights off when no one is in a room, can cut electricity use from lighting by more than 90 percent.[23]

Appliance standards are rapidly improving in the United States, thanks to international leadership, and continuing role-modeling in California, which has just called for significant efficiency improvements in flat-screen TVs. Refrigerators, air conditioners, furnaces, dishwashers, and washing machines are all good bets if an ailing appliance is older than eight or ten years. An especially big target for replacement even before meltdown is the secondary refrigerator—typically ten to nineteen years old and sucking electricity like a leech.

· How to Cut Residential Energy Use in Half ·

When furnaces, refrigerators, and hot water heaters break—or if they are now antiques (more than fifteen years old)—replace them with Energy Star models. Watch for rebates on appliances and fixtures. (If Americans bought only appliances with Energy Star ratings over the next fifteen years, it would be like taking 17 million cars off the road.)

Get an energy auditor (maybe free from the utility or a nonprofit) to prospect for opportunities: leaky window frames, inadequate insulation around electric fixtures, etc. Work with your homeowners association to get an Energy Service Company (ESCO) to do the upgrades and be paid back out of collective savings.

Install a programmable thermostat for heating and cooling, and learn how to use it—it saves a lot of energy. Each degree below 68 degrees Fahrenheit during colder weather saves 3 percent to 5 percent more heating energy, while keeping your thermostat at 78 degrees in warmer weather will also save you energy and money.

If your solar exposure is great, install solar panels to heat your water. Up-front costs may sting, but from then on, your showers and dishwashing will be almost free.

Set the refrigerator thermostat at 37 to 40 degrees Fahrenheit. Clean the condenser coils twice a year to raise efficiency by up to 30 percent.

Install curtains, awnings, and shutters to control heating and cooling, and plant a shade tree in your backyard to reduce AC costs. Shading an air conditioner can improve efficiency by 10 percent.

Wash clothes in warm or cold water rather than hot, and rinse with cold water.

Set up a clothesline. Clothespins aren't hard to figure out!

Air-dry dishes rather than heat-dry them, especially in dry climates. Turn the water heater down to 120 degrees Fahrenheit; insulate the pipes that exit your tank.

Install faucet aerators and low-flow showerheads that deliver a satisfying shower for thousands of gallons less annually.

Bake in ceramic or glass pans that hold the heat better and require 25 degrees lower temperatures, but use a pressure cooker, Crock-Pot, toaster oven, microwave, or stove before resorting to the oven.

Unplug coffeemakers, microwaves, computer printers, and other appliances when they are not in use to eliminate "phantom" power loads.

However, rising demand and expectations continue to outrun efficiency improvements. In the United States, despite overall gains in efficiency in houses and cars, per capita energy consumption increased by 40 percent from 1975 to 2005.[24] The reason is straightforward: with the incremental savings that efficiency provides ever-increasing debt, Americans are choosing larger houses, larger TVs, and more electronic devices. From 1980 to 2001, for example, the number of houses with air-conditioning jumped from 27 percent to 55 percent, probably because of housing growth in the South and Southwest. Across the entire country, the average size of an American home has more than doubled since 1950, from the size of an average European home (1,000 square feet) to the current 2,500 square feet.

Even if a family invests in the most efficient AC technology on the market, it obviously doesn't reduce energy consumption overall if they've just bought a larger house. Demand for electronic devices is the fastest-growing category of electricity consumption, and is also directly related to social expectations. One study predicts that without a culture shift that deflates the prestige of gadgets and wall-sized TVs, electronics globally will by 2030 consume as much electricity as all Japanese and American homes consume for everything. There are already nearly 2 billion television sets and 1 billion computers in use, and over half the world's population now subscribes to a mobile phone service.

Commercial (Service-Providing Offices, Businesses, and Government—author estimates)

30 percent lighting

14 percent heating

13 percent cooling

10 percent office equipment

7 percent water heating

6 percent ventilation

4 percent refrigeration

"We can compost and conserve all we want at home," writes *Time* magazine journalist Lisa Takeuchi Cullen. "But as soon as we hit the office, we turn into triplicate-printing, paper-cup-squashing, run-our-computers-all-night-so-the-boss-thinks-we're-working earth befoulers." A single office worker can easily go through ten thousand pieces of copier paper a year, in cahoots with computers that collectively burn $1 billion worth of energy a year when they are not even being used. Offices, stores, and public buildings consume more than 70 percent of the electricity used in the United States, and are responsible for more than a third of the country's carbon dioxide emissions. Heating, cooling and powering these buildings has become one of humanity's biggest energy challenges.[25]

The challenge is to design and construct (or retrofit) greener buildings that provide light, heat, coolness, and electricity for equipment far more efficiently. At the Ford Motor Company's Rouge River Plant, a 10.4-acre heat-absorbing roof surface was replaced by a "green roof" of hardy plants that keep the building cooler in summer and warmer in winter, reducing energy consumption by 25 percent. Two New York City office buildings—one recently constructed and the other, the iconic Empire State Building, built back in 1931—are also raising the bar of green building design. The 4 Times Square Building, forty-eight stories high and with 1.6 million square feet of office space, was designed with sophisticated energy software to ensure that lighting, windows, and heating and cooling systems work together optimally. Photovoltaic panels producing 15 kilowatts of electricity were integrated right into the sides of the building—doubling as a construction material—and two large fuel cells supply 100 percent of nighttime electrical needs and 5 percent of peak-load needs. The hot-water by-product from the fuel cells helps heat the building as well as its potable water.

The Empire State Building project, which will save building occupants $4.4 million a year, demonstrates that a combination of computer-age logic and upgrades to windows, lights, plug-load controllers, and air-conditioning systems can reduce energy consumption by 40 percent in *existing* buildings—a critical finding, since at least 10 percent of the energy a building uses in its lifetime is consumed in construction and demolition. The U.S. Green Building Council, which administers the coveted Leadership in Energy and Environmental Design (LEED) certification awards for building efficiency, has recently added awards for building retrofits. These include installing automatic shutoffs—occupancy sensors—for lighting, and snooze controls that power computers down automatically after fifteen minutes of idle time, cutting a machine's energy use by 70 percent.

One of the most interesting heating and cooling innovations for a large building is the Eastgate Centre, Zimbabwe's largest office and shopping complex. Convection tubes used by African termites to keep their mounded, high-rise colonies cool inspired this passive cooling design. Taking advantage of large temperature swings from dusk to dawn, the design breathes fresh, cool air into the building, reducing energy consumption by 90 percent compared with conventionally cooled buildings. A similar strategy has recently been used at a London building across from Westminster Palace.

And the British are also front-runners in adopting light-emitter diode (LED) lighting. Buckingham Palace has recently been given a royal makeover, including the conversion to ceiling lights, chandelier fixtures, and exterior lights that last as long as twenty-two years. So stingy with electricity are the LED bulbs that lighting the palace's entire facade requires less electricity than running an electric teakettle.

There's no doubt that compact fluorescent (CFL) bulbs have already led the way to lightbulbs that are semipermanent, more like plumbing fixtures. But as currently designed, CFLs contain mercury, which typically becomes a hazardous waste when the bulb finally burns out. Most CFLs are not dimmable, so they always use maximum power regardless of how much light is needed. Still, they have saved a lot of energy and reduced a lot of greenhouse gas emissions already; from 2001 to 2008, global sales of these energy-miser bulbs more than tripled, from 750 million bulbs to 2.7 billion—before dipping during the recession. Maybe CFLs just need a deposit system that ensures they'll be recycled. And since LED bulbs have a few problems of their own, CFLs are likely to be around for a while. LED light works better as a spotlight rather than a multidirectional light. Although their lifetime is up to four times as long as a CFL's, the quality of light degrades over time.

However, one thing is certain: the Edison bulb, which converts 90 percent of its electricity to heat, is headed for the museum unless it can be radically improved. Various studies suggest that converting the world's fixtures to LED technology would be a quick and cost-effective way of cutting energy use; a complete conversion would slash carbon dioxide emissions from lighting by up to 50 percent in twenty years. In the United States, lighting currently consumes about 6 percent of all energy use. With a boost from federal stimulus funds, lots of cities have already installed the low-maintenance LED bulbs for street and parking-garage lighting. Three major California cities, Los Angeles, San Jose, and San Francisco, have by 2010 installed about a quarter of a million bulbs. The next major market is likely to be office, retail, and government buildings. There are about half a million federal buildings alone in the United States, according to the Earth Policy Institute, and they will pioneer the use of LED lighting.

As a result of these many converging and interacting forces, governmental policies are beginning to yank global energy systems in a new direction. Especially important in the United States are Renewable Energy Standards set by thirty-four states, which mandate that increasing percentages of electricity be generated by renewable technologies in specified time periods. Together, these states consume close to half the country's electricity; when

New York called for 24 percent use of renewable technologies by 2013; Illinois for 25 percent by 2013; Illinois for 25 percent by 2025, and California for 33 percent by 2030, renewable energy as an industry swiftly moved from fantasy to reality. The Environmental Protection Agency's declaration that greenhouse gases would indeed be regulated as air pollutants was another stimulant, as was the virtual guarantee that Congress would pass a climate-change bill, putting a price on carbon emissions.

Another key strategy to support the energy revolution is shifting subsidies away from the coal, oil, and gas industries—which annually amount to $47 billion or more in the United States—and toward renewable energy. Belgium, France, and Japan have phased out subsidies for coal, and Germany intends to phase out the entire industry. Some policy ideas are so ingenious that it's just a matter of time before they are applied. For example, Amory Lovins proposes a "feebate" policy that would charge fees on inefficient new vehicles and rebate those revenues to buyers of efficient models, which would encourage innovation and help shift automakers toward efficiency. Another great idea is to share the profits of efficiency improvements along the whole supply chain, making designers, builders and manufacturers, and marketers stakeholders in innovation.

◆ Key Policies to Keep Clean Energy Growth on Track ◆

Every nation needs a system for putting a price on carbon and other greenhouse gases that doesn't dump higher prices on energy consumers.

Many EU countries have a carbon-taxing or carbon-trading system that penalizes fossil-fuel use but lowers income tax. The emerging cap-and-trade legislation in the U.S. is a start but needs further refinement.

Create secure, long-term incentives and tax credits for renewable energy and efficient appliances and fixtures.

Industries, local governments, and householders will more readily invest in and install efficienct devices and renewable energy with government policies that are consistent and long term. U.S. incentives have been too sporadic.

Increase America's energy IQ with a national outreach campaign like California's Kill-a-Watt initiative.

A 1 percent increase in awareness could save an estimated $20 billion a year in energy costs. California's campaign reduced energy consumption by an estimated 6% to 12%.

Set national Renewable Energy Standards as 34 states and 66 other countries have already done.	A study by the Union of Concerned Scientists estimated that a mandatory increase in renewable energy in the U.S. electricity system to 20% would create more than 355,000 jobs and reduce the national energy bill by $65 billion by 2025.
In all 50 states, decouple utility profits from sales, as Oregon and California have done. Also require utilities to buy renewable energy produced by households and independent energy producers.	Current policies do not reward efficiency, since most utility commissions only allow higher profits from higher sales
Retrofit all local government buildings and permit only LEED-certified new buildings. Then spread this model to residential, commercial, and industrial sectors of the town or city.	Milwaukee's Energy Efficiency task force (Me2) performs audits and efficiency upgrades on homes and buildings in the city. Occupants pay for the improvements in their utility bills, at a rate that approximates energy savings

➤ The View from 2050

It would be fascinating to be alive in forty years, to see if humans had risen to the challenge of reducing fossil-fuel use by 80 percent by 2050, to avoid the most catastrophic effects of climate change. If so, the world would be a different place, socially as well as technologically. Already, we see social changes becoming thinkable. To use less air-conditioning, the suit jacket has become optional in offices around the world. The U.S. Postal Service is considering cutting delivery days down to five. Many workplaces are looking at four-day weeks as an energy and cost-saving measure. Mass transit ridership and bicycling are up, even in the car-dependent United States.

It's been said that we don't typically change when we see the light, but when we feel the heat. We've always known that rising energy costs would eventually supply that heat; however, with a historic, global effort from our generation and the next, we may be able to avoid the unimaginable, life-constricting heat and drought of global warming.

5

Living Wealth: Restoring the Economies of Nature

➤ **New Normal Agenda Point #18:**
Putting a Price on Living Capital

Old Perspective: Nature is, at worst, an evil enemy and at best a warehouse of resources we can convert to cash. Produced capital is more valuable than natural capital because we made it. By the force of technology, will, and human ingenuity, we can displace people, plants, and animals that were original inhabitants and replace them with malls, subdivisions, and electronic gadgets that are far more profitable. Pay no attention to the weeds, pests, toxic chemicals, slash piles, and tailings ponds that are side effects of industry, because that's what money looks like.

New Perspective: Nature is far from being a problem; rather, it's a symphony of tried and true solutions: a source of materials if harvested sustainably, and a "sink" that recycles biodegradable wastes. Letting nature go broke is like swinging wrecking balls against our own houses and places of worship. In many cases, the services nature provides, just in the course of being a living system, have far greater value than the minerals, processed food, and other products that come from the earth's ecosystems. In the emerging era, restoration of natural systems and adoption of sustainable practices will be our civilization's highest priority.

THE HEAVY LIFTING

- Support the transition to a restoration economy by advocating for open-space acquisition; green materials in products; recycling and composting systems that reduce mining, logging, and fertilizer manufacture.

- Support policies that make business pay for ecological damage out of profits.

- Support the completion of the planetary inventory of species.

It used to be that when a given resource became scarce, we could either find a substitute or reduce its scarcity with more powerful and sophisticated technology. If our wells ran dry, we could dig deeper wells. If the fish catch declined, we could drag huge nets along the ocean floor, use sonar to locate dense schools of fish, and (with federal subsidies) buy bigger boats with helicopters and huge onboard freezers. But in a world of rising expectations as well as a rapidly rising global population—another million people are born every four days—we've reached the point of diminishing returns in many of our most critical activities: agriculture, energy generation, transportation, manufactured goods, forestry, water supply, and fishing. High-tech equipment can't increase a fish harvest if the fish aren't there, and deeper wells are useless if an ancient "fossil" aquifer has been pumped dry forever. There's only so much freshwater on the planet, and there are no viable substitutes for it either.

If the earth's climate changes, we can't just push a button and reset it. How did we back ourselves into this evolutionary corner? We created an economic system without an exit strategy, and a value system that protects it. But that system is on a mission to use every scrap of marketable resource. "The economy sends signals that cutting down a rainforest to grow soybeans makes more sense than leaving that forest intact," writes Ricardo Bayon. "It says that building a shopping mall to sell iPods is more valuable than having a wetland that buffers coasts against storms, filters water, and provides nesting ground for birds."[1]

Our technical abilities to thoroughly and precisely extract resources are still "progressing" three hundred years after the steam engine was invented; however, in today's resource-challenged world, technology is far less likely to guarantee profit. Now the limiting factor is diminishing returns from plundered ecosystems and once-rich sources of minerals and water. Without basic changes in the way we do business, we'll go into "overshoot," an ecological term for sometimes-catastrophic miscalculations about nature's ability to bounce back. When a fish catch declines, the price of fish increases, making reduced harvests even more profitable. Continuing to fish beyond sustainable yield depletes species vitality, sometimes resulting in complete collapse, as with the cod fishery in the North Atlantic. Steve Palumbi, a scientist at Stanford University, believes this is the last century of wild seafood.

Why should we care if this might also be the last century for other biological celebrations such as silent old-growth forest, migrations of songbirds and elephants, and pristine mountain lakes? No need to care about such things—unless we have a fondness for life as we know it; unless we have some use for clean air and water, food, flood control, soil fertility, waste recycling, pest control, pollination, raw materials for goods, climate control, seed dispersal, erosion control, recreation, and medicine. A survey of the top 150 prescription drugs used in the United States found that 118 are based on natural sources: plants (74 percent), fungi, bacteria, and snakes.[2] In other words, nature is the club we belong to, and unless its systems are in good working order, we can't thrive as a card-carrying earthlife member.

What can we do to reverse the declining condition of coral reefs, beehives, and elephant habitat? To stabilize a climate kept perfectly in balance for ten thousand years by plants, soil microbes, and an exponentially less consumptive lifestyle? For starters, we can make closer contact with nature by spending more time in it, studying it, telling stories about it. In the medium term, we can tune up and ecoalign our industrial systems, localizing them to add accountability, trust, stewardship, and efficiency. Agriculture is a good example. Though humans first tilled the soil thousands of years ago, we still scar the earth and release megatons of carbon dioxide each growing season, instead of selecting crops that can remain in place permanently, as they did when humans were hunter-gatherers. We travel in vehicles that haven't changed much in more than a century, and still use the lightbulb Edison invented in 1879 (though Australia has already banned it, and the United States will *finally* phase it out between 2012 and 2014 because of its inherent inefficiency).

The choices and leverage points evaluated in this chapter explore methods, systems, and policies that employ "biologic" in place of more-of-the-same, market-driven technologic. We'll look at opportunities to fund natural restoration; policies that preserve existing habitats and ecosystems; personal habits that respect and connect with the systems that generate our products. When it comes to basic knowledge about nature, the average American is virtually clueless—he or she can readily identify a hundred corporate logos but fewer than ten plants that grow right in the region. Nature-focused educators such as David Sobel and Richard Louv, who warn against "ecophobia" and "nature deficit disorder," offer key leverage points for bringing us back to nature. It seems inevitable that in the long run, we will learn to respect biological limits, withdrawing only the interest from nature's accounts, never the principal. As our paradigm shifts, we will resanctify and ritualize nature as a sacred garden, a biospiritual force that shall not be abused.

By becoming more familiar with how nature operates, we will begin to give greater value to mature, resilient, diverse ecosystems—preserving and restoring them for their own sake, and for ours. The following table, which compares the major differences between immature and mature ecosystems, can help us keep nature on the pathway to evolutionary complexity, and can also model the qualities that work in "human ecology," the various systems that constitute civilization.

◆ The Way Natural Systems Evolve ◆

Immature Ecosystems	Mature Ecosystems
Inefficient nutrient utilization (wasteful).	Highly efficient nutrient utilization captures and holds nutrients, letting nothing be wasted.
Competitive, weak links with other species.	Cooperative, in balance, interdependent. No species dominate.
Poor resistance to outside stresses.	Resilient, "unsinkable."
Niche generalists (species have not yet developed specific solutions that provide security and assure food supply).	Niche specialists (species fit perfectly with surroundings, developing camouflage, enzymes to digest local foods, and intricate ways to communicate with one another).
Short, simple life cycles (like an annual flower that starts over from seed every year).	Long, complex life cycles (like perennial flowers).
Low species diversity.	High species diversity.
Nutrients often come from outside the system.	Nutrients come from inside the system.
Food chains mostly linear, simple.	Food chains weblike, use all available wastes.

Immature Ecosystems	Mature Ecosystems
Nutrients are often wasted because of poor soil, lack of dietary diversity, etc., and have to be "imported" from outside the system.	Species have adapted to capture and retain nutrients within the system, reducing the need for nutrients from outside the system.

➤ New Normal Agenda Point #19: Biodiversity or Biobankruptcy? Now's the Time to Choose

Old Perspective: "Survival of the fittest." If humans are intelligent enough to dominate the planet and other species fail to survive, isn't that just the way nature works?

New Perspective: The careless way that we humans meet our needs—from poorly planned housing developments to energy-addicted, industrial agriculture—is destroying the habitats of many other species, and could ultimately result in our own collapse as a global civilization. "Survival of those species that fit" is a more appropriate description of how evolution works.

THE HEAVY LIFTING

- Understand better how nature works and help implement policies and incentives that put a "price tag" on natural systems and resources to reflect their real value to government, business, and civic leaders.

Life on earth is a project that all species have been working on, together, for billions of years. But in our era, humans are not being team players. In fact, we've taken control of the team and begun, foolishly, to dominate the project. Many pro-lifers are outspoken about abortion but strangely silent about species cleansing that's occurring all over the planet as plant and animal populations crash. According to one estimate, the weight of humans and our domesticated animals (livestock and pets) is now more than 95 percent of the total weight of vertebrate animals. Meanwhile, populations of our closest kin, the 5,500 or so mammals identified since 1500, continue to decline. According to the World Conservation Congress, 25 percent of mammal species are threatened by extinction.[3]

Many ecologists argue that other species have a right to exist, regardless of their value to humans. (Ecuador's revised constitution, for example, states that nature "has the right to exist, persist, maintain, and regenerate," the first time a nation has granted such rights.) Even if we humans remain stubbornly in pursuit of economic growth and fail to acknowledge such rights, it would be prudent to do a better job of ensuring their continued existence, because we simply don't know how all the pieces fit together. A good example of our incomplete understanding of ecology is Biosphere 2, a $200 million project in which eight people lived in a closed, human-designed ecosystem for two years (1991–93). Despite the best science that money could buy, the three-acre model ecosystem failed to provide surviv-able conditions. Oxygen levels fell to 14 percent, a concentration normally found at seventeen thousand feet in elevation. Nitrous oxide levels im-paired brain functioning, and pest populations (ants, roaches, and katy-dids) exploded. Aggressive vines spread across Biosphere 2's surfaces, and nineteen of twenty-five vertebrate species included in the experiment van-ished. Clearly, we've got a ways to go before we could survive on another planet. In fact, surviving on our own planet is not a sure thing; the world's teeming microbial populations are not especially impressed with our diplo-mas and economic goals.

Our neophyte status is starkly evidenced by our confusion about the causes of decline in various species and systems. Those who are snorkelers have watched with great sadness and disbelief as coral reefs in Mexico and Central America fade from brilliant colors to black and white. Coral colonies that were here before Columbus sailed in the Caribbean are disappearing from one year to the next, and we don't know exactly why. Viruses, possibly carried in dust storms from Africa, are one possible cause, but the underly-ing culprit is likely rising ocean temperatures. Another globally scaled col-lapse is occurring in bee colonies, and again, the exact cause or causes have not yet been identified conclusively. In Chile, thousands of rare Andean fla-mingos abandoned their nests in 2009, and scientists can't explain why. But they do know that all two thousand of their eggs remained unhatched.

What must the world's brainier animals think of us? Can they feel much gratitude for the diminished habitats and zoo quarters that have become home for so many? Could we really blame them if they somehow orchestrated a rebellion against us? Scientists are uncertain if it's viruses, sonar, or other factors that cause whales and dolphins to beach themselves. However, the evidence is fairly clear that habitat destruction and cruelty are responsible for elephant uprisings in Africa, India, and parts of Southeast Asia. Villages and crops have been destroyed, and thousands of humans have been killed in re-cent years.[4]

Biological researchers like G. A. Bradshaw, who are specialists in ele-phant behavior, attribute the elephants' aggression to a kind of post-traumatic stress disorder caused by poaching, government culling to control populations, and habitat loss. Elephants are a highly social species, living in closely knit families and clans, but their culture is unraveling because of chronic trauma and stress. Says Bradshaw, "The loss of elephant elders and the traumatic experience of witnessing the massacres of their families impair normal brain and behavior development in young elephants." *New York Times* journalist Charles Siebert is less clinical: "The elephant, with such a highly developed sensibility, is not going out quietly, without making some kind of statement."[5]

Fortunately, nature is extremely resilient and ecosystems can often regenerate if given the chance. When gray wolves were reintroduced into Yellowstone National Park they began to once again control an overpopulation of elk, which browse on and often kill young aspen trees. With the population of elk back in balance, the park's aspen groves are now flourishing, along with the beavers that use midsize aspen trunks to build their dams. In turn, the retained moisture from the dams encourages the growth of thirsty aspens. Aquatic life, from insect larvae to small fish, is thriving in the ponds, attracting birds. . . . Nature is stitching itself back together. What does this mean to you and me? Look no further than the mosquito, a carrier of various diseases that affect humans. In a diverse ecosystem, mosquito populations are kept in balance by fish, bats, and birds, but in a dysfunctional ecosystem, pests proliferate.

The demilitarized zone between North and South Korea is another ecological success story, albeit unintentional. Since the fighting stopped in 1953, the DMZ has been virtually off limits to people, resulting in a 150-mile strip of nearly pristine habitat that includes wetlands, forests, estuaries, mountains, coastal islands, riparian valleys, and agricultural fields. This buffer zone between the two countries—still technically at war—is an important refuge for two of the world's most endangered birds: the white-naped and red-crowned cranes. It's rumored that there may even be Korean tigers, one of the rarest mammals on the planet, in the DMZ.

Finding ways to connect strategic chunks of North American habitat with massive wildlife corridors is the primary mission of the Wildlands Network, a consortium of conservation organizations, government agencies, indigenous peoples, private landowners, and scientists. The Yellowstone to Yukon Conservation Initiative (Y2Y), a "one hundred-year vision to protect the wild heart of North America," is one example of the network's efforts to think and act on a grand scale. Imagine a wilderness corridor stretching from Jackson, Montana, to Whitehorse, in the Yukon Territory. The organization hopes to help restore the continent's ecological functions by restoring its flows, with strategies that include the following:

- Supporting the designation of new conservation zones

- Establishing extensive linkages between large natural areas to ensure the continuation of migrations

- Promoting positive public and private incentives that encourage responsible land management

- Helping landowners and land trusts protect critical parcels of private land

- Cooperating with transportation agencies to help remove barriers to wildlife movement

- Working with planners at all levels to create a balance between the needs of nature and of human society

The key question is, who will pay for such sweeping initiatives, or even small pieces of them? Though the first attempts to protect biodiversity on a large scale have been federal programs (see the table at page 157), there is an emerging emphasis on mechanisms that allow various stakeholders (private landowners, tourists, businesses, communities, and states) to enter the "nature market." Organizations like the Nature Conservancy and the World Wildlife Fund are great examples of nonprofits that preserve ecosystems. Ecotourism has become a successful, income-producing strategy worldwide; and certification programs that guarantee shade-grown coffee or sustainably harvested lumber also compensate businesses for the preservation of ecosystems. The Washington, D.C.–based group Forest Trends is a partnership of over fifty companies, governments, conservation experts, and financial institutions that are collectively exploring how biodiversity offsets (tradable credits for ecosystem services created in compensation for losses) can create jobs, preserve species, and offer incentives to preserve and restore forests.[6]

Costa Rica is a bright star in the constellation of biodiversity innovation. In contrast to many other countries that extract resources to the limits of profitability, Costa Rica changed the paradigm, adopting policies that reward many landowners for keeping their forests and rivers healthy and clean. If national resources like watersheds and forests are well maintained, the rivers will be free of silt, and many different citizens will benefit, including farmers, fishermen, dam operators, and various ecotourism entrepreneurs. Even you and I benefit, because healthy forests absorb carbon dioxide.

Costa Rica's Payment for Environmental Services program, implemented in 1997, taxes carbon emissions and rebates those revenues to individuals who protect the forests they own or that surround their communities. The country also imposed a water tax on hydroelectric dams, farmers, and providers of drinking water; the revenue is rebated to upstream villagers to keep their rivers clean. Deforestation has been reversed, and many low-income people now have a small source of income. One-fourth of Costa Rica's land is protected, stimulating the tourist industry; and 95 percent of the country's energy now comes from renewable sources: hydroelectric, wind, and geothermal. Although Costa Rica recently discovered oil within its borders, it banned drilling, which offers further assurance that this little green country will remain pristine and teeming with plant and animal species.[7]

Another huge success in natural preservation is the Canadian Boreal Forest Initiative, achieved by a coalition of environmental groups, Canadian First Nation peoples, nonprofit organizations, and private industry. Under the initiative, 1.3 billion acres of Canada's subarctic woodlands (about one-fourth of the planet's remaining forest, containing three-fourths of its freshwater) are designated for protection and limited sustainable development. At stake are huge pristine chunks of habitat: pine, spruce, poplar, and tundra ecosystems teeming with species such as caribou, wolves, bears, whooping cranes, yellow rails, and warblers.[8]

· Examples of Markets That Reward ·
the Preservation of Biodiversity

Program Description	Where Implemented
Wetlands credits for "no net loss" of wetlands. Those who drain and fill existing wetlands must create equal-value wetlands elsewhere. A wetlands banking system has emerged worth more than $3 billion a year.	The U.S. Clean Water Act provides the stimulus by outlawing destruction of wetlands, unless there is mitigation.
Offset credits for creating habitat for endangered species. Permits are available for displacing endangered species, as long as equivalent habitat is created elsewhere. About 70 "species banks" have been formed by the private sector to provide up to $300 million in credits every year.	The U.S. Endangered Species Act provides the stimulus by outlawing harm to endangered species, unless there is mitigation.

Program Description	Where Implemented
Protection, replanting, and sustainable management of forests. Private landowners receive payment ($20–$65 an acre) to protect the forests on their property. The program is funded by a fuel sales tax, and has already transferred $100 million to landowners.	The Costa Rican National Forest Office and National Fund for Forest Financing.
Offset credits on the international greenhouse-gas market, to protect the Amazon rain forest.	Ecuador and Brazil receive payments from countries like Sweden, Norway, and Germany to reduce carbon dioxide emissions from deforestation and burning.
Private purchase of services to maintain water quality. Payment by Perrier Vittel (private bottler of mineral water) of about $110 an acre for upstream sustainable farming that protects water purity.	Rhine-Meuse Basin, France.

➤ New Normal Agenda Point #20: If it Ain't Fixable, Don't Break It

Old Perspective: It's not important to know what happens in nature, since there's nothing we can do about it. The real value is what nature provides for me to consume. Since nature is "renewable," supplies are limitless.

New Perspective: Each human has a role to play in taking care of nature. At home, work, or church; on the farm; in the campground, voting booth, stock market, or supermarket, we can make choices that protect and restore nature. Nature is not "automatic" but needs to be understood and nurtured, or else our civilization will continue to march toward a chasm of overshoot—a tipping point in natural systems.

THE HEAVY LIFTING

• Create mentor programs that get kids out in nature. Invest time and money in the restoration of nature.

The services provided by the earth's natural systems far exceed the value of the products we buy and sell. One of the most valuable services is protection against natural disasters such as floods, hurricanes, droughts, pestilence, and forest fires. Writes Andrew Simms, author of *Ecological Debt*, "By 2060, economic losses from natural disasters could outstrip global income."[9] This may seem like a radical prediction, but ask top managers in the insurance industry if they support measures to rebuild ecosystems like wetlands and forests, to protect against natural disasters. Ask them if they promote actions to reduce the potential liabilities of global warming. In 2005 alone, Hurricanes Katrina, Rita, and Wilma cost the insurance industry $62 billion, and the potential for natural disasters escalates as flood-controlling forests are clear-cut, wetlands are drained, and greenhouse gases accumulate in the atmosphere.

Storm Cunningham, a strong advocate of natural restoration and CEO of the Resolution Fund, sees huge opportunities for businesses, communities, and investors in an emerging restoration economy. He calculates that restoring 13 million acres of wetlands along the Mississippi River and its tributaries would permanently prevent catastrophic flooding. What would be the cost of this ambitious restoration effort? About two-thirds of the cost of a single flood in 1993, he estimates. Similarly, the restoration of wetlands and barrier islands south of New Orleans could have prevented losses of more than $40 billion after Hurricane Katrina, and is increasingly seen as a wise, preventive investment. Not only would a restored environment protect New Orleans and create jobs, but the restoration would also create natural wealth like birds and aquatic species that help heal a wind-battered landscape.[10]

There is a lucrative market for such services, says wetlands expert Dr. Sarah Mack. Since restoring wetlands prevents carbon and nitrogen emissions that contribute to global warming, offset credits for the restoration can be sold in the world's emerging carbon market. "If we rebuild 30,000 square miles of Louisiana wetlands, that's the equivalent of removing the emissions of 8 million cars, and it translates to $1 billion of the European carbon trade market."[11]

Innovations like these begin to address what is perhaps the greatest dilemma of our time: undervalued resources are overused and abused. Our supply-and-demand mind-set doesn't evaluate the intrinsic worth of ecological systems, which in effect lie *beneath* the bottom line of the global economy. Since the inception of capitalism, the environment has been considered a subset of the economy—an illusion that nature refutes routinely with wildfires in California, or tornadoes that make whole midwestern counties look like landfills. "For eons the price of nature has been close to zero," writes Ricardo Bayon. "Supply typically outstripped demand, and priceless came to mean worthless." As long as our primary economic goal is constantly increasing consumption and GDP, the market will ignore the ecological and social benefits of nature, instead providing pedal-to-the-metal technologies, policies, and services to exploit nature's resources and convert them to "value added" products. However, this obsolete market mind-set is changing, since nature is becoming increasingly scarce and priceless.[12]

The key questions are:

- Will biological and physical scarcity stimulate beneficial changes in human behavior? Will civilization change its priorities because of new biological realities?

- Can we change the direction of our economy, from "Destroy nature, make money" to "Preserve and restore nature, save money"?

Some of the money needed to restore nature can come from *avoided* costs. A landmark 1989 decision by New York City illustrates the value of harnessing nature's services rather than destroying them. The Big Apple had to choose between building a $6 billion to $8 billion water-filtration facility to comply with drinking water standards or spending $1.5 billion to protect and restore the watershed where more than a billion gallons of New York City's water comes from, every day. The city put its money on nature as a filtration system. A restoration campaign to keep two thousand square miles of the Catskill/Delaware watershed clean includes actions like acquiring vulnerable parcels of land; building fences on private land to keep dairy cattle away from streams; and enlisting the cooperation of developers to install catchment basins (sculpted troughs in the landscape) to capture fertilizer runoff.

Partnerships with communities, industry, governments, and nonprofits helps the Wildlands Network promote the critical value of wildlife corridors. For example, acquiring and reforesting a strategically located farm could allow migration from parkland to another, existing forest or access to a river. Sometimes wildlife connections can be provided quite affordably and easily. Writes Storm Cunningham, "Enterprising farmers in Belize simply strung a rope-ladder across a main road, allowing howler monkeys to reach riverside habitat the farmers had restored."[13] The restoration project was funded by profits from a new business: tourists pay the farmers to watch the monkeys in their restored habitat.

Sometimes, restoration is accomplished on a shoestring, by the forces of passion and will. Empathy for Indonesian orangutans inspired Dutchman Willie Smits to join forces with local communities in Borneo to create a sanctuary for his beloved furry friends. In his postuniversity years, he rescued an orangutan from a garbage dump and nursed it back to health. Then he began to rescue other orangutans from bars and nightclubs, where they were captive entertainers. But after discovering how nearby forests were diced up, degraded, and thick with illegal loggers, he decided to create a private forest for the apes, enrolling local farmers to help him replant eight thousand acres of burned-out land. Because the locals will share the renewable wealth of the forest—sugar palms to produce ethanol—they help protect it from poachers. There are already more than a hundred bird species, each of which transfers diversity to the forest via seeds. And the trees' transpiration already produces its own clouds, resulting in 25 percent more rainfall than in surrounding, played-out forests. In the near future, the first of Smits's rehabbed primates will be released into the forest, and the biologist's dream will become a reality.[14]

Everyone has a stake in protecting and restoring natural systems. By supporting sustainable policies and innovative policy makers, individuals amplify their power to create change.

• Funding the Protection and Restoration of Nature •

• Environmental polluters	Oregon and other states have grant programs that redistribute revenues from industrial pollution fines to projects that model sustainable practices. In Oregon, recent awards have protected water quality and native diversity, and have supported sustainable vineyard and farm practices.
General public	In the early 1990s, Finland, Sweden, and Denmark implemented new taxes on pollution and energy and reduced income tax. In 1999, Germany, France, Italy, and the UK also implemented "tax shifts." In Germany fuel use fell by 5%. Denmark collects over 6% of its total tax revenue from green taxes.

United Nations	Under the emerging REDD program (Reducing Emissions from Deforestation and Forest Degradation) the UN will sell carbon credits to nations such as Indonesia and Brazil to comply with international climate-change agreements.
Businesses	The Dole Corporation pledged to be carbon neutral by 2021 in its Costa Rican banana and pineapple operations. The first step was to purchase forest carbon offsets equal to transportation emissions. Many other businesses, including Wells Fargo and Whole Foods, purchase renewable energy certificates to offset their electricity use.
	Argentina is the first country to require companies engaged in potentially hazardous activities to buy insurance to cover environmental damage. About 35,000 such companies will have to comply with the new rules.
Community	Community Forestry Enterprises in Guatemala provides increasingly skilled labor to manage forests at the local level. This increases diversity, reduces poaching, and enables villagers to earn twice the average salary.
	Farmers in Niger "regreened" an area of farmland and forest equal in size to the state of West Virginia after the country's forest service changed strategies, becoming less of a police force and more of a partner and trainer.
Consumer	The U.S. Fish and Wildlife Service produces the Federal Duck Stamp, purchased by hunters for the right to hunt. The stamp sells for $15 and raises about $25 million each year to fund wetland-habitat acquisition for the National Wildlife Refuge System.

➤ New Normal Agenda Point #21:
Increasing Ecological Income:
New Directions in Farming, Fishing, and Forestry

Old Perspective: Since the planet's ecosystems can generate wealth perpetually and since most laws and free-market practices do not steer us toward sustainable production systems, our single-focus goal is to use conventional methods in farming, fishing, and forestry to maximize yield and profits per dollar instead.

New Perspective: The planet's ecosystems cannot deliver wealth indefinitely. In fact, nature is facing bankruptcy. Soils are degrading and eroding, fisheries are being overfished, and forests are being stripped. Only sustainable methods can deliver continuing profits as well as security from potential catastrophes such as climate change and species extinction.

THE HEAVY LIFTING

• Think about a life change that throws nature a lifeline. Not happy with the job you have? Learn about, practice, and teach new ways of harvesting food, fish, and timber that support new industries that support the natural world.

"Everything is connected to everything else," ecologists tell us, after studying pieces of the web that weaves life together. This wisdom, like a Zen koan, is not simplistic but hard-earned, because ecologists sometimes spend whole lifetimes studying the life cycles and niches of one or two species. They emerge at the end of their careers with incredible tales about the abilities, persistence, and interdependence of the species they've come to know. Consider, for example, the life cycles of fungi. One of the planet's most valuable plant kingdoms, only fungi have the specialized enzymes required to decompose materials like the lignin in dead trees. Because they can't move from one tree to another, they made a "deal" with a certain type of mite that carries their spores to other dead trees in exchange for a tasty bite of fungus. Such relationships are not readily observable by the average person, but with a little effort and training, we can begin to see and understand the myriad relationships and connections, taking action to let ecosystems and carbon cycles bounce back. On the other hand, if we don't make nature a higher priority, the human legacy will become a horror movie that just keeps getting creepier.

With better funding for science education and research and a culture that once again values the integrity of whole systems, we will better understand and appreciate how forests absorb carbon dioxide, preventing the earth from overheating. We will see that expanded demand for livestock feed and biofuels is causing deforestation in tropical forests (about the only untilled, arable land left), contributing to a rise in global temperatures. We will understand that the melting of glaciers in the Himalayas cuts off the source of Asian rivers such as the Ganges. This relentless melting makes rice and wheat fields dry up, which in turn puts more tropical forests at risk of being cut down to grow soybeans and grain for a world market—in which demand is quickly catching up with supply. When we notice the price of bread go up on our own shelves, we finally begin to comprehend that in a global market, farms and forests are interconnected even if they are half a planet apart.

Similarly, the global fishing industry is interrelated with farming. When careless practices are used, agricultural wastes like eroded soil and fertilizer and pesticide runoff reduce and degrade fish populations in coastal waters, where the majority of fishing is done. For example, the Chesapeake Bay's fish, oyster, and crab harvests collapsed because of human activity, and it will ultimately cost hundreds of millions of dollars to restore the bay. A half century ago, the bay yielded more than 35 million pounds of oysters a year, but overharvesting, pollution, and sediments from runoff reduced that yield to a mere million pounds a year. Fortunately, the mitigations and benefits of restoration are in plain sight, and a regionwide initiative to control wastewater discharges, runoff from development, and farm erosion is showing signs of progress. As oysters begin to rebound, their capacity to filter and purify the bay increases, and the cleaner water supports higher oyster populations. Another keystone species in the bay, bay grass (a submerged aquatic plant), is being restored on a massive scale, which provides increased oxygen, food, and shelter for newborn crabs and fish, and reduces shoreline erosion by absorbing wave energy.

The point is, nature's complexity is the most valuable asset on earth, and it can regenerate if we let it. Innovations in farming, fishing, and forestry—three industries that impact nature the most—can provide sustainable yields without disrupting nature's resilience. The term "sustainable yield" might be compared to a bank account in which deposits and withdrawals are roughly equal. The principle of the account (the farm, fishery, or forest) remains intact, generating continued dividends.

· Benefits of Sustained-Yield Practices ·

Reduce greenhouse gas emissions.

Agriculture and livestock production and the loss of forests account for more than 40 percent of global greenhouse-gas emissions. Sustainable practices in farming and forestry can reduce the threat of global warming by at least a third.

Promote personal health.

Practices that ensure ecosystem stability generate fewer pollutants and higher-quality produce and fish.

Provide system resilience and diversity.

Sustainable methods protect species and recycle resources and nutrients, letting nothing be wasted.

Provide jobs that are satisfying.

Sustainable practices are more of a craft than industrialized methods. Results are visible and provide a sense of quality and pride.

Use natural momentum and renewable flows of energy and resources.

Instead of trying to overpower nature, sustainable practices conserve resources by letting nature provide pollination, perpetual and clean sources of energy, water and air purification; and healthy food.

According to the Earth Policy Institute, the world's taxpayers pay $700 billion annually to subsidize overpumping of aquifers, clear-cutting of forests, and overfishing.[15]

In effect, we are bankrolling our own demise. By *not* letting the free market work and keeping prices of resources artificially low, we encourage their depletion, assuming there will always be substitutes for what we use up. But what can we substitute for water, for species that have gone extinct, and for primordial topsoil that has eroded into streams, rivers, and oceans?

What if, rather than supporting unsustainable methods of production, nations and industries gave strong incentives to farmers, fishers, and foresters to create mutually beneficial relationships with natural resources? Not only will these restorative incentives benefit the general public (and protect the systems we evolved with), they will also yield long-term benefits for those who work and invest in these resource-based industries. For example, the restoration of forests and wetlands on farms encourages pollinators free of charge, as well as predators that control pests naturally. The renewal of fisheries by providing off-limits marine reserves provides continuing catches; and sustainable forestry practices rather than clear-cutting provide perpetual profits for those in the industry as well as recreational and health benefits for the general population.

WORTH MORE ALIVE THAN DEAD

Following the massive floods, mudslides, and erosion that occurred in 1998 and caused $30 billion in damages, the Chinese government banned logging in the huge Yangtze River watershed, concluding that the flood-control value of the forests was worth three times as much as the lumber. Reports the Earth Policy Institute, "When viewed not just through the eyes of the individual logger but through those of society as a whole, it simply did not make economic sense to continue deforesting. Beijing then took the unusual step of paying the loggers to become tree planters—to reforest instead of deforest."[16] China's heightened focus on the value of forested land triggered the Green Wall initiative to protect land from the expanding Gobi Desert. This modern version of the Great Wall will stretch nearly three thousand miles.

Inspired by the Green Belt movement that won Kenyan Wangari Maathai a Nobel Prize, the United Nations in 2006 launched the Billion Tree Campaign to help restore land and prevent global warming. So far, more than 3 billion trees have been planted in 150 countries, and the goal has now been expanded: plant 7 billion trees—at least one tree for every person on the planet.

Menominee Tribal Enterprises (MTE) in northeastern Wisconsin operates one of the finest examples of sustainable forestry in the world. In recent decades, MTE has managed its 220,000-acre forest based on wider values than maximum yield. More than 2 billion board feet of lumber have been removed from the MTE forest in the last 140 years, yet the volume of saw timber on the reservation is greater than when logging first began. The secret to MTE's success is its focus on quality. Increasing the volume of harvested wood is a primary goal, but this is balanced with improving wood quality, maintaining ecosystem health, providing multiple uses of the forest, and sustaining local communities with jobs and educational opportunities. High environmental standards enable certification from both the Forest Stewardship Council (SmartWood) and Scientific Certification Systems (SCS), fulfilling another MTE goal, higher value per unit of wood.[17]

Urban forestry, too, can play a huge role in increasing ecological wealth.

A study about the value of urban trees concluded that for every $1 spent planting and taking care of trees, communities reap $2 of value in cleaner air, more stable soil, increased tourism, better quality of life, higher real estate values, and lower utility bills. A healthy canopy of trees can reduce ambient temperatures in a city by 5 to 10 degrees Fahrenheit, also reducing the need for air-conditioning, and in a windy city, evergreen trees reduce winter heating bills.[18]

While these trends toward replanting and sustained yield are hopeful, they are currently being erased by rising pressures on the world's forests from increased demand for lumber, paper, and fuel. At the beginning of the twentieth century, the earth's forested area was estimated at about 12 billion acres, but it has since shrunk to about 3 billion acres. A full 20 percent of greenhouse gases is coming from deforestation and the burning of forests—a larger percentage than from transportation or livestock production. Two countries—Indonesia and Brazil—are currently responsible for half of this deforestation.[19]

In the United States, where most old-growth forest is long gone, forest plantations are becoming the standard practice in the wood-products industry, yet recent studies indicate that untouched natural forests store 60 percent more carbon dioxide than plantation forests.[20] Nearly 60 percent of America's forests are privately owned, the majority of these by people fifty-five and older. Vast acreages of forest will soon change hands as aging landowners pass the land to heirs or buyers. Research at the Pinchot Institute for Conservation found that "heirs who will inherit the land are often professionals living far away in cities, have weak bonds to the land, and have little involvement in management of family forests. High taxes are a top reason heirs decide to sell the land." Reducing land taxes and offering incentives to retain, protect, and profit from the land is a sensible strategy for protecting these forests.[21]

GROWING AWARENESS—AND EATING IT

Agriculture, like forested land, offers huge potentials for reducing greenhouse-gas emissions; however, tapping this potential will necessitate changes in standard farming methods. The farming industry will have to move away from conventional, energy-hungry practices and toward more biologically ingenious methods. After all, farming has always been solar-powered, and can again teach us to value and respect ecological income. Until the last century, soil was typically rich in carbonaceous organic matter; however, much of that carbon has been depleted by conventional farming methods including manufactured fertilizer; maximized yields that stifle natural resilience; isolation of livestock from crops (which makes manure a problem rather than a solution); and intensive tillage, which increases erosion and greenhouse-gas emissions.

Massive amounts of carbon can be sequestered in soil if more farmers are encouraged to farm organically. A twenty-three-year study conducted by the Rodale Institute found that organic farming increased soil carbon by 15 to 28 percent and soil nitrogen by 8 to 15 percent. Current use of manufactured fertilizers is estimated at 102 million tons worldwide, much of which is emitted from the soil as nitrous oxide—three hundred times as potent as carbon dioxide as a greenhouse gas. Converting just the U.S. acreage now planted in corn and soybeans would reduce global nitrous oxide emissions by 10 percent. Organic agriculture relies heavily on off-season and rotated cover crops that protect and replenish the soil; wider use of this traditional method would sequester megatons of carbon and make agriculture more productive.[22]

Finding productive ways to till less per unit of food is a global priority, since tillage releases carbon dioxide from soil. While most of our food now comes from annual crops like corn, soybeans, and wheat, researchers at the Land Institute and elsewhere are developing perennial crops that produce grains and oilseeds that won't have to be tilled. "Agroforestry" is a climate-friendly production method that puts trees and shrubs right into farm fields to produce fruit and nuts, medicines, timber, crop fertility, and biological habitat—all on the same piece of farmland. No doubt fruit and nut trees and other perennial crops will provide a higher percentage of the human diet in the future.

Another inevitable change in human diet is a gradual descent down the food chain. Meat production now accounts for almost a fifth of global greenhouse gases. That percentage can be reduced significantly if there are more plants and fewer livestock in our fields and on our plates. There are now more than 18 billion cows, pigs, sheep, goats, chickens, and other livestock on the planet, many of which are fed grains that humans could be eating directly. The fertilizers used to grow grain—and the energy used to manufacture the fertilizers—are leading sources of greenhouse gas. (About one-half of America's farmland is currently devoted to growing feed for livestock.) A growing demand for range-fed beef is a step in the right direction because cattle are healthier and emit less methane when they eat what they evolved to eat. In fact, a 2003 Swedish study found that cattle raised organically on grass emit 40 percent less greenhouse gas than grain-fed cattle.

The conversion of livestock waste to fuel in biogas digesters is an expanding and promising trend, as is injecting manure as fertilizer into the soil to reduce emissions, rather than applying it on top of the ground. Overall, however, the most valuable transformation in the livestock industry will be to decrease its size. Reducing the amount of meat we eat will at the same time improve human health. Like the cattle we fatten with grain, we simply aren't eating what our bodies are designed to eat. Our intestines, for example, more closely resemble an herbivorous deer's than a carnivorous tiger's, yet meat consumption continues to rise, especially in developing countries. The environment can't tolerate our diet either. Erosion, soil depletion, water pollution, global warming, and toxic chemical contamination are end points of our current, mainstream diet—trends that can't and won't continue. As agriculture enters its second ten-thousand-year period, significant improvements are in store.

FISHING FOR SOLUTIONS

The future of the fishing industry looks radically different too. Although total seafood harvest quadrupled in the second half of the twentieth century, the human appetite for seafood is growing faster than the sustainable yield of oceanic fisheries. "Harvests expanded as new technologies evolved, ranging from sonar to vast driftnets that are collectively large enough to circle the earth many times over," writes the Earth Policy Institute's Lester Brown. But it's impossible to think of harvest increases as "progress" when an estimated 90 percent of large ocean fish such as marlin, tuna, and tropical grouper have been eliminated. In an estimated 75 percent of global fisheries, harvests exceed natural regeneration, which inevitably leads to ecological bankruptcy.[23]

As in farming and forestry, misdirected federal subsidies and incentives are a large piece of the problem. Redirecting these subsidies can fairly rapidly increase ecological income and also create jobs. Since small-scale fisheries employ more people per unit of harvest and also have less impact on the environment, why not give a higher percentage of subsidies to them? Subsidizing fuel consumption for ships that travel longer distances is another easy target. Long-distance fishing trips require more energy to keep the catch cold after the harvest. Why not instead reward fishing companies that harvest closer to shore and/or do not use destructive draglines?

Nations with strong fishing industries such as Canada, China, Belgium, New Zealand, and the United Kingdom are starting to shift subsidies from technology to biology, supporting marine reserves that allow fish species to regenerate. Although some fishers oppose putting sections of the ocean off limits, data show that yields actually increase when species are allowed a "time-out" from human predation. Says scientist Callum Roberts of the University of York in the UK, "There is no more effective way of allowing things to live longer, grow larger, and produce more offspring."[24] After a snapper fishery was protected off the coast of New England, the local population of snapper increased forty-fold. In one section of the Gulf of Maine, all fishing methods that put bottom-feeding fish at risk were banned. Population densities, average fish size, and species diversity all rose significantly, and scallop populations increased fourteen-fold within five years.[25]

America's Conservation Reserve Program is another successful use of subsidies that place a value on ecosystem services and regeneration. By taking 35 million acres of marginal, erosion-prone land out of service, U.S. taxpayers are helping reduce greenhouse-gas emissions, because plant cover on the retired acres stores carbon dioxide and isn't tilled. The emergence of carbon markets will substantially raise the value of land and sea that are allowed to regenerate. For example, the World Bank estimates that an acre of rain forest converted to crops is worth $100 to $250. But the same acre might be worth $2,000 if it demonstrably soaks up carbon dioxide and there are buyers of that service. If we program the free market to take us in a sustainable direction, we'll make it.

➤ New Normal Agenda Point #22: Throwing Nature a Lifeline: Personal Choices That Can Turn the Tide

Old Perspective: Individuals don't have to pay attention to the health of natural systems, since our everyday metro-media world consists mostly of human-made designs and devices. Besides, what effect will my decisions and actions really have on "saving the planet"?

New Perspective: Individual actions both affect and are affected by the dominant cultural ethic. The individual's role is to help perfect and be guided by that ethic, for the good of the group (now more than 7 billion strong).

THE HEAVY LIFTING

• Support shifts in subsidies for forests, farms, and fisheries that benefit both the industry and the natural world.

The best solutions for saving the planet are far more profound than simply buying green products or reducing our vehicle miles traveled, although these actions are critical. Even more fundamental is personal awareness of and reverence for the complexity and "rightness" of natural systems. Nature is not a repository of objects that exist for our use, but a living, inter-connected organism; not a list of nouns but very active and very fragile verbs. As individuals, we typically don't make an effort to protect living be-ings until we've had moments of genuine connection, when we see and feel how small we really are and how large and complex life on earth really is. Whatever enables these personal epiphanies is where the restoration of nature begins.

One obvious way to participate is to understand that all of the earth's waste equals food, and to act on that realization by reducing the number of glitches in our lives that prevent "nutrients" from getting back home. Visit a state-of-the-art recycling facility and you'll see materials on their way to second and third life cycles as completely different products: the steel cans snatched up by magnetism and the aluminum cans repelled; the plastic jugs swimming up the conveyor belt like salmon—to spawn new milk jugs, new combs, hoses, and eyeglasses. But individuals can't recycle by them-selves. We need a social structure that demands recyclable products and an infrastructure that collects and markets them.

Before the Second World War, most consumer products were made from natural materials like wood, stone, silk, and glass, but after the war, industrial materials (largely petroleum-based) began to dominate the mar-ket, and our lives. In the 1950s, litter began to coat our streets and lawns because we suddenly had more things to throw away. The appearance of our streets and sidewalks improved only when it became socially taboo to toss your candy wrapper or Coke can. However, judging by the continent-sized island of floating debris in the North Pacific—largely plastic and cig-arette butts—we have by no means banished litter from our lifestyle. "Last year," reports Tom McCann of the Ocean Conservancy, "400,000 volun-teers from more than 100 countries picked up 6.8 million pounds of trash from beaches."[26]

We still purchase (and design) products that are heavily overpackaged, forget to bring cloth bags to the grocery, and use public beaches as huge ash-trays. Fishing boats still discard used nets, and luxury liners still dump trash into the ocean—where sea turtles mistake plastic bags for jellyfish, and sea-birds' intestines become clogged with wrappers and plastic pull tabs.

The solution to this megaproblem is multifaceted: we need an ever-stronger ethic that makes littering at all levels illegal as well as shameful. We need better-designed packaging, made from natural, biodegradable materials. And we need widespread use of laws like those in San Francisco, where the plastic bag was banned, and where residents must now separate compostable trash or face a $500 fine.

Recycling is not just a civic duty, it's the way mature ecosystems work, and we can use natural systems as a mentor for human behavior. (We're "all natural." Though sometimes we behave more like machines.) When Americans collectively fail to recycle more than 50 *billion* aluminum cans a year, the market spawns new aluminum smelters, built on land that used to be habitat— typically near large rivers with hydroelectric plants. What can we do about it? Build recycling securely into our economy, as Brazil has done. Despite rich bauxite deposits that ultimately become profitable aluminum products, this tropical nation recycles 87 percent of its aluminum containers. With a 10¢ deposit on beverages, the state of Michigan recycles 95 percent of its containers, and India is doing its part to reduce waste with a deposit charge about half the cost of a beverage.[27]

LET THEM EAT PLASTIC

Too often, we respond to urgent reports about the decline of nature with a shrug of our shoulders. Since many impacts are embedded within our way of life—the way we manufacture, farm, generate energy, collect used material—we often don't feel there's much we can do as individuals. This collective shoulder-shrugging—a whole civilization deferring responsibility—is potentially fatal; many empires and civilizations before ours collapsed because of a lack of respect for nature. In our times, the throwaway lifestyle seems easy, but it inevitably results in higher taxes, expensive health effects, and degraded landscapes that need to be repaired. These added expenses make our civilization unaffordable.

However, by "saving nature" we make life less expensive while creating jobs, recreation, health, security, a stable climate, and a way of life that requires less maintenance. Yet, because our role as consumers has dominated our lives, we sometimes forget the many other ways we can preserve and restore nature: as teachers, students, farmers, designers, parents, voters, citizen activists, business owners, shareholders, churchgoers, vacationers, petition signers, meal planners, Internet users, and influential friends. In each of these roles, we can weave additional strands into the web of life.

Evidence of the changing paradigm is all around us, as the word "green" begins to redefine our culture. Here are a few high-leverage examples of how individuals play a role in preserving and restoring nature in various aspects of our lives:

Internet user: The Internet is rapidly enhancing the very nature of communication, including the way opinion and advocacy become reality. This new medium, more transformative than the printing press, not only enables political participation, awareness building, and fund-raising for environmental activism, but will inevitably become a means of frequent referenda and pulse taking on key political issues. This may create a more responsive and egalitarian form of democracy than we've ever seen. Individuals can already use the Web to become an expert on issues; sign petitions and respond to polls; download e-books; become bloggers; and network with thousands of people instantly through e-mail and via Twitter, Facebook, and many other sites. In less time than it takes to microwave a dish of potatoes, you can be one of half a million signatories of a petition to stop global warming, plant a virtual tree on the Second Life Web site, or research options for green personal-care products.

Meal planner: Each household's meal planner can be a key player in helping nature bounce back, and cutting meat consumption offers the highest returns. The average American diet, heavy on the meat (more than 200 pounds a year), requires twice as much water and two to four times the land area per person as an equally nutritious vegetarian diet. The livestock industry alone generates about a fifth of global greenhouse gases. Studies have shown that becoming a vegetarian is a more effective greenhouse gas buster than switching from an SUV to a hybrid car. But we don't all have to become vegetarians; we just need to reduce the amount of meat we eat, either with smaller (healthier) portions or with meatless meals. When we learn a new meatless recipe, we are playing a role in changing the ratio of CO_2-absorbing plants to methane-generating livestock. Once again, the Web can help increase our options, offering a wealth of flavorful recipes from all over the world.

Vacationer: Vacations can be great fun for travelers (up to 800 million a year) but sometimes not so much fun for nature. Air travel is one of humanity's most troublesome habits, as is tourism-related development and consumption that can destroy world-class natural areas. Recent research suggests that sunscreen, which may be toxic to algae, may contribute to the decline of coral reefs. Acid rain—partially generated by vehicles—harms the pristine lakes and forests we often visit. Taking vacations closer to home is a start, and combining that approach with purpose-driven vacations is even better. Many vacationers now opt for ecotourism getaways, spending time learning about and rehabilitating ecosystems. A program called World Wide Opportunities on Organic Farms (WWOOF) allows volunteers to learn, hands-on, about farming and gardening while at the same time helping farmers stay in business. Farms and ranches across the country also offer agritourism—a chance to stay, for example, on an olive farm on California's Central Coast and see how olive oil is pressed. Such vacations enable individuals to have an authentic experience that's neutral or even beneficial in its impact.

Employee: Who in his right mind really wants to spend 100,000 hours per lifetime commuting to a job whose products and services harm the environment? Choosing a nature-friendly job can be one of the most valuable ways to make a difference. Ask Steve Golden, now a senior manager with the National Park Service. "Starting in elementary school, I walked to school most days along a brook, stopping to chase ducks or catch frogs. I sometimes arrived at school drenched from falling in the brook, or covered with poison ivy rashes, but these trips were often the highlight of my day," he recalls. Golden preceded his twenty-year career at the NPS with a three-month hike on the Appalachian Trail, from Georgia all the way to Maine, and now he brings his passion to his work. "Every day I partner with people—from the South Bronx to the wilds of Maine—working to save their rivers, trails, and open spaces. I think I may have the best job there is."

Shopper: According to a Natural Marketing Institute survey, certain certification labels that are most familiar have a major, beneficial effect on consumer decisions. Among the early adopters of green products— sometimes termed the Lifestyles of Health and Sustainability (LOHAS) market segment—75 percent are more likely to buy products with green labels such as Energy Star, Recycled, USDA Organic, and Fair Trade. And they will pay more for the quality assurance these labels offer: efficiency, less waste, health, sustainable farming practices, and monetary support for workers. Each label indicates multiple benefits. For example, to qualify for a Fair Trade label on coffee, chocolate, and other products, importers must support fair wages for workers and assist growers in transitioning to organic methods. Similarly, those building and paper products bearing the Forest Stewardship Council logo must obtain their wood from forests that are managed using sustainable methods. By purchasing products with these labels, consumers support sustainable, quality production.

Recycler: Individuals don't recycle; cultures do. I can be a burning soul for the idea of recycling, but if a recycling system isn't set up, I'll ship all my paper, bottles, and cans to the landfill like all my neighbors. Fortunately, my hometown has just implemented a commingled Pay As You Throw program, which means that we can now combine most recyclable goods in a single container, and that we will pay by the bag or trash can for everything we don't recycle. All of a sudden, recycling becomes a kind of consumer sport. If we want to pay less for trash collection, we need to generate less trash, which means buying products with packaging we can recycle, and products that are concentrated, repairable, durable, and designed to resist fashion swings.

If we want to help natural systems recover (partly to keep up with the born-again Joneses) we'll use less paper, and the paper we do use will be at least 80 percent postconsumer recycled. Cloth towels will replace paper towels in the kitchen, and paper plates will become a fad of the past. To insist that Americans can't live without seven hundred pounds of paper a year per person (cumulatively, a third of the world's paper) is to ignore the fact that paper consumption has doubled since 1970. And to further assume that paper must be made from trees is to ignore the fact that the Gutenberg Bible and the U.S. Constitution were printed on hemp-based paper. In the future, a larger percentage of paper can and will be made from agricultural and manufacturing wastes.[28]

Environmental activist: The environmental activism of Kenyan Wangari Maathai won her a Nobel Peace Prize in 2004 for initiating and shepherding the African Green Belt Movement. Maathai's energies demonstrate a cornerstone of activism: identify human and environmental needs and meet them using the focused energies of local citizens to improve their quality of life. She observed that Kenyan women needed firewood, clean drinking water, nutritious food, and income, and that planting trees could help meet these needs. Since 1977, the program has planted more than 30 million trees and trained more than thirty thousand women in trades such as forestry, food processing, and beekeeping to provide income in ways that protect and restore the environment. Of course, we aren't likely to win the Nobel Prize, but we can join the efforts of groups like Environmental Defense Fund, the Union of Concerned Scientists, and the World Wildlife Fund to help change the direction of our culture, including our wayward economy. In the 1990s, activism prompted the giant food corporation Unilever to work with the World Wildlife Fund to establish a system to certify sustainably harvested fish. The resulting Marine Stewardship Council now administers the Fish Forever ecolabel, used in more than thirty nations. Similarly, Home Depot began buying sustainably harvested timber because of shareholder activism. Tyson Foods announced it would no longer use antibiotics in its poultry products, and Red Lobster will certify all farm-raised shrimp as having a minimal impact on the environment. By recognizing and valuing sustainable production, activists are making a huge difference.

House and landscape maintainer: Another inspired individual, Professor Douglas Tallamy, looks at the protection of nature through the eyes of an insect. Entomologist Tallamy has observed throughout his career that native insects don't thrive on non-native plants, and that "because so many animals depend directly or indirectly on insect protein for food, a land without insects is a land without most forms of higher life." The pampered species (such as 30 million to 40 million acres of lawn) we have imported into our private landscapes are aggressive, demanding heavy inputs of nitrogen, herbicides, and energy-intensive maintenance, and providing neither food nor shelter for insects. His passionate, activist response was to reclaim his own ten-acre property in Pennsylvania—replacing all the alien species with natives—and then write about it, in a book titled *Bringing Nature Home.* "This use of our time has put us in intimate contact with the plants on our property and with the wildlife that depends on them," writes Tallamy.

Again, we can't all muster that sort of enthusiasm for insects, but we can begin to add diversity back into our landscapes, even if we risk bewildered gazes from our neighbors.[29]

Educators and students: In a great little book called *Beyond Ecotopia,* elementary-school teacher David Sobel writes, "What's emerging is a strange kind of schizophrenia. Children are disconnected from the world outside their doors and connected with endangered animals and ecosystems around the globe through electronic media." Sobel prefers the less convenient but more relevant method of teaching kids about the nature in their own yards and neighborhoods. To teach children about birds, for example, he likes to craft wings out of cardboard boxes and let his fledgling students become the birds and build nests; only then does he bring out the bird books. He is also adamant about the principle "No tragedies until at least fourth grade," recognizing that when kids are overwhelmed by environmental problems, they don't learn to be comforted and amazed by nature. "Let us allow them to love the Earth before we ask them to save it," Sobel writes. His place-based principles have inspired many educators to ask, "What do children really need?"[30]

➤ **New Normal Agenda Point #23:**
Biologic: Putting Nature Back into Chemical Products
and Processes

Old Perspective: "Better Living Through Chemistry." Manufacturers and retailers wouldn't make and use chemicals that harm people and the environment, would they? Surely somebody is watching.

New Perspective: Of eighty-three thousand different chemicals currently being used, only a few hundred have been rigorously tested. We need a far better system of protecting humans and nature from toxic chemicals and compounds.

THE HEAVY LIFTING

- Use your monthly budget wisely. Support the design, manufacture, and use of products made with natural chemicals, and processes that don't compete with food production or reduce natural diversity.

One mind-set says, "We can *make* it work"; the other says, "Let it work." One says, "Conquer nature, maximize output"; the other says, "Go with the flow, keep the system intact." Since ancient times, one way of thinking has been associated with the military, right-angled efficiency, and increasingly powerful technology, while the other is more closely associated with natural rhythms, crafts, and sturdy villages. At the risk of oversimplification, one mind-set is closely aligned with conventional engineering—technologic— while the other is associated with the emerging field of ecological design— what I call biologic.

Engineers have for several millennia been held in the highest regard, as lifesavers and nature tamers armed with the tools and techniques to vanquish floods, disease, tornadoes, and pestilence. The question is, has the engineering mentality steadily evolved (in partnership with single-goal investors) into more of a threat than nature itself? Rocket inventor Wernher von Braun once said, "It's not my department where they come down." In the pioneer days of space flight, his mission was simply to get the rockets up. In much the same way, the partnership between corporate managers and industrial engineers often strives to get profits and productivity up; never mind where the pollution and social impacts of poorly designed products come down.

Technologic thinkers tend to be problem solvers, not problem avoiders. If you want to get from point A to point B, they can muscle you up a superhighway, but it's not in their job description to preserve the view, or the native grasses and birds. Technologic is not just an engineering trait; it's also a familiar characteristic among economists, urban planners, and politicians who prefer to fit the world into their plans and theories rather than adapting the plan to meet the needs of people and nature. A good example of technologic is the control of agricultural pests. Scientists on the agribusiness payroll have genetically engineered commodity crops like corn to be resistant to herbicides, allowing those chemicals to be used with abandon to control weeds. A more holistic, biologic approach builds pest resistance into the whole system to prevent weed infestations, by rotating crops, keeping the right seed eaters happy (insects and birds), and using precisely applied amounts of water and organic fertilizer—enough for the crop but not for the weeds.

The manufacture and use of other industrial chemicals—for products ranging from packaging to building materials—will more frequently begin with ecological design in the new millennium. There are still many obstacles to designing with nature, not the least of which is that soft, or green, chemistry requires learning new chemical pathways—effectively a different language. After the world's first commercial oil spurted out of the ground about 150 years ago, the patterns and pathways of industry were totally restructured and quickly became standard procedures. It was suddenly far more profitable to use long-dead organisms (in oil and natural gas) than recently living organisms (in plants, whale oil, livestock) to make dyes, chemicals, fertilizers, paints, inks, solvents, construction materials, and energy.

When the gas-powered automobile beat out the first electric cars, oil became a universal currency. While three out of four consumer products were still made from natural materials (like wood, minerals, cotton, rubber, beeswax, silk, and glass) as late as 1950, by 2010, three out of four products were made primarily from petroleum and its by-products. No wonder we've depleted our rich, oily trust fund so quickly! But future generations may well regard our first primitive chemistry experiments as baby talk. Having learned the basic vocabulary of chemistry, we now must decide what we want to say. What exactly do we want chemicals to accomplish? Where should these chemicals come from, and where should they end up?

The truth is, the petrochemical industry, with about $600 billion annually in global sales and more than 6 million employees, is on shaky foundations. When the inevitable peak of oil production arrives (next year? in five years?) demand for oil will exceed supply, and its cost will skyrocket, along with the universe of products that are made from or powered by it. But that's not the only reason why green chemistry and nature-inspired products are flowing into the mainstream. New advances in biology have lowered the cost of making products with plants and microbes. Using sunlight, naturally occurring molecules, and microbial catalysts, researchers are eliminating many negative side effects of chemical manufacturing. Still, as *Los Angeles Times* journalist Marla Cone observes, "Virtually everything we buy, breathe, drink and eat contains traces of toxic substances. The names are confusing; the list, mind-boggling: Bisphenol A in plastic baby bottles and food cans. Phthalates in vinyl toys. Polybrominated flame retardants in furniture cushions. Formaldehyde in kitchen cabinets. Radon in granite countertops. Lead in lipstick. 1,4-Dioxane in shampoo. Volatile organic compounds in hair spray."[31]

Our lives are on a collision course with the chemicals we create; an average newborn baby's body contains nearly three hundred compounds, according to recent analyses of umbilical cords, including mercury from fish, flame retardants from household dust, pesticides from backyards and nearby farms, and hydrocarbons from fossil fuels. Company managers fear lawsuits, recalls, and sudden changes in regulation, and are rethinking. While smaller labs and companies like the Draths Corporation have the flexibility to innovate, even huge corporations BASF and Rohm and Haas are interested in creating safer substances that won't seep into human bloodstreams, endanger wildlife, or pollute resources. Another stimulant for biologic chemistry is government regulation that has put limits on such by-products of petrochemicals as sulfur and mercury. Bioproducts offer a strong potential for reducing greenhouse-gas emissions, since during growth, plants absorb carbon dioxide. Using plant and microbial molecules avoids the high temperatures, pressures, acids, and heavy metals typically required to break the tight molecular bonds in petroleum. In many cases, green production pathways are no more expensive than petro pathways. So, what variables need to converge to shift both the supply and demand sides in a green direction? We can learn a lot from the widespread adoption of soybean ink to replace ink made from fossil fuel. In the late 1970s, oil supplies were unreliable and prices were volatile. The Newspaper Association of America researched more than two thousand different vegetable oil formulations to find a cost-effective alternative that performed as well as petroleum-based ink.

The ideal ink had to have certain performance and environmental properties to satisfy different stakeholders: Press operators wanted good absorption but minimal bleeding through the paper, to stretch a pound of ink further. Newspaper managers wanted supply dependability, lower paper and ink consumption, compatibility with existing equipment, good public relations, and bright colors. State and federal regulations were becoming increasingly strict about volatile organic compound (VOC) emissions, which are unhealthy to breathe and a precursor to urban smog. The general public wanted a highly recyclable newspaper, produced with ink that was environmentally friendly.

Soybean ink met all these criteria, and more. The *Cedar Rapids Gazette*, in the heart of soybean country, was the product's earliest adopter. Recalls Joe Hladky, the paper's publisher, "We were getting 10 to 12 percent more copies for the same amount of ink, and because soy ink is non-toxic, we didn't have to pay a premium to haul hazardous waste ink. Soybean ink has only 3 to 15 percent volatile organic emissions compared with 36 to 40 percent from conventional inks, so overall, we could smell the difference, see the difference, and track the difference in costs." Today, more than a third of U.S. newspapers use soy ink for the entire newspaper, and 90 percent of the country's ten thousand newspapers use colored soy ink because the colors are more vibrant.[32]

· Principles and Benefits of Green Chemistry ·

Prevents waste by design rather than having to treat it or clean it up later.

Intentionally designs substances that possess little or no toxicity to human health and the environment.

Chemical products are designed to break down after their function is achieved rather than persisting in the environment.

Processes can be performed at ambient pressures and temperatures, which is radically different from conventional chemical production. Separation and purification steps use less energy, and renewable materials are used, rather than petroleum.

Reduces or eliminates the need for hazardous solvents, reagents, and catalysts in chemical production.

Can reduce the potential for chemical accidents during production and use, including releases, explosions, and fires.

Specific design goals are more easily achieved: for example, chemicals are durable enough to do the job but are not "immortal." Chemicals can avoid being overengineered so one size fits all, and can be deliberately designed for a commercial "afterlife."

Each green process or product will have to pass similar testing to overcome the industrial inertia that characterizes the chemical-products industry. "Many chemical companies still take a stance of 'let's just let this green thing blow over,'" says Yale chemistry professor Paul Anastas, known as the father of green chemistry. In a report commissioned by twelve of the largest chemical companies, consultants concluded the industry was "fiercely defensive," with a "bunker mentality" similar to the attitude initially taken by the tobacco industry. Being first to the market is usually a stronger design criterion than being the greenest product on the market. Still, given the havoc created by chemicals that are a bad fit, and the inevitable high costs of oil, the industry will without a doubt continue to turn darker shades of green. A new California law is leading the way. By 2011, the state and its industries must identify hazardous chemical ingredients, regulate their use, and search for sustainable alternatives.[33]

Another strong driver of innovation is the power exerted by corporate giants like Wal-Mart. With 200 million customers and sixty thousand suppliers, Wal-Mart sends ripples of change throughout American industry when it demands a product without toxic chemicals. Life cycle analysis (LCA) enables manufacturers to determine where a chemical comes from, what sort of impacts it will have on people and the environment, and what will happen at the end of its life. Even comparatively small companies amplify their influence by being members of organizations like the Outdoor Industry Association, which helps suppliers deliver products that are free of toxic side effects to very particular megabuyers like REI, Nike, and Patagonia.

A next-generation start-up, the Draths Corporation, was recently awarded $21 million in venture funding to make nylon and other widely used products with renewable resources and natural feedstocks rather than by conventional methods. Chemist John Frost, formerly of Michigan State University, calls his process a "sweeter route to nylon" because it begins with naturally occurring sugars from plant starch. The biologic pathway Frost discovered avoids the creation of benzene, a cancer-causing compound. And as long as there's sunlight, there will be a renewable supply of interwoven, moldable, elastic, durable, stable nylon to form into sheets, rods, fibers, pipes, tubes, and coatings. Related technologies could also provide sustainable solutions for the $80 billion-a-year chemical aromatics industry, which includes such common products as paints, coatings, and other widely used materials.[34]

Elevance Renewable Sciences, named one of *Business Week*'s Top 10 Most Successful Startups of 2008, offers further evidence that the $3 trillion chemical industry is beginning to experience systemic change. Using a Nobel Prize–winning technology (olefin metathesis), the company uses natural oils to create a wide range of chemicals, including waxes, cleaners, lubricants, additives, adhesives, cosmetics, fungicides, textiles, motor oil, and disinfectants. The company chose the bee as its logo because the overall mission is to use raw ingredients like soybean, canola, corn, and sunflower oils to make "honey," without harming the source.

➤ New Normal Agenda Point #24: Nature, Weather, and Water

Old Perspective: Because the earth is a closed system, water is endlessly recycled, and we can never run out. Nature provides rain and snow just when we need water to convey our wastes, shampoo our hair, grow our crops, and cool our power plants. The rest is abundantly available for wildlife, wildflowers, and rainbows.

New Perspective: Because the earth is a closed system, there is only a finite amount of water available. Populations continue to expand, and water demand per capita also continues to expand. Weather patterns are changing, ecosystems are drying up, and the value of water must be reassessed.

THE HEAVY LIFTING

- Use water more efficiently at home and urge leaders in agriculture and industry to follow suit.

- Crusade for placing a higher cultural value on all those things that enable our support system—nature—to produce clean, affordable water: wetlands, streams, rivers, and lakes.

- Influence local authorities to charge higher prices for water because of emerging scarcity.

- Influence local, state, and national government officials to implement more rigorous and innovative water policies, from changes in subsidies to rebates, regulations, and restrictions.

A Costa Rican saying, "When it rains, everyone drinks," is wonderfully egalitarian, and also plausible in a country where ten feet of rain a year isn't unusual. Most of the world's countries are not as richly endowed with both rain and rain forest as Costa Rica, and this remarkable little country has optimized its assets. A generation of Costa Rican leaders has preserved and reclaimed more than a third of the country's forests, understanding that they increase quality of life, the number of tourists, and the reliability of rain. How do trees increase rain? In effect, solar energy powers plant growth and evaporation from leaves to "pump" water through tree roots, trunks, and leaves into the atmosphere, where it forms moisture-heavy clouds. In *Plan B 3.0*, Lester Brown explains what happens next:

> *The world's forests are conduits for transporting water inland. In a healthy rainforest, only about one-fourth of the rainfall runs off into rivers and back to the ocean. The other three-fourths evaporates and is carried further inland, where the process is repeated. If the rainforest is burned off and, for example, planted to grass for cattle raising, then the cycling of rainfall is dramatically altered; three-fourths of the rainfall runs off and returns to the sea the first time it falls, leaving little to be carried inland.*[35]

The hydrologic cycle is far more than an Earth Science 101 assignment! Water is undeniably the signature and lifeblood of the planet, inextricably connected with weather patterns. Therefore, as nature's abundance and diversity decline, so do the purity and dependability of water. Without widespread support for wise water use, corporate control of water will inevitably increase, as huge companies buy, sell, pump, treat, and trade it on the open market. What many have seen coming for years is already here. Extended droughts have resulted in restrictions on lawn watering, and in dire actions such as the conversion of sewage directly into drinking water with high-tech filtration systems like the one Los Angeles recently constructed. Energy-hungry desalination plants dot the coastlines of arid Middle Eastern countries (there are more than fifteen thousand such plants worldwide), while in places like the high plains of eastern Colorado, legally binding water rights become meaningless as aquifers like the Ogallala (which are not rechargeable) continue to dry up. In California, water previously used on vegetable crops is now piped to cities, glossy green with thirsty lawns and exotic landscapes. On every continent, glaciers and ice shelves are melting, channeling precious freshwater to the oceans. Warns the World Economic Forum in a 2009 report, most glaciers in the Himalayas and Tibet—which provide water for 2 billion people—will be gone by 2100 at the current rate of melting. Another alarming connection between climate change and water use is that the warmer the world becomes, the faster water evaporates from canals, reservoirs, and soil.

Here's the bottom line: although the total volume of water on our planet is estimated at about 340 million cubic miles, only 2.5 percent of that is *fresh*water. The most critical question for humanity right now is,

How can we learn to use that 2.5 percent more wisely? A corollary question is, How can we stabilize the climate our civilization and its crops evolved with? The first step is to get the prices of water and energy right, so that they reflect overall value—not just to us but to future generations and to the world's 1.5 million other species.

Though we are just one (very exploitative) species among millions, humans capture, use, and waste most of the planet's water. By tracking the water we withdraw from rivers, lakes, and aquifers through the pipelines to its various uses, we find many opportunities to get more value from each drop. Worldwide, agriculture uses roughly three-fourths of freshwater withdrawals, while industrial and household uses are the next largest categories. Especially in developing countries, up to 40 percent of water is lost by leaky pipes, mismanagement, and corruption. Specific water-consumptive industries are livestock, aquaculture, mining, and power plants. In fact, in the United States, 39 percent of all freshwater withdrawn is diverted to cool fossil fuel and nuclear reactors. When it goes back into the watershed, it contains thermal and some chemical pollution. A rapid transition to renewable energy sources like wind and solar can reduce power-related uses, though geothermal energy and biomass energy sources are very water consumptive. "Bottom-of-the-barrel" fossil-fuel sources like tar sands and oil shale also use huge quantities of water per unit of fuel.

There are many opportunities to make the food system more water-efficient, some embedded in the extravagant American diet. Although the average person consumes about a gallon of water a day (in both water and food), it takes five hundred times as much water to *grow* what we eat every day. It costs about 1,800 gallons of water to produce a single pound of beef, and 1,000 tons of water to produce a ton of grain. (For this reason, it might be said that when the United States exports a million tons of grain every year, it is not only exporting topsoil, but also water.) Since roughly three-quarters of the grain used in the United States is fed to livestock, it becomes clear that eating lower on the food chain will also conserve billions of gallons of water. Efficient application of irrigation water is another key opportunity. While drip irrigation technology is many times more efficient than furrow or sprinkler systems, only 4 percent of irrigated land is drip-irrigated in the United States, and even less in China and India (1–3 percent). Organic farming is also water conservative, since maintaining a higher percentage of organic matter in the soil holds water like a sponge, requiring less irrigation.

The average American's "water footprint" is roughly 500,000 gallons a year, according to the U.S. Geological Survey, including his or her share of agricultural, commercial, residential, manufacturing, and other uses. The typical household spends as much as $500 per year on its water and sewer bills. The EPA's WaterSense Web site explains how simple actions in the home such as installing water-efficient toilets, showerheads, and appliances can win back more than $170 a year. High-efficiency toilets have come a long way in recent years, in both performance and water conservation. When remodeling a bathroom, building a new home, or simply replacing an old, leaky toilet, a WaterSense label makes sense.

Toilets that offer a dual flush option add a level of choice and logic— why use even 1.6 gallons of water to flush urine when 1 gallon will do it? In fact, an increasing number of Americans are asking, Why use water at all? They opt instead for waterless, computer-controlled toilets that compost waste instead of sending it to energy- and chemical-intensive treatment plants. At the Cobb Hill Cohousing community in Hartland, Vermont, twenty-three residences have for the last eight years used high-tech compost toilets with tanks in the basement that receive a precise amount of aeration. Longtime Cobb Hill resident Susan Sweitzer reports no major problems or inconvenience, "Documented water use per day per person in the community is twenty-three gallons . . . less than a fourth of the national average.

It's not hard to imagine a water tax on certain water-intensive industries in the future, or at least a water bill that escalates in price proportional to water consumed—the exact opposite of many utility agreements, in which the price goes down as use increases. While the most effective way to reduce industrial water use is to reduce the overall throughput or volume of products flowing through the economy, there are several high-leverage targets. For example, since paper manufacturing is one of the most water-intensive industries, personal actions like paper recycling and junk-mail reduction can significantly lower the water footprint. In turn these actions cascade into lower regional water consumption, avoiding the huge expense of building new water- and wastewater-treatment plants.

Processed food uses far more water in its manufacture than fresh food because of all the rinsing, cleaning, and cooling of machinery, chemical procedures, packaging manufacture, and so on. However, meat is the most water-intensive food because its water footprint includes feed, sanitation, and drinking. And it takes thirty-seven gallons of water to manufacture a single cup of coffee! A cup of tea is a bargain, at about eight gallons per cup; but either beverage in a café container is the water equivalent of many five-gallon buckets. Pharmaceuticals, metals-heavy technology, petroleum refining, and bottling are other industries that use large amounts of water, and because of increasing costs as well as public pressure, many companies in these industries are adopting methods that are far more water-efficient. It's clear that technology can play a major role in water efficiency, and three other variables are also critical: (1) higher prices for water because of emerging scarcity; (2) more rigorous and innovative policy measures in agriculture, industry, and public use—from changes in subsidies to rebates, regulations, and restrictions; and (3) a new ethic that makes conserving water the right thing (the only *sensible* thing) for individuals and organizations to do.

One indication that we are willing to pay more for water is the recent upsurge in sales of bottled water. In 1976, the average American drank 1.6 gallons of water; by 2007 that number had jumped to 30.6 gallons. Americans now purchase more bottled water than either milk or beer.[36] Many studies have indicated that we pay far too much (both economically and environmentally) for the convenience and symbolic value of bottled water— forty thousand semis are on the highways every week delivering this profitable product—yet with a shift in awareness and style, our enthusiasm for purchased water can be channeled to more effective ways of ensuring continuing supplies of clean water. Without a doubt, nature is the most reliable treatment plant on the planet, though we present continuing challenges in our current way of life. Writes environmentalist Donella Meadows, "Living communities have attuned themselves over tens of thousands of years to the ebbs and flows of water produced by nature. When we change those ebbs and flows, we endanger not just isolated species, but whole ecosystems. . . . Whenever water is dammed, drained, piped, dumped, channeled, chlorinated, polluted, diverted, warmed, cooled, or otherwise manipulated, someone's home is upset. Species are threatened. Communities are destroyed."[37]

When we destroy natural communities by neglecting water quality, we then have to resort to bottled water, fish farming, and expensive treatment plants. How can we educate ourselves to understand that water and nature are infinitely more valuable than money? That understanding grows out of an ethic, sometimes a passion, which becomes central to the way we live our lives. Teril Shorb and his family moved to central Arizona partly because they liked having wildlife living nearby—wild javelinas, deer, foxes, coyotes, tarantulas, and a rainbow of birds, from scrub jays to roadrunners. "We put out a wet welcome mat in the form of a shallow steel pan of water, which was used mostly by birds for bathing. The pan was usually three-quarters full the next morning," says Shorb.

But then extended drought came to their region, and the "pan index" changed. "We put out more pans," he recalls. "By day javelinas sip daintily, and dozens of juncos and white-crowned sparrows perch on the rim, bending low to dip thirsty beaks. Desert hares, gray foxes, a coyote, wasps, beetles, and other wild creatures are regular visitors to the pans." The Shorbs began to realize that water is about life and death, and they began to reduce their own water footprint to offset what they gave to the animals. They installed low-flush toilets, consolidated washing chores, and replaced dying, exotic landscape plants with native species. They began to drive fewer miles for entertainment, and to buy fewer consumer items. Their paradigm was changing, and with it, their lifestyle. "Conserving water is a small sacrifice compared to the enormous joy of seeing wild creatures at the little steel water holes; our backyard oasis. Looking out for other-than-human beings in our natural neighborhood is our way of responding positively to global climate change."[38]

From passions like these spring civic and political actions. There are now thousands of local groups that have organized to clean up streams and rivers, or plant trees in neglected and abused watersheds. In Shapleigh, Maine, citizens recently voted at a special town meeting to grant rights to ecosystems but deny rights of personhood to corporations. The ordinance they passed is intended to protect the town's groundwater resources from the reach of Nestlé, producers of Poland Springs bottled water and related products. Says the resolution announcing the ordinance, "We won't back down. We are the stewards of this most precious resource, water, and we want to protect it for future generations. The right to water is a social justice issue and we believe that citizens will do a much better job of protecting this resource than a for-profit corporation."

6

Where We Live to Consume, or Where We Come to Life?

Before World War II, fewer than half of Americans owned cars, and only about half owned their own houses. But in the 1950s the American Dream began to take shape, on TV screens and streets all across the country. Houses and subdivisions became the epicenter of a political and economic idea, in which mass consumption would deliver not only prosperity, but also freedom, social equality, jobs, economic growth, and, most of all, happiness. What a Dream it was! As the American population doubled, so did the size of houses and yards, even though family sizes were steadily shrinking.

However, by 2009, the great house expansion seemed to be over. For the first time in fifteen years, the average size of homes *under construction* began to fall, according the National Association of Home Builders—from a cavernous 2,600 square feet to a still quite adequate 2,300 square feet. It's likely that trend will continue as energy costs rise and a higher percentage of the population becomes elderly. In 2000, about a third of U.S. households included children, but by 2030, only a fourth will. Now, the challenge is what to do with homes that are bigger than people want and need. Many homeowners are renting out rooms, and new buyers are converting houses into homes for autistic children or halfway houses for released prisoners. A century ago, many Victorian mansions in both the United States and the UK were subdivided into apartments. However, in today's world, zoning ordinances and homeowners association bylaws limit the number of unrelated people who live in one dwelling. Why shouldn't some of these rules bend, to permit restaurants and stores right on suburban and once-suburban streets?

Another trend in new housing is toward denser neighborhood patterns that are more in keeping with human anthropology; they provide rich social connections and cooperative opportunities. By clustering homes together, builders can create parklike open spaces instead of redundant yards. The success of minimovements like cohousing (now more than 120 communities strong) and the larger pattern, new urbanism, are models for a new way of living—really, a return to housing patterns familiar to our grandparents—in which more needs are met right in the neighborhood.

➤ New Normal Agenda Point #25: Where to Live?

Old Perspective: Choose an exclusive location and as large a house as you qualify for, to attain "the good life," because the house is a symbol of success.

New Perspective: You'll get just as much satisfaction from a smaller, well-designed house, and as much prestige from being a person who cares about others, supports a greener lifestyle, and knows his or her neighbors. These are the new icons of success.

THE HEAVY LIFTING

- Before buying a house, perform an extensive resource audit that asks the following questions: Does it have good solar exposure? Is there good garden soil that will allow the development of a plot of vegetables? Are the appliances energy efficient? How good is the insulation? Will the windows conserve heat in the winter and keep out heat in the summer? Is public transit readily accessible? Do the size and design of the house match the things you like to do? For example, is there space for a workbench that will allow you to do woodworking? Is there enough space for yoga or exercise equipment? If you're a crafter, is the natural lighting good enough or do you have to install energy-efficient lighting?

How can we make sensible, sustainable choices when buying a new house? What criteria should guide our decisions? What benefits, both monetary and nonmonetary, will result from the choices we make?

While most developers and realtors tend to focus on "the most house for the money" (square footage, lawn size, and asking price), forward-looking home buyers carefully consider wider questions such as: What are the opportunities for installing renewable energy (e.g., solar electric and hot water, or geothermal energy with a ground source heat pump) in this house? What sort of investment would it take to bring the windows, furnace, and insulation up to optimum efficiency, and over the course of a decade, how much money would be saved? How will the landscape contribute to sustainability—for example, will shade trees reduce the need for energy-intensive air-conditioning? Are there opportunities to develop a garden and small orchard in the backyard, for the freshest, most local food possible?

The true value of the house we choose will depend on deeper considerations than whether it looks like a magazine cover. While privacy, convenience, and resale potential—central aspirations of the American Dream—do have value, so do many other qualities, like a sense of place and the pursuit of health. Really, the most essential questions of all are, Who do I want to *be* in this new house? Is this a good place for building an active, fulfilling life?

For example, Marie and Steve Zanowick were considering a move to British Columbia in their retirement years, and wanted to base their decision on a much wider foundation than price and appearance. Says Marie, "A Canadian broker found out we were interested in land and said he could show us some great properties on golf courses and in fancy suburban neighborhoods. But what was more important to us was having direct, walkable access to town and knowing that our water supply was clean and reliable."

The most sustainable house is not just where we live and generate half a pound of trash a day, but where we *come to life.* The house we choose should be not simply a "consumer unit," but the center of a productive existence, meeting basic needs like security, safety, comfort, expression, and social contact. It does not have to be large, but it should enable a large *life,* rich with people we love and respect, activities that engage us, and opportunities to be in natural settings.

Try working with a green real-estate agent, maybe one trained by a company like EcoBroker International. EcoBroker provides a curriculum of energy and environmental training for agents who care about the environment and wish to help their clients benefit from energy efficiency, and green and healthier features of homes and buildings.

· Suggestions for Choosing a House ·

Check for good solar exposure that will enable installation of photovoltaic (electric) and solar hot-water systems.

See what kind of soil the property has, to optimize gardening opportunities.

Have an energy auditor examine the house for efficient windows, insulation, furnace, and other features before you buy.

Find out if the house is within walking and/or bicycling distance of a public transit stop.

Talk to members of the homeowners association, if there is one. Are there opportunities for cooperation as well as lively social gatherings? Is there a community gathering place such as a local school, church, or clubhouse?

Find out if there are public parks, streams, and bike trails nearby. Are stores, cafés, and restaurants within walking or biking distance?

See if local government has shown support for sustainability measures, such as water conservation, sustainable supplies of potable water, pay-as-you-throw recycling, slow streets, and incentives for independent businesses. How can you have a sustainable house unless it's in a sustainable community?

THINKING OUTSIDE THE BOX OF YOUR HOUSE

Although many Americans are accustomed to the idea that exclusivity and separation are essential ingredients for the "good life," there's a growing interest in living in vibrantly healthy neighborhoods that include people from all walks of life. Says neighborhood designer Peter Calthorpe, "It's time to redefine the American Dream. Certain traditional values—diversity, community, frugality, and human scale—should be the foundation of a new direction."[1]

Calthorpe has now designed many neighborhoods that have stores, parks, and services like health clinics right down the street. More than six hundred new towns, villages, and neighborhoods following principles of new urbanism are planned or under construction in the United States, restoring the human scale and fabric of many metropolitan areas.

And Americans are curious about this type of neighborhood. Gallup, Fannie Mae, and Roper polls report that about two-thirds of Americans would reduce the size of their trophy home in exchange for a great neighborhood. Intuition tells them that a more efficient, supportive neighborhood will save time, money, stress, and human effort, improving their quality of life. Yet, many existing neighborhoods were engineered for consumption, not efficiency; for cars, not people. They were built to provide retreat, not community. The standard suburban neighborhood may provide a benefit like a quiet, relatively safe place to live, but if also comes with huge costs: social isolation; long commute times; neglect of elderly, young, and low-income people who can't drive; increased air pollution and traffic fatalities from all the driving (car accidents occur three times as often in suburbs as in cities); loss of farmland; vanishing open space; and added expense for longer runs of pipes, wires, cables, roads, maintenance, and delivery.

What are the benefits of a neighborhood where "everybody knows your name"? Put simply, this kind of neighborhood meets more human needs. Safety, security, and support are dramatically increased as compared with a lushly hedged McCastle. Residents of successful neighborhoods often drive less, consume less, and spend less time in front of TV and computer screens because neighborhoods generate their own wealth, such as potlucks, discussion groups, community gardens, and shared programs like food co-ops or community-supported agriculture (buying produce from a local farmer). Because such neighborhoods have a high "parks-to-pavement" ratio and more destinations within walking and bicycling distance, residents tend to be healthier.

Says health expert Richard Jackson, "The diseases of the 21st century will be chronic diseases like diabetes, obesity, asthma, and depression, that steal vitality and productivity, and consume time and money. These diseases can be moderated by how we design, build, and maintain our human environment."[2] These tangible benefits are actually *measurable*: in a closely knit community, levels of serotonin (a natural antidepressant) are higher, so the neighborhood is collectively more optimistic and energetic.

➤ New Normal Agenda Point #26:
What Size House or Apartment Is Ideal?

Old Perspective: In the cold war with the Joneses, a large house was the ultimate symbol of success. The average size of an American house expanded from roughly 1,000 square feet in 1950 to 2,300 square feet in 2008, and U-Store-It lockers expanded even faster.

New Perspective: Small is beautiful when a house is well designed, especially when it's located near amenities we need—groceries, banks, parks, libraries, and restaurants. Large houses are expensive, not only to buy, but to heat, cool, landscape, and maintain. And a large house is always hungry for more stuff.

THE HEAVY LIFTING

- Make a realistic assessment of the size house you really need, rather than envisioning a house that exists only as a symbol—to impress others. Make a checklist of how you will *live* in the house to help with this. Assess your needs in terms of number of people in the household and what activities will take place in the house. Consider carefully how much maintenance you will have to do to keep the house in good shape. Consider the suitability of the house for later life, if you plan to retire in place.

The decision to live in a smaller, more efficient, more conveniently located home offers huge opportunities for increasing one's quality of life while reducing the consumption of resources. Says Shay Soloman, author of *Little House on a Small Planet*, "Live in less space but have more room to enjoy it. Does that sound like a contradiction? On the contrary, living small frees up your mind, your wallet, and your soul."[3] Admittedly, there are psychological roadblocks to overcome. The house is a perceived symbol of success in our world (ironically, it's also a refuge from a world so preoccupied with material success). But a person who lives in a smaller house than he or she can afford probably has a healthy level of self-confidence and plenty of time, and may also desire to do more with his or her life than consume.

I recently toured a series of small, well-designed houses and was struck by the "livability" that features such as skylights, interior glass partitions, and built-in shelving gave the houses. They felt like sailboats, with everything in its proper place. The beautifully kept landscapes outside the homes interconnected with the interiors, making the yard an extension of the living room. I could often see diagonally from one corner of the house to the other, through glass partitions, which conveyed a feeling of spaciousness. As I walked through the 900- to 1,500-square-foot houses, I realized that it's not really space that we want, but a feeling of spaciousness.

Small houses save energy, time, and money. Money saved in construction can be used to incorporate favorite materials, shapes, and patterns, from tile counters and wainscoting to bamboo floors. These touches add charm and a down-to-earth feeling. Concludes Sarah Susanka in the bestseller *The Not So Big House*, "It's time for a different kind of house that is more than just square footage; a house where each room is used every day. A house with a floor plan inspired by our informal lifestyle instead of the way our grandparents lived."[4] (In 1901 the average size of a family was 4.9 people, while by 2006, it had shrunk to 2.6 people). Yet, in our world, fewer people need more space. Sarah Susanka fervently believes that the typical American house has too many bathrooms and too large of a living room to be comfortable and cozy. "It is less like a nest than a massive storage container."

· Why Small Houses Are Beautiful ·

Use fewer building materials: Says green building expert David Johnston: "Forty percent of all the stuff we make and use in the U.S. goes into buildings, with all the associated pollution and impacts." By living in a house with a human scale, we prevent the destruction of habitat, conserve resources, and teach ourselves how to live without kitchen gadgets and tabletop knickknacks.

Use fewer resources: For example, the large size of a U.S. house, with its long pipes, wastes hundreds of gallons of water a year—just waiting for the hot water to arrive.

Require less time and money for payments and maintenance, which can be spent on other things, like vacations, special people in your life, or continuing education. The average annual utility bill is $1,500 and climbing quickly—so just in fuel bills, the small house yields continuing dividends.

More likely to be found in places (like first-ring suburbs) that are near the things we need—stores, schools, theaters, banks, and so on. So there may be considerable savings and a higher quality of life from reduced transportation. Some banks are now offering "location-efficient mortgages" for that reason. We're a better financial risk if we save on transportation costs.

Are often homier and more intimate. They make people feel less stressful and less overwhelmed. We should take a cue from beavers' dams, birds' nests, and bears' dens, none of which are larger than is necessary.

Reduce the stress of constant maintenance and insecurity about theft, deterioration, and isolation. The less flamboyant our houses are, the safer we are, statistically.

Can be fixed up just the way we want them, since there is less space to decorate and furnish.

Enable us to focus on nonmaterial forms of wealth, like taking care of family and participating in civic activities. Small, comfortable houses encourage humility, lack of pretense, and creativity. They confer a sense of "doing the right thing."

Source: David Wann, *Simple Prosperity*. (New York: St. Martin's Press, 2007), 192.

➤ New Normal Agenda Point #27: Landscaping for Dollars and Sense

Old Perspective: A house's landscape is mostly for appearance, not function. Why conserve water and energy when these resources are so cheap?

New Perspective: A landscape can be functional and productive, meeting some of our needs for fresh food, energy conservation, recreation, and contact with nature.

THE HEAVY LIFTING

- If you're going to eat locally, you should also be planting locally. Start by observing the weather, natural lighting, and soil conditions on your property. Then choose landscaping options that fit those conditions and are proven winners in your area.

The way we landscape our yards plays a major role in the altitude of our utility bills! If we plant the right trees, shrubs, and vines in the right places, we can keep our houses cool in summer and warm in winter, by design. We can reduce winter heating bills by as much as a fourth, and summer cooling bills by half, at the same time reducing air pollution and noise, providing habitat for wildlife, and increasing the resale value of our houses.

Computer models from the U.S. Department of Energy show that just three trees, strategically placed around a single-family house, can save an average household between $120 and $275 in heating and cooling energy costs annually. The National Academy of Sciences estimates that America has 100 million potential tree spaces on urban streets and yards, and probably many times more in rural areas. Buying a shade tree when it's an eight-foot sapling costs about as much as an awning for a large window, and provides more interesting shading for many years.

A good first step is simple, no-brainer observation. Track the sun's path on your property and house throughout both summer and winter days to pinpoint strategic places for deciduous (leaf-bearing) trees and shrubs. Notice how sunlight heats up pavements, walls, and roofs, and how it penetrates windows in all seasons. Make special note of how the sun strikes the house between 9:00 a.m. and 3:00 p.m. in the winter—your only opportunity to warm up your living room with passive solar energy. Also, notice which directions the winds blow in from, so you can position wind-deflecting shrubs and trees in the right places. Remember, if the outside temperature is 10 degrees Fahrenheit and the wind speed is 20 miles per hour, the wind chill is a very uncomfortable (and expensive) -24 degrees! A study in South Dakota found that windbreaks to the north, west, and east of houses cut fuel consumption by an average of 40 percent.[5]

The most effective way to keep your home cool is to prevent heat buildup in the first place, so keeping hard surfaces cool is important. Trees and vines create cool microclimates around walls, pavements, and other hard surfaces that reduce ambient temperatures dramatically. Planting shrubs, bushes, and vines next to your house creates dead air spaces that insulate your home in both winter and summer. Leave at least a foot of space between full-grown plants and your home's wall.

"Use a large bush or row of shrubs to shade your patio or driveway," suggests Steve Cramer, a Colorado extension agent. "Plant a hedge to shade a sidewalk, or a trellis for climbing vines to shade a patio area." He also suggests using fences, windbreak plantings, and shade trees to provide a "sun pocket" on the south side of your home where outside activities can take place during sunny and cool but still comfortable fall and spring days.[6]

Studies conducted by the Lawrence Berkeley National Laboratory documented summer daytime air temperatures to be 3 to 6 degrees cooler in tree-shaded neighborhoods than in treeless areas. As a general rule, provide shade by planting deciduous trees in an arc around the east, south, southwest, and west sides of your home. This blocks sun in the summer but lets it come through in the winter, when leaves have fallen.

Locate windbreaks—often consisting of evergreen trees and shrubs—on the north and west sides of the home, where sunlight is scant in the winter and winds are usually strongest. The best windbreaks block wind close to the ground by using trees and shrubs that have low crowns (leaves and branches). Research has shown that a windbreak will reduce wind speed for a distance of as much as thirty times the windbreak's height. But planting your windbreak away from your house a distance of two to five times the mature height of the trees will keep your home even cozier. Using shade effectively requires you to know the size, shape, and location of the moving shadow that a tree casts. For example, if you want to plant a shade tree for your yard but don't want it to block sun into your house, a fifty-foot-tall tree planted one hundred feet from the house will work. Location of shade trees also depends upon the shape of the tree crown, the height of the roof or walls, and avoiding overhead wires and underground pipes. Deciduous trees with high, spreading crowns can be planted to the south of your home to provide maximum summertime roof shading. Trees with crowns lower to the ground are more appropriate to the west, where shade is needed from lower afternoon sun angles.

Shading and wind breaking may be the most evident methods of conserving energy in a landscape, but certain other approaches can help save energy in a larger sense. For example, if you replace bluegrass turf with low-maintenance shrubs, grasses, and trees, you may reduce the energy connected with mowing the lawn with a gasoline-powered mower. There's energy "embodied" in fertilizer, pesticides, and water, too. These materials require petroleum feedstocks, manufacturing energy, transportation energy, and pumping energy long before they arrive at our houses. And concrete, one of the materials that heats up the quickest in your landscape, requires a lot of energy in its manufacture. By substituting skill, knowledge, and good landscaping design for these energy-intensive materials, we can reduce the heat load on the planet itself.

Plant an "edible landscape." Cut back on the amount of time you spend maintaining the lawn and spend it instead watering tomorrow's breakfast. I'm not suggesting that you get rid of your lawn completely, because lawns do work pretty well as ground covers. They do keep mud off the carpet. But they also consume a lot of resources, chemicals, and time, to produce a final product that's typically sent to the dump. Americans pamper 30 million acres of lawn that cumulatively consume millions of bags of fertilizer and reservoirs full of potable water. Each time we mow, it's the pollution equivalent of a 150-mile car trip.

What if just one-fifth of your lawn became a miniorchard, grape arbor, and strawberry patch? You don't need to be an expert to grow fruit; you just need to envision your yard in a different way, and do a little research. By reallocating money for a few well-chosen varieties, and blowing off a few weekends, you can create a Garden of Eden in one corner of a yard that looks good enough to eat. (That's you, lying in a hammock strung from the grape arbor to the semidwarf apple tree, picking mulberries while you read this book.)

➤ New Normal Agenda Point #28: Choosing Density, Diversity, and Design over Sprawl

Old Perspective: The words "density" and "diversity" describe places where quality of life is low, crime is high, and privacy is compromised. Living in dense, diverse neighborhoods and communities is undesirable because it takes away our ability to be exclusive and apart from the others. Cultural and income diversity make us feel insecure. Given the choice, wouldn't everyone want to live in low-density suburban surroundings?

New Perspective: The quality of life in a given community is determined by quality of design, by pride of place, and by whether care is being taken to meet human and natural needs well. With transportation and its infrastructure becoming more expensive, biological habitat being destroyed, and the American ecological footprint getting increasingly larger, it's time to try new patterns of design that are more sustainable. Density and diversity can provide many quality-of-life benefits, both private and public.

THE HEAVY LIFTING

- When looking for a new home, don't just look at the house and its surrounding land. Consider the neighborhood. Walk the streets and walkways built for community and sustainability. Consider the number of front porches, small front yards, common open spaces, stores, bike paths, and efficient houses in the area.

- Support community development in local politics by advocating for developers who present designs that take into account the needs of humans and the needs of nature.

Whether we realize it consciously or not, the intrinsic motivation when we choose which community to live in is to meet fundamental needs. Millions move to the suburbs trying to find good schools; less congestion, crime, and noise; decent access to work; a sense of being closer to nature; and certification of "upward mobility." They are trying to fulfill certain core values such as responsibility to family, freedom of choice, expression of individuality, a sense of community, and appreciation of nature.

The question is, How well do suburbs actually supply these sought-after qualities? For example, do they supply freedom of choice in housing? Not exactly. Mandated by law to be low-density, the suburbs offer "a limited range of choices in the style and location of new housing—typically, single-family homes in automobile-oriented neighborhoods built on what was once forest or farmland," in the words of design expert Donald Chen.[7]

But there's a growing movement in the United States and globally to build and rebuild neighborhoods that make sense ecologically and anthropologically. For example, more than six hundred new-urbanism neighborhoods have been built or are being planned in the United States. The goal of new urbanism, first enunciated in the early 1980s, is to create new design patterns—in both urban infill and new suburban developments—that result in friendlier and more livable, walkable, and sustainable communities. The charter of the Congress for New Urbanism advocates changes in public policy and development practices to create culturally and economically diverse neighborhoods and communities; pedestrian- and transit-friendly streets; and public spaces that celebrate local history, climate, ecology, and architectural traditions.

Far from being just a bunch of good words, these well-articulated goals are finding responsive ears in local governments and professional associations. They help redefine what makes neighborhoods and communities great, often stimulating much-needed changes in policy. For example, these principles have in many cases encouraged city zoning departments to allow houses to be closer to sidewalks, increasing interactions between residents and pedestrians. Higher-than-typical housing densities enable transit stops to be economically viable; and parking requirements that allow fewer spaces encourage more bicycling, walking, and transit.

· Selected Elements of New Urbanism ·

The neighborhood has a discernible center. This is often a square or a green and sometimes a busy or memorable street corner. A transit stop would be located at this center.

Most of the dwellings are within a five-minute walk of the center, an average of roughly one-quarter mile.

There are a variety of dwelling types like houses, row houses, and apartments, so younger and older people, singles and families, the poor, and the wealthy may find places to live.

At the edge of the neighborhood, there are shops and offices of sufficiently varied types to supply the weekly needs of a household.

An elementary school is close enough so that most children can walk from their home.

There are small playgrounds accessible to every dwelling—not more than a tenth of a mile away.

The streets are relatively narrow and shaded by rows of trees. This slows traffic, creating an environment suitable for pedestrians and bicycles.

Parking lots and garage doors rarely front the street. Parking is relegated to the rear of buildings, usually accessed by alleys.

Certain prominent sites at the termination of street vistas or in the neighborhood center are reserved for civic buildings. These provide sites for community meetings, education, and religious or cultural activities.

The Holiday neighborhood project in Boulder, Colorado, highlights some of the lifestyle-changing benefits of new urbanism. One of them is a significant reduction in average car-miles and car-hours. To make Holiday a walkable, pedestrian-oriented community in a city that's dominated by cars, project developers introduced a palette of concepts that literally got people back on their feet. They designed gardens, pathways, and other interesting spots to linger in throughout the site. A greenway that extends from one side of the three-hundred-acre neighborhood to the other is the backbone of that strategy.

The greenway cuts through the two-acre "park at the heart" and also through a live/work cluster of residences called Studio Mews, where pedestrians watch artists and craftspeople create in their live/work studios. The project further reduces transportation by incorporating a few stores, recreational opportunities, great linkage with Boulder's bike trail system, and great access to public transportation.

Many resource-saving measures were included in the Holiday project by design, functioning automatically to save energy, water, or materials. For example, when construction was completed, the Wild Sage Cohousing neighborhood received an EPA energy rating of Five Star Plus—the highest rating given—on all of its thirty-four homes. (Cohousing is a design approach adapted from Danish architecture in which residents have private homes but share public amenities like a common house, playgrounds, and community gardens.) Clearly, the design team created a winning combination of building elements and features. Other resource-saving aspects of the neighborhood rely on human behavior, such as reduction in the number of car trips, consumption and disposal of products, and overall participation in recycling. If Wild Sage is equal to or better than the average cohousing neighborhood in the United States (there are now about 120 built), residents will drive 30 percent less, pay 50 percent less in utility bills, and use 40 percent less water.

Although Holiday's homes are only two-thirds as large as average American houses, "affordable doesn't necessarily mean 'cheap,'" says architect John Wolff. "Building at thirty units per acre is probably the most sustainable thing a developer can do to conserve land, water, and energy. If you build at the typical suburban density of three units per acre, you'll need ten times as much land, ten times as much infrastructure for water, sewer, utilities, roads. . . . So if you can build compact, livable, affordable communities and still get the same qualities as at the lower densities, then you get the best of both worlds."[8]

Changes that people make to save resources are reinforced by a neighborhood culture that rewards such behavior. For example, at Wild Sage Cohousing, a community workshop is located under the common house, which eliminates the need for every household to have a full set of tools. "Why have thirty-four table saws when one is sufficient?" asks architect Bryan Bowen. A similar benefit is the guest room at Wild Sage—a resource that eliminates the need to heat and maintain thirty-four private guest rooms. Chris and Jules Hauck, early residents of Wild Sage, found that their new lifestyle had a narrower radius. "Everything we need is within a very small universe," Chris told me in an interview. "We take the kids to school by bike, we can walk to shops, and we can take the bus to the bank. By having a smaller radius of activities than before we use fewer resources, and we also have more opportunities for exercise and direct contact with nature and with people." The couple compared the Wild Sage home with their previous home in Texas. "We had to travel an hour by car to get to just about everything, and we ate up a large part of our average day just surviving. At Wild Sage, we've given up our second car, and we have much more time to be with our kids." The Haucks have also given away their TV set in favor of such activities as playing guitar and learning to dance the tango.

· Ten Steps to Carbon-Neutral Homes · at Wild Sage Cohousing Community

1. Energy 10 Base: A computer program, Energy 10, generalizes the energy use of building components based on 1997 UBC requirements and typical energy use of appliances based on Energy Star values. This program enables a comparative look at the efficiency and cost of insulation, glazing, and electrical plug loads.

2. Orientation: The first step in lowering energy use is to place the building properly in the site. By evaluating sun, shade, and wind, a building can be oriented to take advantage of these natural site forces to reduce energy use. South-facing windows increase energy absorbed from the sun, while shading decreases cooling loads in the summer.

3. Insulation: The next step is to buy extra insulation and reduce infiltration. Basic conservation strategies modeled in Energy 10 also include wise building orientation, appropriate glazing, reduced infiltration, and high-efficiency mechanical equipment.

4. Daylight: By using natural light, electrical loads can be substantially reduced during daytime hours. This study found that use of daylighting techniques reduced lighting loads by 20 percent.

5. Efficient Lighting: Replacing existing bulbs with compact fluorescent lamps decreased lighting loads by 50 percent. More sophisticated systems can include dimmable ballasts, occupancy sensors, photocells, and timers.

6. Energy Star: New Energy Star guidelines were enacted in January 2004 by the U.S. Department of Energy, and can reduce plug loads by 54 percent over conventional appliances.

7. Hot-Water Conservation: Steps as simple as lowering the temperature on the washing machine and hot-water heater can have an impact on energy use. Water-efficient showerheads, faucets, and appliances are readily available with little increase in cost.

8. Solar Hot-Water Panels: Solar collectors take advantage of the energy provided by the sun to heat water that is used for domestic fixtures and appliances. By collecting solar energy we can substitute a sustainable resource for the traditional coal-fired electrical sources. Using solar collectors for hot water reduces total gas loads by 20 percent.

9. Solar Heating Panels: Using solar panels for heating further reduces gas loads by an additional 80 percent.

10. Renewable Energy Sources: By purchasing electricity that was produced with renewable energy such as wind, solar, biomass, hydro, and other clean energy sources, Wild Sage or any other development can attain the goal of Zero Energy.

➤ New Normal Agenda Point #29: More Emphasis on Public Values, Less Obsession with Private Gratification

Old Perspective: Each individual must "make it on his or her own," competing with all others in the market to maximize monetary wealth.

Public values, funded by taxes and administered by all levels of government, are secondary to private values because we need to "get government off our backs" and get a slice of the American Dream.

New Perspective: Why not structure and maintain a society that taps into human strengths like cooperation and mutual support? When operating as intended, government *is* the people; to keep it off our backs, we need to take part in it, safeguarding and pampering it like a Thoroughbred racehorse.

THE HEAVY LIFTING

- Say hello to a neighbor you've seen but never talked to.

- Go to city council meetings.

- Volunteer to be on a citizen task force.

- Shop locally.

- Promote more comprehensive recycling practices and community-funded public art.

A recent study by the National Science Foundation documented that one-fourth of all Americans have no one they can confide in or celebrate with. In the rest of the population, the average number of confidants has fallen from three to two. Certainly, where we live can play a major role in connecting with other people, if we put a higher priority on creating housing that optimizes social interactions rather than warehouses and isolates occupants. As a central symbol of success and status, the American home is the perfect place to begin creating a new ethic; a new standard for defining success.

If we want to create a truly restorative, just, and sustainable society, our current way of living rides the wrong values in the wrong direction. If we don't understand the real value of nature—as a system that we are part of, that purifies air and water; provides disease resistance; maintains soil fertility; and provides pollination, beauty, serenity, and all the other quintessential services—we won't make the effort to protect it. We'll continue to overvalue private assets and neglect public assets in nature and culture.

The taxes we pay for our mainstream lifestyle are not just monetary but also psychological, emotional, and temporal. Private mobility, which has been promoted as the ultimate luxury, cascades into public congestion and massive public expenditures for new highway lanes. (We now average thirty-six hours per year lost in the oblivion of gridlock.) Obviously, private consumption results in other public environmental impacts, as resources are stripped to meet the demands of the Dream. But we don't see the slash piles or mine tailings, and truthfully, they rarely occur to us. The demand to live on large lots, closer to nature, often destroys the nature we hoped to be near. But we don't notice when a chorus of cricket chirps is reduced to a sparse, desperate quartet.

Since 1950, the amount of public space in our communities—parks, civic buildings, schools, churches, and so on—has decreased by one-fifth, while the average amount of square footage in new homes has roughly doubled. And the percentage of income spent for house payments, house heating, cooling, and "stuffing" our private realm increased from one-fifth to one-half, according to the American Planning Association.

What this all means is that we're turning our backs on the commons, letting it degrade while we catch the next episode of *Imaginary Lives*. As we continue to disinvest in public spaces, instead funneling resources, time, and money into our private lives, we get spoiled. Time spent in the privacy of our cars and homes reduces time available for active involvement in public decision making and community building. We look for a sense of community on TV and on vacation, but we're unfamiliar with how to create it in our own neighborhoods—even though polls strongly indicate a trend away from exclusivity and privacy and toward community.

For example, a "private country club" was preferred by only 18 percent of respondents in one poll, while 64 percent preferred a "small cluster of convenience stores nearby." A dramatic entrance appealed to only 8 percent of respondents, while 64 percent preferred a "small neighborhood library." Only 12 percent requested walls around the subdivision, compared to 46 percent who wanted little parks nearby. In question after question, respondents expressed a greater desire for the conveniences of neighborhood life than for the amenities of middle-class suburbia.

Civic life is suffering from our demand for privacy too, yet our species is a natural fit with cooperative decision making. Barn raisings and Habitat for Humanity raisings; church philanthropic projects; holiday festivals and block parties; demonstrations and protests; volunteer activities like PTA and Red Cross; neighborhood watches, community gardens, and lively discussion groups—all these activities remind us that we belong to an extended family that needs and values our participation. European citizens invest far more readily in public values like health, education, and infrastructure like bike paths and public transit; and the data prove it.

Especially eye-opening is data compiled by John de Graaf, director of the nonprofit Take Back Your Time (Timeday.org), which advocates legislative and lifestyle changes to provide more discretionary time. The data compare the United States with fourteen European Union countries in key quality-of-life indicators, demonstrating that many of our economic and cultural priorities are out of step with what humans actually need. Despite the familiar aspiration to be (or at least appear) optimistic, it's clear that health care, safety, personal security, equality, education, and leisure time are faltering in America. "A thirty-year trend of income tax cuts for the rich has decreased quality of life overall in the U.S.," says de Graaf. "In contrast, Western European countries invested in their social contracts. Strategic investments in health-care, education, transportation, and common space reduced the need (and desire) of individuals to maximize their own incomes."[9]

Compared with the fourteen EU countries, the United States is in the top third in the following:[10]

gross domestic product (1)

average home size (1)

health-care spending (1)

defense spending (1)

lowest taxes (2)

car ownership (2)

But we're worst in the following:

child poverty (15)

poverty rate (15)

infant mortality (15)

obesity (15)

murder rate (15)

incarceration rate (15)

traffic fatalities per capita (15)

ecological footprint (15)

water usage per capita (15)

air pollution/CO_2 emissions (15)

voting rate (15)

paid family leave/sick leave (15)

vacation days per year (15)

We're beginning to examine carefully the *value* we get for the huge amounts of money we spend and owe. By changing a few key priorities and perspectives, we can take better care of our kids, the environment, and ourselves, discovering a mother lode of *real* wealth woven right into our everyday lives, in, for example, where we live.

➣ New Normal Agenda Point #30: What Are Buildings *For*?

Old Perspective: Let the market decide how buildings should be built, according to return on developers' investments. Builders should not be responsible for building healthy, durable, energy-efficient buildings, because if the market doesn't want them, high-quality buildings are just a waste of (developers') money.

New Perspective: As in the medical profession, builders must design and construct buildings that "do no harm." To ensure high-quality, long-lasting buildings, they should respond to incentives like Leadership in Energy and Environmental Design (LEED) and Energy Star certification, which can inform and guide the market. New-paradigm building codes, tax incentives, and zoning decisions can upgrade the stock of new and existing buildings, making America's Great Indoors more livable. The market can't yet imagine the benefits of green buildings because there are not enough examples.

THE HEAVY LIFTING

- Become an active player in the construction and renovation of the buildings you use. Make sure that construction companies, carpenters, painters, plumbers, and electricians working on these projects use products and building techniques that will make your home, school, church, and workplace more efficient and people-friendly.

- Form building committees that will help provide access to public transportation, raise funds to install solar-energy panels, preserve green spaces, and assure Internet access for all.

What do we want buildings to do? A question this basic begins to redefine how we should design, construct, and operate them. In times of resource scarcity and climate change, we want buildings constructed with nontoxic and recycled materials. We want to feel great in the houses and buildings we use, with lots of sun and good ventilation. Many studies document that well-designed buildings can raise employee productivity by up to 30 percent and eliminate expenditures to find qualified employees. The SAS software firm, for example, has designed facilities that provide on-site child-care centers, employee health-care centers, fitness centers, and wellness programs. Staff turnover is 3 percent in an industry that averages 20 percent, and a few years ago the company received 27,000 applications for 945 job openings. The bottom line is that SAS saves an estimated $50 million a year in recruitment and training costs. At a specially designed green Wal-Mart store in Kansas, sales reports documented higher sales on the side of the store that had natural daylight from skylights.

We want buildings to be energy efficient and to use as many renewable energy sources as possible. Most building-related policy making occurs at the local level, and some progressive cities and counties have regulations and guidelines that achieve particular goals, such as limiting the number of huge houses that consume huge amounts of energy. For example, to receive a building permit, any new project in Boulder, Colorado, must comply with the Green Points ordinance concerning building and landscape elements—from foundations and plumbing through air quality, indoor air quality, and solar energy. Says green building expert David Johnston, primary architect of the Green Points system, "It keeps housing costs and sizes down so more people who work in the community can afford to own a house here."[11] Aspen and Telluride, Colorado, also have regulations to keep houses to a reasonable size, especially since in many cases, these monster homes are simply getaway skiing chalets for the wealthy and don't add a sense of community.

As Johnston points out, buildings are one of humanity's greatest impacts: "Forty percent of all the stuff we make and use in the U.S. goes into buildings, with all the associated pollution and impacts," he says. "Thirty-five percent of all the raw energy we use—the oil, natural gas and coal—is directly attributable to buildings, and sixty-six percent of all the electricity that's generated is used in buildings, primarily for heating, cooling, lighting and appliances." We are also using approximately 70 trillion board feet of softwood (a board foot is a one-inch board, twelve by twelve inches) in our buildings every year to build houses. So buildings are not only one of the world's greatest impacts but one of its greatest opportunities for reducing resource use and meeting human needs better.

Alex Wilson, for twenty-five years the editor of *Environmental Building*

News, is an advocate for building codes that assure the safety and continuity of function in hospitals, office buildings, and schools. "With the increasing frequency of power outages, we need codes that mandate natural cooling designs in hot areas, and solar heating in cold areas. A standard for a solid HERS rating (a method of rating energy efficiency in homes) might stipulate that the home would never fall below 55 degrees, for example."[12]

One of the most effective incentives for building and rebuilding projects is the LEED Green Building Rating System, developed by the non-profit U.S. Green Building Council, which provides a suite of standards for environmentally sustainable construction. Since 1998, LEED has certified more than fourteen thousand projects in all fifty U.S. states and thirty countries. The system establishes a common standard of measurement, recognizes environmental leadership in the building industry, stimulates green competition, and raises consumer awareness of green building benefits.

A recently completed building in Golden, the Science Technology Facility at the National Renewable Energy Lab, received the highest rating of LEED certification—Platinum. The multistory building was designed to fit into the gently sloping side of a mesa, where care was taken to minimize disturbing the natural terrain and to conserve and manage water resources. Architectural features such as natural lighting, evaporative cooling, and efficient motors, fans, windows, and lighting reduce the building's energy requirements, saving 41 percent in energy costs. Eleven percent of the building materials were from recycled materials, and 27 percent of the construction materials were manufactured within five hundred miles of the building site, minimizing effects on land and air quality.

Another nongovernmental incentive for an excellent built environment is preferential mortgage rates offered by banks who take location and energy efficiency into account when setting the terms of a loan. If a house is located near services that residents need, less driving will be necessary and borrowers' ability to make payments is more secure. Likewise, an energy-efficient home means borrowers will be less of a risk. Many cities now have no-growth or slow-growth ordinances specifying when and where new buildings can be built. Some have set boundaries to urban growth in order to preserve farmland and create higher-density, more diverse neighborhoods.

Policies like these require us to be aware of the bigger picture: the direction we want our built environment to take. They can help America improve its overall quality of life and at the same time use far fewer resources.

• Boulder Green Points Checklist (New and • Remodeled Buildings Must Comply)

Construction/demolition and use of recycled materials	29 points
Land use and water conservation	25
Framing	30
Energy code measures	113
Plumbing	5
Electrical	10
Insulation	34
HVAC	51
Solar	79
Indoor air quality	48
Innovation	10
Total possible points	**434**

➤ New Normal Agenda Point #31: From Suburbia to Superbia: Making Existing Neighborhoods More Sustainable

Old Perspective: Carefree, car-dependent consumption is a way of life. What defines "the good life" is mindless consumption—having anything and everything we want. The suburbs are ideal units of consumption, offer retreat from a chaotic world, and bestow the sense of playing the game successfully.

New Perspective: Conservation, care, and cooperation are a way of life. Although suburbs *at their best* do offer a world of wonderful benefits, there are also many social, economic, and environmental impacts. Since we have finite supplies of energy, water, land, raw materials, and social stamina, we won't be able to finance suburbia for much longer in its current form. Simply put, the suburbs—where houses have on average doubled in size since the 1950s, and where driving per capita has tripled in the same time period—are the best possible invention for mindless consumption. They may well be the largest single environmental impact the world has ever known.

THE HEAVY LIFTING

- Become a neighborhood activist. Cooperate with those who live on your street and town to make social and physical changes in your neighborhood through discussion groups, cleanup projects, tool sharing, and parent-guided "walking buses" to school.

The existing suburbs need to be remodeled, and since they are already occupied, this effort needs to be driven by residents, with the blessing and support of municipalities. Even in the land of private, green-lawn luxury, we can rediscover our cooperative nature with a grassroots effort to find and establish strategic centers among the sprawl.

The problem is that few people fully perceive the costs of their flawless suburban kingdoms, and besides, they are too busy to consider making changes. The idea of extra activities typically seems intimidating. But suburban makeover activities can be fun and can ultimately give more than they take. Some of these actions can replace unproductive, current activities in our lifestyles—they are substitutes rather than add-on activities, so they won't take up additional time.

Another typical reaction from suburban residents reflects the mythology of the American Dream. "I've worked hard to get where I am," goes the myth, "and it's okay for me to do whatever I want." One of the primary reasons I wrote this book was to help establish an everyday ethic that challenges that myth. When a rebellious teenager has the "whatever I want" attitude, isn't he or she encouraged to think again? The care and feeding of a one-third-acre lawn, for example, typically costs $600 or more a year, requiring lawn equipment, ten pounds of pesticides, twenty pounds of fertilizer, 170,000 gallons of water, and forty hours of mowing labor. According to the Audubon Society, the pollution generated by an inefficient gas-powered lawn mower in those forty hours is equivalent to driving a car fourteen thousand miles—more than halfway around the world.

What, specifically, can be done to begin the Extreme Makeover of the suburbs described in depth in the book *Superbia! 31 Ways to Create Sustainable Neighborhoods*? This massive grassroots effort begins with a very simple first step: saying hello to a neighbor you've never spoken to. Then a "what if?" dialogue begins on sidewalks, decks, and living rooms across America. Said poet Carl Sandburg, "Nothing happens unless first a dream." In this case the dream is a reshaping of the suburbs as well as formless, forgotten urban areas into a new American Dream.

· Superbia! Checklist ·

Easy Steps

Sponsor community dinners.

Establish a community newsletter, bulletin board, and community roster.

Establish a neighborhood watch program.

Start neighborhood investment clubs, community sports activities, and restoration projects.

Form weekly discussion groups.

Establish neighborhood babysitting co-op.

Form an organic food co-op.

Create car- or vanpools for commuting to and from work.

Create a neighborhood work-share program.

Create a mission statement.

Create an asset inventory.

Bolder Steps

Tear down fences: open backyards to create communal play space and a space for neighbors to mingle and a community garden.

Plant a community garden and orchard.

Establish a neighborhood composting and recycling facility.

Plant shade trees and windbreaks to create a more favorable microclimate.

Replace asphalt and concrete with porous pavers and greenery.

Establish a more edible landscape—incrementally remove grass in front lawns and replace with vegetables and fruit trees.

Start a community-supported agriculture program in which neighbors "subscribe" to local organic farms' produce.

Create a car-share program, purchasing a van or truck for rent to community members.

Begin communitywide retrofitting of homes and yards for energy and water efficiency.

Solarize residents' homes.

Boldest Steps

Create a community energy system.

Establish alternative water and wastewater systems.

Establish a more environmentally friendly transportation strategy.

Create a common house.

Create a community-shared office.

Establish weekly entertainment for the community.

Narrow or eliminate streets, converting more space to park and edible landscape, walkways, and picnic areas.

Retrofit garages and rooms in your homes into apartments or add granny flats to house students or others in need of housing.

Establish a mixed-use neighborhood by opening a coffee shop, convenience store, and garden market.

Promote a more diverse neighborhood with multifamily dwellings.

Source: Dan Chiras and Dave Wann, *Superbia! 31 Ways to Create Sustainable Neighborhoods* (Gabriola Island, British Columbia: New Society, 2003).

➤ New Normal Agenda Point #32: Celebrating and Preserving Our Places

Old Perspective: What defines a great place is the size of its largest mall and good access to the freeway. Since most of our time is spent indoors, climate is not important, and neither are local history and tradition. No citizen participation is necessary to make a place great as long as the town or city has corporate cash cows to help pay the bills.

New Perspective: What defines a great place is "social capital"— the networking and trust that accumulate in a town or city with a long-term vision—and good bones: the buildings, infrastructure, and natural features that help make a place livable. The more social capital we spend, the more we have, but spending it means we have to make time for community, not just consumption.

THE HEAVY LIFTING

- Become active in city government and run for a seat on the city council.
- Participate in community celebrations, pancake breakfasts and parades.
- Form committees and activist groups that will help preserve traditional architecture
- Volunteer to help disadvantaged kids.

Says James Kuntsler, author of *The Geography of Nowhere*, "The twentieth century was about going and going, but the twenty-first century will be about staying in places worth staying in."[13]

A place worth staying in usually has great schools, a low crime rate, and a high level of social capital—the networking, trust, and participation that cement a community together. It has a good supply of affordable housing for the people who live and work there, like the nurses, firemen, and merchants. A person feels safe in a great, human-scaled place. There are public spaces where people and cars are kept separate—pedestrian walkways, and places to listen to music and see local art.

The goal is to create a community culture that puts the pieces together, not only identifying what the community needs but how best to meet those needs in resourceful, synergistic ways. We find good restaurants there—the kind that proudly post their menus on the front window and encourage patrons to enjoy leisurely meals. The library has a good collection of books and Internet access, and the community hospital is well staffed and well funded. Though we may not think of it as we walk down the street, a thriving community makes the most of its natural and social assets, generating a minimum of stress and waste, and at the same time, a high level of trust and tradition. A great place knows how to preserve, renew, and recycle its resources and doesn't burn itself up. For example, by keeping money in the local economy, communities build self-reliance to handle sudden challenges like surging energy prices or natural disasters.

How does a place become truly great? Through a combination of choices made by leaders and energetic citizens. Let's look at some examples of towns and cities that value what they have and celebrate it.

Bethel, Maine, no stranger to snow, celebrates it with tourist-friendly winter festivals that include rides in a horse-drawn sleigh and, this year, a world-record snowwoman (122 feet tall and 13 million pounds).

In Brattleboro, Vermont, residents value the slow pace of life, the maple syrup, pastures, and covered bridges. Faced with the challenge of preserving their agricultural heritage and their beautiful landscape, residents of Brattleboro created a local tradition that really captured New England's imagination: the Strolling of the Heifers, a New England version of Pamplona's Running of the Bulls. Up to fifty thousand people attend this three-day, volunteer-run June event to celebrate regional agriculture with a parade, music, farm-fresh food, workshops, and farm tours. The Brattleboro Food Co-op carries five hundred different cheeses, most of them from Vermont, and every month a producer of the month is spotlighted at the store. Says the co-op's manager, "Sometimes people have a hard time getting through the store because they keep running into people they know."

In Bloomington, Indiana, bicycles are an icon of daily life. At the Community Bicycle Project, "gently used" bikes are donated, rebuilt, and resold— road-ready. Volunteers "earn a bike" working with the project, at the same time learning the valuable skills of bicycle repair and maintenance. Repeatedly awarded the Tree City USA distinction, Bloomington is also becoming known for creating wildlife habitat in naturalized backyards and parks. More than two hundred homes are certified by the National Wildlife Federation as providing Backyard Wildlife Habitat—a form of diverse landscaping that includes native plants and offers food, shelter, and habitat to animals.

In tiny, artisan-focused Dixon, New Mexico, about half an hour from Taos and an hour from Santa Fe, houses and farms were built fairly close together to make use of meticulously maintained *acequias*—irrigation ditches fed by snowmelt. The town blossoms the first weekend in November when the annual studio tour begins. Stone sculptors, vegetable farmers, grapevine-wreath weavers, garlic garland braiders, winemakers, chocolate makers, and many other artisans open their homesteads to visitors to demonstrate how they practice their crafts and honor their traditions.

Mayor Ann Campbell, a forty-year resident of Ames, Iowa, is committed to making her hometown greener and healthier. A signer of the U.S. Mayors' Climate Protection Act, she's worked with city council to purchase hybrid vehicles for the city, construct public buildings to LEED energy-efficiency standards, and maintain the quality and performance of the Cy-Ride bus system, which provides 4.5 million bus trips a year, largely to Iowa

State University students who all have bus passes paid for through activity fees, significantly reducing the carbon footprint of Ames. A peak moment for civic energy in Ames came in 2006, when the city hosted the Special Olympics USA Games. "We were so proud when eight thousand volunteers stepped forward to make this event even more 'special,'" says Campbell.

In Viroqua, Wisconsin, which has one of the densest populations of organic farmers in the country, the economy was challenged by the size and marketing clout of corporate farms. In self-defense, growers banded together to create a market niche for organic food. From its original membership of seven farmers, the Organic Valley Cooperative has grown to more than 1,200 family farms.

Viroqua retailers faced a similar crisis when Wal-Mart came to town in the late 1980s and seven businesses went broke. Viroqua rallied, becoming "the Town That Beat Wal-Mart" by revamping small-business inventories to sell merchandise that Wal-Mart didn't. The town took advantage of business consulting paid for by the state, learning how to conduct market surveys and how to bring Main Street back to life. The Temple Theater, built in 1922, was restored by the energy and donations of hundreds of past and present residents, and since 1989, Viroqua has seen fifty-six new businesses start up, creating more than 150 new jobs.

7

Revolt of the Munchkins: Value, Not Volume, in the Market

The Egyptian pharaohs must have taken comfort in the belief that their stuff would be available for their use in the afterlife; clothing, perfumes and cosmetics, games, musical instruments, and sacred works of art are always found in their tombs. In today's cyberlife, it's iPods and cell phones we want to take with us, according to funeral managers across the country. As caskets are lowered into the ground at many services, a familiar if muffled ring tone can be heard—as if the deceased is just about to pick up and tell you what he's up to (not much). Days later, loved ones continue to call—until the battery runs down—so they can at least hear that well-worn message, ". . . I can't take your call right now. . . ." Given sufficient space, some would no doubt want to be buried in their sports car, or have their cherished La-Z-Boy chairs and flat-screen TVs right beside them (in case some game is so compelling that they come back to life to see it). One thing is for sure: a typical American's identity is wrapped up in what he or she owns.

Since the 1950s, the American lifestyle has been zooming ever further off the consumer charts. With each increase in salary or additional household earner, Americans buy more powerful cars; bigger TVs; and more gadgets, couches, and toys than can possibly fit in even supersize houses. We're simply doing what our culture tells us to do. With 2.3 billion square feet of self-storage space in the United States, every American could fit under the aluminum canopy of the U-Store-It universe;[1] and what we don't use or store, we pitch. Every day, Americans generate 10 billion pounds of garbage, and every day, six hundred semis take out New York City's trash—up to three hundred miles away.

Now countries like Brazil, China, and India are queuing up at the consumer buffet. One study found that at an income level of about U.S. $2,500 per person, many Indian households have only basic lighting and a fan. At $5,000, TV access becomes standard and many have hot-water heaters. At $8,000, most Indian citizens acquire consumer goods such as washing machines, DVD players, kitchen appliances, and computers. This is all very reasonable; however, as incomes continue to rise, the trouble begins. Consumption of meat, cars, paper, air-conditioning, and air travel starts to close in on American levels.[2] The stark reality is that 7 billion people simply can't consume at American levels, no matter how hard they've worked to get there.

Writes Erik Assadourian in the 2010 Worldwatch Institute *State of the World* report, "If everyone lived like Americans, Earth could sustain only 1.4 billion people. Even at middle-income levels—the equivalent of what people in Jordan and Thailand earn on average—Earth can sustain fewer people than are alive today."[3] There's only one viable solution: to meet in the middle. The world's overconsumers need to consume less and live more fully, modeling a satisfying lifestyle, while those not yet meeting basic needs continue to reach for moderate consumption levels. But this very obvious solution is fighting a very strong current indeed: most of the world's dominant institutions—in business, government, media, and education—have adopted consumerism as a central organizing principle, convinced that high levels of consumption equal high levels of well-being and powerful status as nations. In most of the world's cultures, loud advertising, celebrity endorsements, and gaudy logos on clothes are now completely normal. America's greatest export—the credit card—has in the past few decades become a symbol of affluence in Brazil, Mexico, India, China, South Korea, and many other countries. Although Turkey's culture traditionally regarded debt as extremely shameful, the dam burst three decades ago. Since 1980, the number of credit cards there has grown from ten thousand to more than 38 million—still just one-thousandth of the 3.67 billion credit and debit cards in the world.

➤ Peak Consumption, Now What?

One percent of gross world product is now spent to prime the pump of advertising. Product hawkers dropped $643 billion in 2008 for advertising, and in countries like China and India, advertising expenditures are growing by 10 percent each year. Yet, many Americans have reached a saturation point with advertising, with thousands of ads dancing in front of our faces like fruit flies every day on the Internet, pop-up ads are getting harder to wrestle off the screen, prompting cuss words we didn't know we knew. TV viewers scramble to hit the mute button when ads come on, or purge them with TiVo. In desperation, advertisers are spending more to disguise advertising by placing products in TV and movie scenes. (Average daily TV viewing time in the industrial world: 3.5 hours. Movie tickets sold worldwide in 2006: 8 billion.) In 2004, companies spent $3.5 billion for product placement, four times the amount spent in 2000. Yet, PepsiCo's decision not to place its usual ad during the 2009 Super Bowl—the epicenter of the commercial TV universe—is a symbol of shifting ad strategies. PepsiCo will instead spend its money on Web advertising. Other companies are drafting volunteers to pitch products to friends—essentially actors on the stage of consumerism. These "brand agents" (now about a million strong in the United States) receive free beverages, electronic devices, or fashion accessories to pitch, blog, and conduct surveys about "their" products. In 2008, U.S. businesses spent $1.5 billion to outfit these business-friendly battalions.

Weapons of mass distraction like these separate us from the work we need to be doing—namely, creating a more sensible, secure future for our kids and ourselves. Our daily lives are smothered by thoughts and routines connected with stuff. One study calculated that the typical American will spend eight months opening junk mail, six months sitting at red lights, one year searching for misplaced items, four years cleaning house, and five years waiting in line—all activities that relate at least in part to our lives as consumers.[4]

As I write this, international climate-change talks are very much about levels of consumption—whether deemed too high or too low. In the United States, there are apparently no cultural limits for consumption, yet if humans are to reduce our greenhouse-gas emissions by 83 percent by 2050—what scientists say will be necessary to prevent runaway warming—the products we design, make, and buy will play a central role, since they are so filled with energy. A plastic bag, for example, is essentially lightweight energy, expended when the oil it comes from is pumped, delivered, and refined; when high temperatures are required to manufacture it; when machines cut handles in it and print logos on it; when it's delivered to the warehouse; and finally when it's taken to the landfill—sometimes in a matter of days.

Industrial products are designed, manufactured, consumed, and cast aside as if life itself were an assembly line. And because consumers don't feel that we have a choice, we take what we can get. After all, the producers own the resources and set the prices. Yet, there are many signs that buyers are beginning to wake up, get the information we need on the Internet and elsewhere, and challenge the sellers to negotiate.

Over the last half century, one of the strongest cards in the sellers' hand was consumer naïveté. Even after countless reports on the toxicity, planned obsolescence, and environmental impacts of the products we use, we continued to trust dedicated, underpaid nonprofits and government agencies to protect us. But how many cases of lead poisoning or smoking cars does it take to get even their attention? Now the electronic revolution has equipped us to be citizen-researchers and reporters. We're able to read product reviews online at sites like consumerreports.com and goodguide.com, culling useful information and instantly conveying it to friends and bloggers.

➤ Challenging the Assumption of Consumption

In the book *Ecological Intelligence,* Daniel Goleman delves into the potential of a transparent market, in which buyers know exactly where a product comes from and how it was produced. Armed with bar-scanning, twittering, Web surfing cell phones, consumers can access a universe of summarized data, playing an active role in protecting their children and defending the environment. Greater accountability can result in higher-quality products, he believes, citing the example of Eosta, Europe's largest distributor of organic produce. This $100 million business ranks fruits and vegetables according to how well they are grown, in terms of environment, health, and social responsibility. The company's "trace and tell" approach enables consumers to track each fruit or vegetable back to its grower, and see what kind of ranking it got from Eosta. If a certain grower has installed drip irrigation to conserve water or supports local schools with low-profit produce for lunches, the price of his produce could be higher. A three-digit number on the sticker of each item can lead the consumer to a streaming interview with the very farmer who grew it. "We're trying to build awareness bridges," says Eosta founder Volkert Engelsman, "so customers can know about our growers."[5]

Goleman recounts another example of transparency—a corporate paradigm shift spurred by consumer activism. During a severe drought in 2004–5 in the Indian province of Kerala, some farmers committed suicide and many villagers ran out of water while a Coca-Cola bottling plant continued to draw water from a deep aquifer. Every day, eighty-five truckloads of Coke were very visibly shipped from the plant, each containing more than ten thousand bottles. The outcry of local villagers and a key court decision in Kerala forced the plant to close down for seventeen months. As media reported the story and sales took a dive, Coca-Cola senior managers began to rethink their relationships with communities as well as with consumers. Observes Goleman, in a world where 40 percent of people don't have safe drinking water, environmental obliviousness is not an option. The huge corporation convened meetings to discuss water in each of its twenty-three global divisions, issuing three-hundred-question surveys to each branch manager. These meetings launched a companywide focus on water.

Working with experts at the World Wildlife Fund, the company began to see the limitations of its old way of thinking. The company had previously viewed water only in terms of its use in products, cleaning, and processing. The WWF expanded that myopic view by analyzing a bottling plant's total water footprint, from suppliers through distributors and retailers. Sugarcane, it turns out, requires some of the most intense water use of any crop; it takes more than two hundred liters of water simply to grow the sugarcane that goes into one liter of Coke. Insights like these shifted the scope of thinking about water from the single watershed a bottling plant draws on to all those watersheds tapped at any point in the company's supply chain.

As a result of these new insights, Coca-Cola has begun to install rainwater-harvesting systems to recharge local groundwater supplies, mandated that all plants return their wastewater to the local watershed clean enough to support aquatic life, and changed company policy. "We should not cause more water to be removed from a watershed than we replenish," announced the company's CEO.[6]

To change the overall direction and goals in the marketplace, we need to think holistically, as Coca-Cola is beginning to do. In a sense, products and services are contracts between the selling team and the buying team. The selling team for a manufactured item consists of the supply chain (extractors, refiners, suppliers of component parts, packaging suppliers, etc.), business advocates and associations, the product manufacturer, advertisers, distributors, wholesalers, and retailers. The buying team is the customer (whether a household, business, or school) as well as delivery, maintenance, and disposal/recycle personnel, and the various agencies and consumer organizations that serve the interests of the general public. This long yet incomplete list of participants in the life cycle of a single product is a reminder of the inertia and vested interests embedded in the existing way of conducting business. In the emerging economic paradigm, several game-changing goals will be agreed upon, for the good of everyone. Products and services should be streams of quality from start to finish, and policies and technologies should serve that goal. Higher quality can and should cost more, resulting in no net loss to the economy—if society accepts one key aspect of a new producer/ consumer paradigm: less clutter in our lives, but better-designed objects and services. Fewer things but better.

To create a marketplace that functions optimally, commerce needs to weave webs of interdependence, as in an ecosystem. Packaging designers need to think like consumers and design for recycling. Manufacturers need to create relationships with suppliers to deliver high-quality materials and components. Manufacturers also must adapt their processes, so new designs can come into the market. Consumers need to become cooperatively active once again—boycotting dangerous products and communicating to designers and producers what we want. Recyclers need to promote their services through government agencies and political activism, making sure "technical nutrients" get back to the producers.

➤ New Normal Agenda Point #33: Choosing Value over Volume

Old Perspective: The goods and services we buy are worth all the time we put in at work to be able to afford them. They show the world that we are right in step—and maybe a little bit ahead—with styles and fashions, and that our lives are successful. The things we buy may not always be natural, but they are normal, and they are familiar.

New Perspective: We've been duped by the marketers, who play our psyches and emotions like slot machines. But we have options, and we intend to use them.

THE HEAVY LIFTING

- Don't just click and buy. First, check the reliability and quality of products and services on the Web.

- Consider using "products of service" that you are in effect leasing rather than owning. This leaves the responsibilities of maintenance and eventual recycling to the producer.

- Buy American when possible because it makes more sense socially and ecologically.

The evolution of the global marketplace was not the natural product of an automatic, self-adjusting free market. Key aspects were deliberately and—it must be said—deviously shaped by public-relations experts like Edward

Bernays and Victor Lebow, with our naive, candy-shop consent. Bernays imported the psychoanalytic theories of Sigmund Freud (his uncle) to the market about eighty years ago, expressly to tap human emotions such as shame, outrage, insecurity, and loneliness. For example, under contract to the tobacco industry in 1929, he orchestrated an ad campaign to prove conclusively that the human psyche can be bought. After consulting with a psychologist about such things as oral eroticism in women, Bernays hired debutantes to smoke cigarettes in public, even though smoking was at that time largely a man's habit. The female troupe strutted down Broadway in Manhattan's Easter Parade, defiantly displaying their "torches of liberty" as symbols of liberation from male dominance. Publicity photos were sent to the world's largest newspapers and magazines, and instantly caught the attention of millions. (Only nine years earlier, a long, proud history of activism had won the vote for American women, and feelings about women's equality were still very strong.) This publicity stunt hit the jackpot: a global taboo about women smoking disappeared overnight, cigarette sales boomed, and the PR industry became the supply side's secret weapon, like a Stealth bomber or Warrior drone. The economy was increasingly fueled by dissatisfaction, but consumers remained naively unaware.

In the book *Propaganda,* Bernays wrote, "The conscious and intelligent manipulation of the habits and opinions of the masses is an important element in a democratic society. Those who manipulate this unseen mechanism of society constitute an invisible government which is the true ruling power of our country."[7] This statement is all the more disturbing because it rings so true. Public relations is really psychological manipulation. PR experts aren't selling just a product, but a stage set come to life. As PR analyst Victor Lebow observed in the 1950s, although a particular ad campaign might not be successful, "it will contribute to the general pressure by which wants are stimulated and maintained. Thus its very failure may serve to fertilize the soil."[8] As TV messages became engraved in our minds and belief systems, the victorious PR industry knew it had raised a bumper crop of consumers.

REVOLT OF THE MUNCHKINS

Although tuning up the market with information and efficiency is critical, what the world really needs is a social movement with teeth: *consumer disobedience*. At this moment in history, we seem less Americans than Munchkins, living in the shadow of a Wicked Witch economy that pervades and dominates our lives. We need a Good Witch economy! Think how good it will feel when we stage a social revolution—creating a society that empowers humans rather than bleeding us dry. A standard response is "But that would be the end of the economy as we know it" A large percentage of the planet's dispossessed and/or enlightened people would counter, "Exactly."

Here's some of the damage the wicked witch has wreaked just in recent years: Between 1987 and 2006, total debt in the U.S. credit market quadrupled, from $10 trillion to more than $40 trillion. What did we buy with all the borrowed money? Billions of electronic devices, millions of tons of cheap fast food, and with it, oceans of pop and bottled water. We paid more for education as tuition went sky-high; more for energy as the price of oil rose; and more for health care as expensive technology, sedentary lifestyles, and questionable insurance practices converged. And then there were all those huge, refinanced houses and shiny new cars.

Now there's a rumbling in America's consumer ranks—like a collective upset stomach—related to what we've just consumed. If it's any consolation, we can count on less consumption in the near future, even if the recession begins to melt away. An aging population will need to spend less and save more for retirement, with people's pensions gutted and many of their investments devoured by unemployment. The average American already carries as much personal debt as he or she can manage—currently about $16,000 not including mortgage debt. Even more troubling for economists are data on average retirement savings. The baby-boomer generation in the United States (now aged forty-six to sixty-three) has managed to save an average of $38,000 for retirement, according to federal data—not counting pensions and Social Security. Among households in the golden years (sixty-five and older) with retirement accounts, the median combined balance of all household retirement accounts was just $60,800 in 2007. As if this weren't alarming enough, Social Security beneficiaries will rise in coming decades to 84 million from the current 50 million, and the number of Americans on Medicare will rise from 44 million to 79 million. This will cost taxpayers $50 trillion in the next seventy-five years—about $170,000 per person.[9]

ENTER THE FLYING MONKEYS

However, the most significant constraint on consumption is the coming scarcity of key resources that are essential for survival. When demand for oil, water, and arable land inevitably exceeds supply, almost everything will go up in price. The best escape route is to change the very structure of our consumer paradigm, in favor of moderation and efficiency rather than excess and waste. From the dizzying heights of peak consumption we are now beginning our descent to a more ingenious, affordable, admirable civilization. The high-leverage actions presented in this book are tools for dismantling our current paradigm and designing and building a better one. Like Toto in *The Wizard of Oz*, I've tried to pull the curtain back to reveal that the great and powerful Oz is really just an illusion. Our economy is a Ponzi scheme: we borrow money from the future to make payments in the present—hoping that growth will cover us.

When we begin to understand how badly we've been duped—and as inflation bares its teeth—we'll begin to practice consumer disobedience because we won't have anything to lose. (We saw glimpses of that in the worldwide food riots of 2007–8.) First we'll take the baby steps of consumer empowerment; then we'll become a visible, self-assembling movement; then the paradigm will shift. This is inevitable, and highly desirable, because our current way of life is just far too expensive.

One small but telling example of consumer disobedience is the recent increase in haggling in America's chain stores. Equipped with oceans of information on the Web and pushed from their comfort zone by a slowing economy, Americans are relearning the ancient art of bargaining for televisions, cameras, couches, rugs, clothing, and all the rest. It's working, in small stores and large. Says marketing professor Priya Raghubir, "In the past, when you tried to get a deal it was an embarrassing thing that you did if you couldn't afford to pay. Now it's about being a smart shopper." A spokeswoman for Home Depot supports the trend of haggling, because flexibility by the sales staff creates a more customer-friendly environment that feels more like a local store than a megastore.[10] Even small actions like these remind us of our collective power. We don't have to buy! If we break our addiction to hyperactive spending and arrange a culturewide cease-fire with the Joneses, all we really have to lose is a lot of insecurity, debt, and stress.

BEYOND PEAK CONSUMPTION: TOOLS FOR SWEEPING UP THE MESS

Throughout our current economy, we do it for the money. For example, two-thirds of U.S. schools get kickbacks from vending-machine companies that typically peddle junk food. Politicians get caught in webs of lobbyist favors and campaign contributions with strings attached. Municipalities bribe chain stores to move to their towns to increase sales tax revenues. Landscapes become littered with billboards, jobs are sent overseas where labor is one step above slavery, and products are deliberately designed to fail—for the money. Further cementing the consumer paradigm are the forty-hour workweek, which makes us rich in money but poor in time, and subsidies to increase yields at the expense of nature. The overall assumption is consumption. However, if we begin to think the unthinkable—collectively ramping down our consumer expectations—there are many tangible ways to steer our economy in a bold new direction that can supply *greater* satisfaction with less material growth.

For example, while taxes are not generally thought of as enjoyable, they can at least be far more *useful* if they provide social incentives and direction. Revenues should be collected from those who benefit. User fees maintain toll roads, and surcharges on car batteries and recyclable beverage containers (in eleven states) directly finance the recycling of these materials. In the Netherlands, Sweden, and Switzerland, surcharges for cell phones enable manufacturers to recycle them with designed-in precision. As mentioned previously, many European countries have lowered income taxes but increased taxes on pollution and resource consumption. This makes sense because they are rewarding resource efficiency and removing penalties for work at the same time. Most EU countries have also decoupled health care from employment and have guaranteed equal pay for part-time work. These paradigm-shifting policies give citizens and employees a choice: more money for consumption or more time for life.

Given the heavy burden that meat production puts on the earth, why not tax it, encouraging a diet that is more appropriate for an omnivore species? Why not tax advertising, a form of social pollution? In the current paradigm, consumers pay for advertising in the prices of products. Every year, the average American spends $900 to be buried in an avalanche of ads. Why shouldn't the producers pay all the costs of advertising, financed by greater in-house efficiency? Polaroid inventor Edwin Land believed that marketing is what you do when the product is no good. Why not rely on the quality of products to provide word-of-mouth promotion, especially in a given region? Why not increase online consumer feedback about products, but decrease annoying online advertising? This would necessitate designing different revenue streams for TV and Web media; a higher proportion of subscriptions (user fees) would finance these. Why not explore the possibilities of value-added taxes for products, in which all beneficiaries in the supply chain are taxed for their share of the environmental and social impacts the product creates?

Why not aspire to ever-higher goals in the making and marketing of products, as architect and systems thinker William McDonough advocates. In the book *Cradle to Cradle* and many articles on values-driven design, McDonough envisions "a world in which all the things we make, use, and consume provide nutrition for nature and industry—a world in which human activity generates a delightful, restorative ecological footprint." With a designer's optimism, McDonough writes, "The destructive qualities of today's industrial system can be seen as a fundamental design problem." One of his most useful and immediately achievable concepts is leasing more and owning less—relying on producers to service, maintain, and recycle products.

> *Instead of assuming that all products are to be bought, owned, and disposed of by "consumers," products would be reconceived as* services *people want to enjoy. In this scenario, customers (a more apt term for the users of these products) would purchase the service of such a product for a defined user period, say ten thousand hours of television viewing, rather than the television itself. They would not be paying for complex materials that they won't be able to use after a product's current life.*[11]

When customers are done with the TV or want a different model, the manufacturer replaces it, says McDonough, taking it back to the factory, breaking it down, and using its complex materials (there are more than four thousand chemical compounds in a typical TV) for new products. Replaceable carpeting is another example. "Millions of pounds of potential technical nutrients are wasted each year in the carpet industry alone, and new raw materials must continually be extracted." Customers who want new carpeting pay the hidden costs of extraction in the purchase price, and if they are environmentally concerned, they are "taxed with guilt as well, about disposing of the old and purchasing the new."[12] At the core of McDonough's vision is the quest to fit into a technical metabolism in sync with nature. When carpeting is designed to be recycled into new carpeting, very little is wasted. The cost of a service-based product? About the same as our current throwaway products, because value is recouped in recycling, less advertising and marketing, and lower R & D expenses once nontoxic, safe, and durable products are developed. "One of our ideas for a new design would combine a durable bottom layer with a detachable top. When a customer wants to replace the carpet, the manufacturer simply removes the top, snaps down a fresh one in the desired color, and takes the old one back as food for further recycling."[13]

Of course, a high-quality carpet that is bought and sold in the traditional way would be a first step, but what McDonough proposes is systemic change that will occur only when we finally understand why the current system is so dysfunctional, and so expensive. At the top of the list is the lack of appreciation for what nature has already invented. We force-fit our clunky inventions (like the steam engine, invented in 1712, which we are still using) onto the living fabric of nature, destroying designs that are proven by evolution. In the new era of green design, we'll know better!

· Items on This Year's **Shopping List** ·

Some of the Things I *May* Buy This Year	Benefits
An e-book reader	Some analyses give e-book readers like Kindle, Nook, or Sony Reader a smaller footprint than printed books. One report estimates that each represents about the same emissions as 15 books bought at stores or 30 purchased online. If I spring for one of these devices, I'll hope for a life span of more than a year before the model changes. I don't want to be pressured to upgrade!
Food/beverage packaging	I refuse to buy bottled water and instead use a few stainless-steel containers to keep filtered tap water in. Among my current packaging peeves are aseptic containers for beverages like Rice Dream—too complex to recycle—and frozen-food boxes with an outer coating that also can't be recycled. On the upside, companies like Eden Foods are designing cans that don't contain potentially hazardous plastic lining.
Apples, bell peppers	The difference in flavor between organic and conventional produce is unmistakable. And the nutritional content is proportional. I love Honeycrisp apples from my own state(!) and bright red bell peppers from my own garden. However, these two items, both high in vitamin C, are among the most heavily sprayed products on factory farms and fruit plantations.
New refrigerator	Though it's still a fantasy at this point, if book royalties are good this year, we'd love to install at least 1,000 watts of solar electric capacity. (We have great solar exposure and already have a solar hot-water panel.) Solar electricity will power a Sunfrost, one of the world's most efficient, easiest to maintain, and silent fridges.

Some of the Things I *May* Buy This Year	Benefits
Window coverings	Last year, we installed double-thickness, honeycombed Venetian blinds on all but three windows, and I'll get the other three this year. They hold the heat in at night in the winter and keep it out in the summer, with just a little effort and watchfulness from me. I take part in keeping my fuel bills low by watching where the sun is.
Rain gear	I'm still using a jacket I bought at Patagonia eight years ago. When a zipper broke, they fixed it for nothing. I'll go back there because of their quality and their genuine environmental and social practices.
Heirloom seeds and drip irrigation	This year, two new things will happen in the community garden. I'll experiment with heirloom seeds (you can save seeds for next year) that have good yields in my region. I'll try Johnny's Selected Seeds or Seeds of Change. For drip irrigation, I'm going with T-Tape, which drips water slowly at 8-inch intervals.
Running shoes	Not that I run a whole lot these days, but if I decide I need another pair of plastic shoes, I'm going to compare New Balance's prices, because they are currently the only athletic shoe manufactured in the U.S.
Gandhi's sandals and glasses; Revolutionary War coins	No, I don't have the big bucks to buy objects like these (Gandhi's belongings recently sold for $1.8 million), but what I cherish about them is that they are symbols of people who stood up for what they believed in and changed the world. I don't have to own Gandhi's spectacles to value them greatly from a distance.

➤ New Normal Agenda Point #34:
Designing with Nature

Old Perspective: Design is a colorful, entertaining way of making life easier and more fun. Good design makes everything seem like a party or a vacation.

New Perspective: Design is one of humanity's greatest strengths— and responsibilities. It's a powerful tool for making the world more sustainable, safe, engaging, fair, resource efficient, and nature-friendly. The best designs are collaborations among producers and users, informed by biology, psychology, and anthropology.

THE HEAVY LIFTING

• Be aware of what constitutes good design. Communicate with designers (industrial designers, architects, city planners, artists) in e-mails, blogs, letters, and phone calls about your ideas for better design.

• Widen personal conversations to include the importance of design. Watch labels for Fair Trade, Energy Star, Forest Stewardship Council, USDA Organic, and similar certifications. Support the rebirth of the federal Office of Technology Assessment to enable a wider forum about the desirability of technologies and designs.

DESIGNED TO FAIL

I had an unsettling thought the other day as I wrestled, scissors in hand, with the fortresslike plastic packaging around a new electric razor. I wondered if anyone had accidentally taken his own life trying to unwrap a consumer item like this one. If a person's flustered grip on the package slipped, I thought, those sharp scissors could plunge into vital organs. Cause of death: thick, stubborn packaging.

I knew the packaging was as much for the manufacturers' and retailers' benefits as for mine, and I resented that. They were making the money; I was spending the time—first the work time to buy the expensive razor, then the fluster time to penetrate its package. I'd bought the electric unit because I was tired of buying and throwing out blades. I wanted something that lasts longer than refrigerator leftovers.

I hoped to do less damage to my checking account and to the environment with the electric razor, but considering all the electricity the razor would use and all the energy that had gone into its manufacture, I wasn't completely certain. Still, it did feel better than the prospect of tossing another five thousand blades (and all their packaging) before I die.

I thought about the man who got me into this shaving jam to begin with—King Gillette, who, at the end of the nineteenth century pondered what sort of business he should launch. Why not design and sell an essential but flawed product that would need replacing after a few uses, providing a steady stream of profits? In 1895, while he shaved with a dull razor, inspiration struck, in the form of a minor neck wound: blades that could be simply thrown away when they got dull. In a sense, Gillette and people like him were responsible not only for disposable razor blades but also for the whole calculated, costly, disposable culture we're tangled up in. To obtain the "convenience" of those throwaway blades, how many hours do we spend prowling supermarket aisles in search of new cartridges? How much hidden time do we spend in the car and at work? And of course, it's not just razor blades but computer equipment, frozen dinners, paper towels, tape dispensers, batteries, even cars and houses, all of which typically are designed for short, often shoddy lifetimes. It's easy to conclude that a large part of our economy is shaped by intentionally bad design that leaves us dissatisfied. Which, in turn, makes us all the more eager to seek comfort in consuming.

Throughout our hyperindustrial era, many products have been not only designed for short lives, but also discovered accidentally, or designed using erroneous logic. For example, the father of synthetic fertilizer, German scientist Justus von Liebig, based his flawed deduction that plants need only three basic nutrients on simplistic experiments in which he burned plant tissue and examined what was left. But the combustion destroyed most of the chemical compounds. (Doh!) Liebig didn't realize until the end of his life that he had made a colossal mistake, which spread into the world like a Trojan computer virus but infinitely worse. Synthetic fertilizers boost yields the way candy boosts energy—temporarily. Both soil and human bodies have reserves of the other essential nutrients, but when those reserves are depleted crashes result, in both cases. In 1843, the scientist-designer wrote remorsefully that he had sinned against the wisdom of the Creator. What seemed at first like a technological miracle was largely responsible for a global population explosion as well as billions of acres of used-up soil.

Scientist Thomas Midgley repeatedly received prestigious awards for his chemical designs, primarily leaded gasoline and Freon (or CFCs). For more than half a century, Midgley's power-boosting ethyl additive caused five thousand deaths annually from lead poisoning, while CFCs, which damage the earth's ozone layer, almost wiped out the planet's critical shield against solar radiation. Although the severe health effects of leaded gasoline were known back in the 1920s, the auto industry was able to keep the lid on and the lead in until 1986—by spending millions of dollars to reassure the public and bribe the politicians. After ethyl was banned, levels of lead in the blood of Americans declined more than 75 percent.[14]

Industries that profited from making and selling CFCs also spent millions to defend their coolant and aerosol products. DuPont chairman Irving Shapiro commented in 1975 that the ozone-depletion theory was "a science fiction tale . . . a load of rubbish . . . utter nonsense." But thorough, peer-reviewed research proved otherwise.[15]

Accidental designs are part of evolution, but they need to be assessed and approved by both technicians and sociologists. Those that are a poor fit should be rejected, which is why the world's customers should be informed enough to tell one another which ones are losers. The invention of synthetic colors brightened the world's appearance but also opened a Pandora's box of toxic chemicals. In 1856 (at the age of eighteen), English chemist William Perkin was looking for a way to synthesize quinine, a natural compound used to fight malaria in Africa. He was astounded to see the color purple emerge in his murky laboratory soup of coal tar wastes. (Until that time, colors had been derived from plants, insects, shells, and minerals.) Within the year, chemists all over the world were mixing a pinch of this, a pinch of that, trying to synthesize colors, fertilizers, fabrics, and other cheaply produced "carbon copies."

The chemical pathways that resulted have become standard practices in the petrochemical industry; however, new trails are now being blazed in laboratories all around the world. For example, a Canadian company and a German company collaborated to reroute the chemical pathway to an end product of polyester. Researchers analyzed every ingredient and procedure in conventional polyester, selecting dyes and chemicals that are not health or environmental hazards. Most important, they got rid of the industry's standard catalyst—antimony—a carcinogenic metal that is also toxic to the heart, lungs, liver, and skin.[16]

INTELLIGENT DESIGN—BY HUMANS

The good news is that driven by regulations, consumer demand, fear of future lawsuits, and a green-themed business environment, design in general is beginning to become more intelligent. As opposed to accidental design that doesn't know where it's going or who will use it, next-generation design is analytical and packed with relevant information. The Proctor and Gamble Company examined the energy impact of its detergents and discovered that washing machines were the largest single energy user in the whole laundry system—production, consumption, and disposal of detergents and packaging. Since most detergents work effectively only in warm water, a lot of energy is used to heat the water, so P & G researchers went back to the lab and invented a detergent, Ariel Cool Clean, which works in cold water, saving energy without any loss in performance. Says P&G's sustainability Web site, "We combine two key strengths—consumer understanding and science—to deliver sustainable innovations that don't require tradeoffs in performance or value." Is this mission statement "greenwash"? Partly, but it's also an ethical direction and, possibly, a self-fulfilling prophecy.

These kinds of opportunities exist in all types of design—we just need cultural instructions to look for them. This is truly the design profession's greatest moment. The challenges we face require radically redesigned production systems, landscapes, and structures, all sensitive to changing variables like energy, health, climate, and resource availability. We need an inspired new generation of whole-systems designers to express changing values in designs. Society should grant the design profession the social status of doctors and lawyers—calling for pride, skill, and integrity in the design field. As with the age-old physician's oath to "do no harm," we need a designer's oath (a Leonardo's da Vinci ethic) to "design nothing harmful." Designers reflect cultural direction, and their designs are responses to directions they receive from the culture, often intuitively. In this moment of massive change, we need democratic, values-driven design because we are not just designing gadgets and packaging but also redesigning the civilization that contains them. In the Renaissance, the highest mission of a designer was to glorify God; in our time, the highest mission is to fit the world like a glove fits a hand.

If we integrate values such as efficiency, moderation, and fairness into our designs, with tools such as precision, prevention, and participation, we stand a chance of creating a realistic, affordable civilization. However, if we integrate the spoiled assumptions of our current era into our products, buildings, and landscapes, we'll lock ourselves into a future that is literally designed to fail.

Ideally, our designs will be so well conceived that fewer regulations will be necessary. For example, if we design products that are fully recyclable and a collection system that makes recycling effortless, it will become almost impossible *not* to recycle. If we use eco-intelligent ingredients and procedures throughout the industrial sector, we will radically reduce many environmental and health impacts that have plagued us for centuries. In effect, we will integrate the law right into the product. As William McDonough phrases it, "If a factory's effluent is cleaner than its influent, it might well prefer to use its affluent as influent." (This statement is far from theoretical. McDonough worked with a European company that chose thirty-eight environmentally friendly ingredients from a field of thousands to make fabric out of, resulting in a process that literally filtered the water.)

Just as an architect needs to know the characteristics and constraints of a building site before designing a house, designers of all types need to work with biologists and sociologists to make sure their designs are in sync with natural and cultural constraints. "We can't practice architecture without knowledge of forestry and energy issues," wrote Paul Hawken in the foreword to my book *Deep Design: Pathways to a Livable Future.* "Chemical engineering without epidemiology and biology is inexact and lacking, and transportation systems that don't take into account community, family and climate are not systems at all." All those who use a given design have a right, even a responsibility, to have an opinion about the design and to express it in public, at city council meetings, in corporate focus groups, and, most conveniently, on government- or nonprofit-sponsored Web sites. The Internet enables easily accessed commentary about designs. Like scientific papers, designs and technologies should be peer-reviewed. Both experts and everyday users should be able to choose what enters our world, and what doesn't. Products that prove harmful—whether physically, environmentally, or socially—should get very low grades, even if heavy, misleading advertising made them popular initially.

Since cheap supplies of energy and materials are no longer a sure thing, designers need to be socially as well as technically competent. For example, state-of-the-art batteries for electric vehicles and elsewhere contain lithium, an element that is most abundant in Bolivia, a country the United States is currently not on great terms with. The heavy rare-earth metal dysprosium, which makes electric motors up to 90 percent more efficient, is also geographically perplexing; 99 percent of all dysprosium comes from two hundred mines in China.[17]

The opening scene in *2001: A Space Odyssey*—in which a prehistoric human flings a primitive tool skyward—is a symbol of the human destiny: with an ingenious brain and hands to match, it was inevitable that we would be designers. However, the practice of design lost some of its standing when it became a servant of the market. In the near future, enlightened designers won't just say, "Here's what you can have"; instead, they will wisely ask, "What do we need? How can design make our lives better, not just busier and more expensive?"

DESIGNING LIKE OUR LIVES DEPEND ON IT

A civilization on the cusp of megachange needs to prioritize its design goals and to channel public, private, and nonprofit resources toward those goals. At the top of the list are systems that:

- prevent climate change

- preserve, conserve, and restore water supplies

- minimize pollution and health impacts

- effectively and humanely prevent unwanted birth

- make recycling automatic

- restore farmland and forested land

- optimize social capabilities as well as needs

This is not a trivial to-do list, is it? Some of the big-hitter human activities that are especially in need of redesign are energy production, wastewater treatment, and the manufacture of automobiles, cement, and plastic. Fortunately, designers all over the world are immersed in research that is yielding major breakthroughs.

Society's instructions to engineers and designers concerning energy production are explicit: "Go green. Get the carbon out of our fuels and power plants, right now." As energy guru Amory Lovins has phrased it, we need a history-shifting "undiscovery of fire," and we will have it. Joining innovators in the transportation and electrical-power sectors—which account for about two-thirds of greenhouse-gas emissions—are other heavy hitters like the cement and plastics industries. Engineers in both industries are learning how to incorporate carbon dioxide into their products rather than dumping it into the atmosphere. The cement industry accounts for 6 percent of global CO_2 emissions (twice as much as the aviation industry), and that figure is going to get higher as Asia and Eastern Europe continue to build infrastructure. (Some analysts predict that the cement industry could become a larger contributor to climate change than the entire European Union by 2030.) The Calera Corporation in California is challenging a cement-making paradigm that has remained constant for more than 2,300 years with a process that's similar to the way coral reefs self-assemble. Calera injects carbon dioxide emissions from power plants into seawater, which creates a chalky carbonate that is added to gravel and water to make concrete. This process avoids the need for the high temperatures typically supplied by coal-fired kilns, creating a cement that is 40 percent solidified carbonate by weight.

The industrial production of algae for fuel is also being assessed as a way to scrub CO_2 emissions from power plants. Algae may prove to be the most efficient way to produce biofuels, so why not create a partnership between power plants and biofuel factories? The Raytheon Company and others are currently running pilot programs to see if algae can efficiently absorb carbon dioxide, then be made into a biofuel. Though ethanol from corn was originally thought to be a serendipitous substitute for gasoline, it doesn't significantly reduce greenhouse gases; too much gas-emitting energy is used when the corn is fertilized, harvested, and processed. Many scientists rank the power density of algae far higher than that of corn and other prospects like cellulose-rich switchgrass. Other advantages of algae are that its production doesn't compete with food and feed crops for prime farmland, and that it can be grown wherever there's sunlight and water, for example in deserts, where land is cheap, or at wastewater treatment plants, where algae growth and harvest could help purify the water as well as power the plant.

A company in Venice, Italy, is using synthetic natural gas made from algae to power electricity-producing turbines. The carbon dioxide released by the combustion goes back into the process, to stimulate the next generation of algae. A San Diego start-up company, Sapphire Energy, proposes to use existing infrastructure—pipelines, refineries, and vehicles—to produce a fuel that has the same molecules as conventional fossil fuels. Their product has already been flight-tested by various airlines and given good grades: it combusts at lower temperatures than conventional jet fuel and has 4 percent better mileage in the tests.

However, as an industry, algae-based biofuel faces stiff political competition. So far, the eighteen senators from nine corn-growing states have consistently voted to subsidize corn-based ethanol. However, the current federal mandate for biofuels is 1 billion gallons by 2020, and it's quite possible that algae can become part of that equation.

A third technological innovation that meets high-priority needs is plastic that incorporates CO_2 right into the product. Currently, 10 percent of oil consumed in the United States is used for plastics manufacturing and packaging. The plastics industry is also responsible for heavy emissions of greenhouse gases and toxic substances found in products like baby bottles, vinyl toys, coatings in tin cans, and flame retardants. The Novomer Company, in upstate New York, may have a new kind of plastic that could radically transform the industry. According to CEO Jim Mahoney, the manufacture of polypropylene carbonate (PPC) reduces petroleum usage per unit by at least 50 percent while also converting CO_2 from pollution into valuable materials. As in the biofuel and cement processes mentioned above, the CO_2 could come from power-plant or industrial scrubbers. It's not hard to imagine an "industrial ecology" facility at which these four industries share and optimize resources like CO_2, waste heat, electricity, and distribution pipelines.

DESIGNING WITH NATURE

A new movement in the world of design, called biomimicry, is destined to change the way our world functions. By developing a genuine understanding of how the world's species meet their needs, designers can draw on a living catalog of inventions. Says Janine Benyus, who wrote one of the first books on the subject and is now a biomimicry consultant and educator, "You take an engineering problem like how to lubricate or adhere to something, and you find examples of how nature has solved that problem. If you look carefully, you can always find technologies shaped by natural selection that hold the answers." Dietar Gurtler, an engineer with the company then known as DaimlerChrysler, used that very approach, studying the shapes of fish to design an aerodynamic compact car. Says Gurtler, "Evolution has formed creatures that are very economical with energy."[18]

Similarly, Oregon State University professor Kaichang Li studied the way mussels cling to surf-battered shoreline rocks, and discovered that they exude threads of protein as an adhesive. He had a flash of insight: why not add amino acids to soybeans to create a water-resistant, nontoxic adhesive? Several years later, many homes and buildings became less toxic when one of the country's largest plywood manufacturers replaced cancer-causing formaldehyde in its adhesive resins with soybeans.[19]

Paint companies have mimicked the self-cleaning technique of the lotus leaf, which maintains its solar exposure even in swampy conditions; the microscopic structure of its top layer makes dust particles stick to raindrops, which then drip off the leaf. And inspiration for one of the most familiar fasteners in the world, Velcro, came in 1955 when amateur inventor and mountaineer George de Mestral pulled burrs from his dog's fur after a walk. Under a microscope, he saw small hooks in the burr's clingy seed surface, and tiny loops in the dog's fur and his pants. He named his invention from a blend of the words "velour" and "crochet."

The world desperately needs alternatives for the flush toilet, another of humanity's biggest blunders. What do you have when you put a drop of clean water into a gallon of sewage? Sewage. What do you have when you put a drop of sewage into a gallon of water? Sewage. Now for the critical question: What do you have when you put billions of gallons of industrial wastes into sewage, every day? A system that prevents the recycling of nutrients back into agriculture. However, the bioinspired Living Machine, perfected by bioneer John Todd, is a solar aquaculture system that looks like a greenhouse. A succession of organisms like snails, cattails, microbes, fish, and even roses purifies wastewater as well as or better than conventional wastewater-treatment plants. (The state of Indiana has certified this technology as legal treatment.) The synergies between this naturalized system with no noticeable odor (I've toured a few) and apartment buildings, office buildings, and neighborhoods could, with start-up subsidies, make our way of life far more affordable overall, providing technical jobs and a very important balance between what we consume and what we grow. The missing link in this open loop may be more perceptual than actual: health concerns. Surely, microbiology, vermiculture, and compost science are sufficiently advanced to change the wastewater paradigm, too.

Population? Maybe the most pressing design need of all. As physicist Al Bartlett has pointed out for years, many desirable aspects of our culture—such as peace, law and order, high-yield agriculture, accident prevention, medicine, and environmental protection—make population swell to a breaking point, while abortion, war, disease, murder, famine, and pollution control population. Houston, we have a problem. Population expansion can be held in check only with a blend of social transformation and technology. Again, given the rapid advance of genetic biology, shouldn't we soon be able to "turn off" the reproductive gene and later turn it back on? The bigger challenge might ultimately be social: shouldn't we able to decide collectively that one child per family is perfect?

Design should take its marching orders from cultural consensus. If society continues to specify that only nature-compatible design is acceptable, all future humans will regard us as an era that found its way out of a very dark forest.

• General Qualities of a Good Design •

Does the design incorporate three key levers for change—precision, prevention, and participation?

Will users be able to understand the design, maintain it, and be satisfied with it?

Does the design increase rather than limit the users' options?

Is it designed with the future in mind, including the product's use, reuse, and disposal?

Is the product safe to use, reuse, and recycle—not requiring protective equipment during production or consumption?

Does the design leave opportunities for imagination and creativity? (Can these qualities be an interactive output rather than a predesigned input?)

Does it increase users' self-reliance and self-worth rather than creating dependency and insecurity?

Does the design optimize existing infrastructure, and materials that are recyclable?

Does the design enhance creative thinking?

Does the design allow point-of-sale recovery of materials such as packaging?

Is the design produced in an eco-friendly process, considering proximity to treatment facilities and efficient transportation systems as well as integrity of existing ecosystems?

Does it have educational potential?

Are materials and systems flexible enough to allow upgrades and retrofits?

Does it minimize the use of off-site electricity for heating and cooling?

Is it burdened with "embodied energy" in extraction, refining, manufacturing, shipping, and disposal costs?

Does it take advantage of supply-chain partnerships that minimize environmental impacts at every link in the supply and use chain?

Is it designed for diversity, flexibility, and "fit"?

8

Social Alchemy: Creating a New Normal

S ocial change is natural, and inevitable. Without it, we wouldn't be here. Yet, paradoxically, intelligence and adaptability can be liabilities as well as assets. Our scientific knowledge is now sufficiently advanced to cause some real trouble. For example, we've become the best producers, marketers, and consumers in the universe. We cleverly find ways to survive even unnatural acts and designs like diets of processed food and the wrath of toxic buildings—at least in the short term. But knowledge is only one facet of human ingenuity, and many believe it's time to rely on a richer mix of instinct, intuition, and wisdom. In the book *The Power of Limits,* Gyorgy Doczi makes an important distinction between knowledge and wisdom: "Wisdom is a pulling together, knowledge a taking apart. Wisdom synthesizes and integrates; knowledge analyzes and differentiates. Wisdom envisions relationship, wholeness, and unity. Knowledge accepts only that which can be verified by the senses, it grasps only the specific."[1] From the days of Galileo and Descartes and even before, humans have been extremely strong on exploration and knowledge. Taking the pieces apart to find the monetary treasure that lay inside, we began to understand what makes life tick. Now it's time for wisdom to reassert itself with ancient insights about life: it doesn't just "tick" like one of our machines; it pulses with life. It's usually advantageous to leave living systems in place, especially if they are mature systems that have worked so hard, so long, to perfect themselves in relation to other species. Taking them apart unravels all the weaving, all the trials and errors, that ensure a good fit. The wealth inherent in systems (which, for example, regulate climate and create breathable air) far exceeds the largely symbolic wealth we accumulate in safe-deposit boxes, stock portfolios, and stuffed garages.

Let's hope that a hundred years from now, the world's citizens aren't shaking their heads and asking, "Why didn't they DO something?" In a way, we're innocent—we're just playing the game the way it's set up. But wisdom tells us we need a new game. (I hope this book has left readers with some ideas about the shape and purpose of a new game.) The impacts of our lifestyle are familiar to historians who track the decline of overextended empires throughout history: resource stocks fall, and wastes build up. Technologies are brought online to compensate for the loss of services that nature once provided free. Scarcer, more distant resources are exploited, and more capital is allocated to the military and industry to access and defend these resources. Protest flourishes (sometimes it's terrorism; other times, it's more aptly called revolution). Natural systems become less resilient and more prone to disaster. We see all these symptoms in our troubled times, but we don't yet see how huge the cracks are—we prefer to look the other way. Surely some new technology or charismatic leader will come along, or God will intervene.[2]

The truth is, we need to act on our own behalf, and on behalf of our kids and grandkids. We can either make wiser, deep green choices or watch helplessly as the future unfolds in shades of brown, gray, and black. In our hearts, we know this is true; we just haven't accepted it as a culture. Unfortunately, our sharpest instincts won't kick in until we recognize the scope of the problem, and there is much static and social inertia that prevent this recognition. Elisabeth Kubler-Ross identified the five stages that accompany the process of dying: denial, anger, bargaining, depression, and finally, acceptance. Regarding the decline and inevitable death of our current paradigm, I'd say that many humans are moving through the bargaining phase, though many are obstinately stuck in denial and others are quite angry—for example, at governments that are "on our backs" or at billionaire CEOs who somehow pay no taxes. Many are saddled with depression about the changes that will be necessary; but fortunately, many others have already rolled up their sleeves and accepted the death of our excessive lifestyle as a natural, inevitable, desirable event, and have begun to move on, just as the pioneers of early American history did. Let's throw our support to the accepters, who have risked sticking their necks out, and who can lead us to a more sensible way of life.

➤ Corporate Muscle

Companies go through transitional phases too, as they leave behind obsolete, irresponsible, and inefficient ways of producing goods and services. A company's wake-up call can be stimulated in many ways, including enlightened leadership; grassroots protest either from within the company or by the general public; pressure from media; changes in regulations; and changes in costs or availability of resources. At Interface, a carpet manufacturer, President Ray Anderson credits the "persistent and aggressive voice of a single customer" (author and activist Paul Hawken) with the company's turnaround. Walmart CEO Lee Scott launched a yearlong exploration of corporate impacts—including visits to remote supplier locations like Turkey—after years of environmental and civic muckraking. Nike began its mission toward sustainability with an embarrassing photo in *Life* magazine that showed a twelve-year-old boy in Pakistan stitching a pile of Nike soccer balls. From the awareness phase, companies like these create a vision of how they can improve. They have retreats, establish prototypes on a small scale, and examine the life cycle of their products and how each supplier conducts its business. Finally they begin integrating the vision into everyday practice. The overall goal is not only a more sustainable product but also a transformed company culture, with a new sense of identity and more efficient procedures. In short, "the way we do it here" changes, which perpetuates a quest for excellence. Given the huge amount of capital that companies now control, the steady transformation of industry is one of the most powerful levers of change the world has ever seen. It's up to us as citizen-consumers and investors to expect and demand this corporate cultural shift.[3]

It's often assumed that powerful individuals are the heroes of change, as in the mythological stories that helped shape our civilization. In our times, that assumption is itself a myth. More likely to change the course of history are great ideas that various stakeholders in a network find beneficial. For example, renewable energy is finally moving forward as an industry because policy-makers, investors, start-up companies and even oil companies have formed a network that is mutually empowering. With the combined forces of capital, information, public support and evolving technology, renewable energy has become not only socially acceptable but financially secure.

➤ Baboons and Spittoons: Evidence That We Can Change

Neuroscientist Robert Sapolsky documents social alchemy in his work with baboons, a species typically identified with aggressive, male-dominated behavior. The Stanford University scientist has studied Kenyan baboons for years, observing that alpha males have their pick of females while bullying subordinate males into a state of constant stress. But in one troop the culture began to shift when a tourist lodge opened nearby and began to dump half-eaten scraps and leftovers near the baboons. The alpha males insisted on first pick of these freebies, but their aggression did them in. They ate contaminated meat and died of tuberculosis. The remaining males refused to perpetuate aggression as a way of life. They were lovers, not fighters, and began reciprocating when females groomed them. Even more unusual, the males groomed other males rather than bullying them. Typically, adolescent baboons leave their birthplace to join other troops, but have to fight to gain status. However, in this born-again troop, new arrivals were treated much more congenially. The baboon sisterhood began grooming them within six days, in contrast to the usual stressful three-month waiting period. The baboons had changed their deep-seated culture, "editing out" a highly aggressive hierarchy. Being subordinate in this group was no longer more stressful than being dominant. Sapolsky concludes that the determinant of stress (in both baboon and human cultures) is not what rank an individual achieves, but whether the larger society treats all individuals with respect—even those with low status.[4]

Many human cultures have also shifted behavior patterns, sometimes out of necessity. Cuba, for example, was forced in desperation to shift its agricultural practices (essentially going organic) when oil and fertilizer supplies from the Soviet Union were cut off. This "Special Period" of transition, with its accent on cooperation, provides the world with a model of self-reliance that may prove useful in coming years. Costa Rica, Bhutan, the United Kingdom, and several Scandinavian countries have reinvented key aspects of their cultures within the past generation, and even the profligate U.S. culture has shown a capability for change. During World War II, for example, Americans accepted the rationing of essentials like tires, gasoline, fuel oil, and sugar. Automobile factories stopped making and selling cars for private use and instead manufactured tanks and armored cars. Highway construction stopped, and women marched into factories by the millions to build aircraft and operate cranes. Everything was recycled, from bottles to bones, and two-thirds of the nation's vegetables were produced in 20 million Victory Gardens. Camaraderie blossomed, both on the war front and the home front during this unique and heroic period, illustrating a key theme of this book: as material wealth declines, more intrinsic forms of wealth often increase.[5]

Tobacco is another example of a dramatic shift in American norms. During the eighteenth and nineteenth centuries, the use of chewing tobacco was so common that the floors of public places, including government offices, were "slippery with tobacco juice." Even into the early twentieth century, sidewalks and floorboards of trains and buses were coated with spit, since hitting the sandbox or spittoon was considered unnecessary. Throughout the twentieth century, despite billions spent by the tobacco industry, cigarettes lost their movie-star allure and fell into disgrace. They were banned from many restaurants and other indoor places, and now even the last refuges are disappearing: The University of Kentucky recently banned cigarettes from the entire campus—not only indoors but outdoors as well.

The United States has taken at least three direct hits on its cultural identity in the last decade. And what have we learned? 9-11 taught Americans that not everyone in the world idolizes us. Although we initially responded to that attack by pulling together as neighbors and families, when the president told us to go shopping and then invaded the wrong country, we lost an opportunity to use the moment as a fulcrum of change. The flooding of New Orleans by Hurricane Katrina and the BP oil spill revealed flaws both in engineering and in government response to the needs of people. And the Great Recession that began in 2007 revealed deep character flaws in the financial system, demonstrating again that our political purpose—to represent the public good—needs to be reclaimed. Yet in 2010, significant indicators of change became apparent. For the first time since World War II, the number of cars scrapped exceeded the number purchased. The number of farms in the United States increased for the first time in decades. The number of cars manufactured in the United States fell 2 percent in 2009, from a peak of a quarter million cars. While there are still nearly five vehicles for every four licensed drivers in America, this drop is an indicator of several underlying trends, according to resource analyst Lester Brown: market saturation, ongoing urbanization, economic uncertainty, oil insecurity, rising gasoline prices, frustration with traffic congestion, mounting concerns about climate change, and a declining interest in cars among young people. These are the kinds of liabilities that together tilt a culture in a new direction. Referring to the last variable in the list, Brown writes, "Many of today's young people in a more urban society learn to live without cars. Many don't even bother to get a driver's license. This helps explain why, despite the largest U.S. teenage population ever, the number of teenagers with licenses is now under 10 million, after peaking at 12 million in 1978."[6]

➤ When Benefits Exceed Risks

Humans are not dummies; we won't abandon even a burning building until we know there's a safe place to jump. When the perceived benefits outweigh the risks, a culture begins to shift. The evidence is growing that even we comfortable Americans may be willing to jump as the smoke begins to burn our lungs. For example, when gasoline hit peak price levels in 2008, the number of cars on the road fell dramatically, especially in areas with well-run public-transit systems. In Boston, traffic on turnpikes declined by 600,000 cars in one month, causing officials to urge public-transit passengers to travel at off-peak hours. *Time* magazine writer Amanda Ripley compiled a list of benefits of higher-priced gas, to the delight of many environmentalists who have advocated higher gas taxes for years. With the sting of $100 fill-ups comes fewer deaths from car accidents, Ripley reported, because fewer cars are on the road. Several reputable scholars estimated that traffic fatalities in the United States would fall by a third if gas prices remained at $4 a gallon— that's one thousand lives spared every month. Decreased levels of air pollution would spare another two thousand lives a year, and insurance premiums would fall too, since those who are driving less might qualify for lower car-insurance rates.

One researcher estimated that a permanent $1 hike in gas prices would cut obesity by 10 percent, saving billions of dollars a year, because people would walk and bike more and eat out less. The environmental and social costs of sprawl would stall; there would be more police officers on foot patrols and bicycles; and the sales of superefficient cars would continue to climb. To reduce transportation costs, many globalized jobs would come back home—a very attractive benefit when one adult in ten is unemployed. Some employees would be offered four-day weeks as employers consider the benefits of heating and cooling buildings less. In short, high gas prices, and other culture-shifting events, often create many positive opportunities.[7]

Is massive change possible, even in America? Of course it is. After all, if it weren't, how did all these suburbs get here? In the late 1940s, the automobile industry was ready to roll. Land was available, the construction created millions of jobs, a federal mandate created the interstate highway system, and suburbs spread across the land like fields of poppies. Seventy years later, other factors are converging that will result in a remodeling of America to fit the times. Whole new industries will spring up: soil prospecting to find fertile, farmable soil under aging split-levels; suburban remodelers; vanpool operators; technical consultants who maintain residential solar, wind, and compost toilet systems. In today's suburbs, energetic gardeners are already planting in the backyards and even front yards of their neighbors, sharing the produce; devices are being installed to slow traffic; restaurants are appearing on the cul-de-sacs and curvilinear streets of suburbia; and neighborhoods are reenergized by all the people who now work at home.

Cities are rezoning to allow single-family McMansions to become multifamily homes. The city of Baltimore has made a special project out of making alleyways more beautiful and more useful—creating gardens and gathering places for neighbors where there were once only trash containers. In Detroit, an eighty-acre farm will be created in the hollowed-out part of the city that is now vacant lots, with full city approval and encouragement. Chicago is piloting the installation of rooftop gardens and green spaces, and in Portland, Oregon, citizens are reclaiming public streets for use as spaces for kiosks. One neighborhood in Seattle has reimagined itself as a cooperative Ecovillage, while in Boulder, Colorado, a neighborhood is trying to make the car an alternative form of transportation, with various walking, bicycling, solar-powered vehicles, and public-transit innovations. America's small cities, once hubs of manufacturing and still blessed with town centers, are ready to be put back into service as regional centers of culture and industry.

➤ Cold Turkey Sandwiches

There are many tools we can use to create and normalize a new paradigm, but the first step is invariably to bring down the old paradigm, as if it were a statue of Stalin. "You keep pointing at the anomalies and failures of the old paradigm," suggests systems thinker Donella Meadows. "You come yourself, with assurance, from the new one; you insert people with the new paradigm in places of public visibility and power. You don't waste time with reactionaries; rather you work with active change agents and with the vast middle ground of people who are open-minded."[8] A key piece of this transition is to accept responsibility ("If not us, who?") and admit, collectively, that the current system is out of control, like an addiction. (For example, we do have a 200-billion-gallon-a-year addiction to petroleum.) When a new pathway at last seems safer and saner than the one we are on, we make a collective leap of faith—a paradigm shift.

A typical 12-step program combines public disclosure of the addiction; humility, and recognition of a greater power; support from sponsors to examine what went wrong; and finally acceptance of a new code of behavior. This is a successful formula because it throws out the old paradigm and assures the abuser that a new one will work far better. Essentially, a program like this converts embarrassment and shame into pride—or sin into redemption. Few story lines in history or mythology are more powerful than this one. Mythologist Joseph Campbell observed that throughout the last millennium, the height of buildings reflected what we valued. The cathedral first became the tallest building, expressing a hope that God would supply comfort and meet humanity's humble needs. Then government buildings became taller, symbolizing a belief in liberty, democracy, and collective power. The needle-shaped Burj Khalifa tower in Dubai, more than half a mile tall (taller than the combined heights of the Empire State Building and the Sears Tower), symbolizes our current hope—that the commercial world can best supply comfort and meet our needs. Maybe cities of the future will bring building height back down to earth, acknowledging that mountains—and nature—will, and should, always be the world's most formidable structures.

➤ Tools for Change

Half the battle in shifting cultures is deciding which direction we should go. For example, when it becomes clear that we need to reduce obesity, we make that an overarching goal. All over the country, actions are taken under that banner: calories per serving appear on restaurant menus, trans fats are outlawed, and school boards mobilize parents to walk neighbor kids to school. In cafeterias, trays are not used, to encourage students to take and eat less. Similarly, when the overarching goal is energy efficiency and conservation, it's on everyone's mind, from top-level corporate managers to homeowners sitting at their kitchen tables. For example, Dan Riker tracks the energy his appliances and lights are consuming with a device hooked up to his fuse box. He can see the information on a meter in his kitchen or online. Says Riker, "In general, we think knowledge is power. And, indeed, in this case, knowledge is *less* power. My six-year-old son was looking at our little meter, which normally is at 200 watts, and this thing shoots up to 1,800 watts. He says, daddy, look. And it was simply the toaster, you know, turning electrical energy into massive heat energy to singe this toast." Observing another spike in the graph, Riker discovered that the motor in his furnace was old and inefficient, and replaced it.[9]

It's clear that "green" products, designs, and behaviors have become a dominant, overarching goal. The challenge is to motivate the mainstream to follow through, converting intentions into actions. The research of environmental psychologist Doug McKenzie-Mohr offers ample evidence that behavior change is best accomplished with social support, commitment, and empowerment. People will gravitate to actions that have high benefits and few barriers. Adopting one behavior frequently means rejecting another. For example, adopting composting as a household routine means rejecting the alternative—throwing away valuable food and yard wastes that could become a rich soil amendment. In effect, we are substituting the satisfaction of being part of a natural cycle for the ease of disposal, with no net loss of satisfaction.

McKenzie-Mohr calls his approach "community-based social marketing," a behavior changing method that incorporates various motivational techniques, including persuasive social contact, commitment, modeling of behavior changes, evaluation of what could be lost, and appeals to autonomy, generosity, money savings, time savings, stress reduction, responsibility, and accountability. While these techniques work well to motivate behavior change at the individual level, they are also a good model for how to change the culture of a community, or even of a civilization.

Despite billions of dollars spent to disseminate information about recycling or energy conservation, the results are fairly dismal. One information campaign after another fails to realize that what motivates people is appeals to values—who we are, not just what we do. We change behavior because we want the respect of others; we want to be part of something big; we want to show that we are "doing the right thing," or just that we know the current trends. We participate in recycling when it's easy to do; when others are doing it (or our children badger us into it); and most important, because it makes us feel good about ourselves. We can't do it alone, even if we know how many football stadiums our state's garbage fills in a year. There are four basic strategies to motivate the behavior of individuals, communities, and even civilizations:

- Increase the benefits of the target behavior.

- Decrease the barriers to the target behavior.

- Decrease the benefits of the competing behaviors.

- Increase the barriers of the competing behaviors.

Pioneering efforts to increase recycling in the state of Washington illustrate these strategies well. Policy innovators realized that if they could reward residents for recycling and penalize them for throwing trash away, recycling might increase. They began to charge for waste disposal based on the number of cans of garbage put at curbside. The brightly colored containers with recycled material were picked up for free, or for a minimal charge. When the program was implemented in the early 1980s, Seattle residents averaged 3.5 cans of garbage per household each week. Twelve years later, recycling had become as strong a part of the community culture as high-quality coffee; residents were now averaging only 1 can of garbage.

➤ Fostering Sustainable Behavior

In *Fostering Sustainable Behavior,* McKenzie-Mohr shares many anecdotes about what actually changes behavior. In one carefully staged experiment, the experimenter set up his towel, radio, and personal things at a beach. After a few minutes, he asked the people near him if they would watch his things while he went in the water. In nineteen out of twenty different experiments, caretakers pursued a fake thief who was part of the experiment, compared with only four out of twenty when the experimenter left without asking for their protective help. In almost every documented effort to change behavior, a commitment to vote or to recycle resulted in much higher participation. Especially binding is a written commitment, which apparently has the power of a contract. When community residents were urged to try riding a bus to work, commitment was an even stronger factor than financial incentive. Commitment is strongest when it is a public commitment. A person's desire to keep his or her word is strong, and is amplified in proportion to the number of people who know about the commitment.

Personal contact is a key motivator too: when neighbors who serve as "block leaders" of a project go door-to-door to explain the project, participation is generally twice as high as when leaflets alone are distributed. Momentum and active participation also play key roles in changing behavior. People are much more likely to contribute time or money if they have already contributed and were told they were "generous." In one study, residents were first asked to display stickers on their car windows that said "Be a Safe Driver." Everyone agreed to this harmless request, and amazingly, as compared to another group (that didn't display the stickers), three-fourths later agreed to have a large, ugly billboard that said "Drive Carefully" placed on their lawns. They were already safe-driving advocates who had gotten past their inhibitions to display stickers.

Research into behavior change tells us not only how personal behavior can shift a culture, but also how rapid changes in a culture can motivate and empower personal change.

➤ Finding the Hidden Benefits in Behavior Change

Whenever the benefits of and barriers to implementing any decision are examined, the decision maker should look behind the curtain for hidden benefits. For example, choosing an Energy Star–rated refrigerator is a great decision because in the past ten years the efficiency of refrigerators has increased by up to 25 percent. But there are considerations beyond the efficiencies of a single product. For example, a suite of efficient appliances makes renewable energy far more viable. Before considering installing solar electric panels on the roof of a house, it makes sense to reduce your home's electrical consumption, and refrigerators are a great place to start. An extremely efficient refrigerator emits far less droning noise because the compressor comes on less frequently—a subtle but tangible benefit. State-of-the-art fridges also have great humidity and temperature control in the vegetable and meat drawers, so food remains fresh much longer. This is significant for health reasons and also quality-of-life reasons. If the produce you chose last week is still fresh this week, you don't have to hustle back to the supermarket as soon, and you can also reduce the amount of food you throw away (the American average is 10 to 15 percent).

If a household's washing machine is finally on its last legs, a front-loading washer is probably worth the price premium because a horizontal-axis washer not only uses less energy but also less water, and is easier on clothes as well. Similarly, the often-higher price of organic produce is justified by values beyond cost: it delivers better nutrition because it's grown in mineral-rich soil. Buying organic avoids pesticide residues and uses less water back on the farm because loamy soil stores water like a sponge.

As we consider funding further developmental work on promising technologies like fuel cells, we should include values beyond their cost per kilowatt. Fuel cells are a clean, silent source of energy that can be installed right in our neighborhoods. This avoids the need for transmission lines and eliminates power "line losses" as electricity travels from the power plant. In fact, the use of fuel cells on a wide scale in a region can help eliminate the need to build another coal-fired power plant altogether. As a bonus by-product, fuel cells produce pure water, which might be used in landscaping a neighborhood park. My point is, there are often benefits that counterbalance cost, if we take the time to account for them.

For many of the choices presented in this book, we can't expect the comfort of familiarity and routine to be motivating factors. Instead, we'll rely on our capacities for quick adaptation. The unfamiliar soon becomes familiar. By definition, innovation and change are different from what preceded them, so standard operating procedures for buying, cooking, looking for a job, looking for a house, commuting, designing, and investing will be reinvented, as they have been already, many times. For example, eating meat one day less a week may mean that we make an effort to find a few classic meatless recipes and make them part of our repertoires. Asian, Latin American, and Mediterranean cuisines all offer meatless entrées that rely on other sources of protein like nuts, beans, and high-protein vegetables and grains.

The changes suggested in this book are not add-ons but replacements for procedures and actions that are not optimally efficient, healthy, or socially engaging. Social factors (such as advertising, TV, and widespread adoption of the "good life") got us into this mess, and social factors can get us out. We'll get to a more sensible way of living by telling and retelling a story that promotes a joyfully moderate, less stressful, sustainable lifestyle. We'll build a new civilization the way we built the current one: with incentives, social rewards, changing styles and designs, new kinds of technologies, and new ways of meeting our needs. It's time for a cultural revolution. Let's hope we have the vitality and courage to participate in a movement of consumer disobedience that demands quality over quantity, localization rather than globalization, and time affluence rather than the poverty of constant, stressful deadlines. Let's choose less aggression and more empathy; more respect for public places, including the environment, and less obsession with individual ambition and accumulation.

The future is waiting. It's time for us to stop seeing the world as it is, and begin to see it as it should be.

Notes

Introduction: Once Upon a Paradigm, When Growth Was King

1. Donella Meadows, "Leverage Points: Places to Intervene in a System," http://www.thesolutionsjournal.com/node/470.

2. "World Changing, staff Earth Day: 10 Big, Really Hard Things We Can Do to Save the Planet," April 22, 2009, http://www.worldchanging.com/.

3. Thomas L. Friedman, "The Inflection Is Near?" *New York Times,* March 7, 2009, http://www.nytimes.com/2009/03/08/opinion/08friedman.html.

4. "Paul Hawken Shares His Views" by Kamal Patel, Sept. 25, 2009, http://www.worldchanging.com/archives/010556.html.

5. Dacher Keltner, *Born to Be Good: The Science of a Meaningful Life* (New York: W.W. Norton, Austin, Texas 2009).

Chapter One: The Software of Civilization

1. Jim Rubens, *OverSuccess* (Austin, TX: Greenleaf Books, 2009), 40.

2. Mark Shwartz and Lisa Share, "Robert Sapolsky Discusses Physiological Effects of Stress," *Stanford Report,* March 7, 2007, http://news-service.stanford.edu/news/2007/march7/sapolskysr-030707.html?view=print.

3. Malcolm Gladwell, *Outliers: The Story of Success* (New York: Little, Brown, 2008), 6–9.

4. Margaret Wheatley, "The Future," in *Imagine: What America Could Be in the 21st Century,* ed. Marianna Williamson, 403–4 (Emmaus, PA: Rodale Books, 2000).

5. Ibid. *Imagine: What America Could Be in the 21st Century,* ed. Marianna Williamson (Emmaus, Pennsylvania: Rodale Books, 2000), 128

6. Elizabeth Rosenthal, "Fast Food Hits Mediterranean; a Diet Succumbs," *New York Times,* September 24, 2008, http://www.nytimes.com/2008/09/24/world/europe/24diet.html?_r=1&th&emc=th&oref=slogin.

7. Rubens, *OverSuccess,* 43.

8. Jonah Lehrer, *How We Decide* (New York: Houghton Mifflin, 2009), 184.

9. Adam Smith, *The Wealth of Nations*. (Petersfield, Hampshire, United Kingdom: Harriman House, 2007), 53.

10. Tim Jackson, "Motivating Sustainable Consumption," January 2005, http://www.comminit.com/en/node/219688/306.

11. Alan Durning, Social Contract Journal vol. 3, no. 3 (Spring 1993), excerpt from *How Much Is Enough?* http://www.thesocialcontract.com/artman2/publish/tsc0303/article_242.shtml.

12. Dale Southertin, Alan Warde, and Martin Hand, "The Limited Autonomy of the Consumer," in *Sustainable Consumption,* Dale Southertin et al., eds. (Cheltenham, United Kingdom: Edward Elgar Publishing, Limited, 2004), 32.

13. Kevin Phillips, *Bad Money* (New York: Penguin, 2009), 54

14. Lester Brown, "Early Signs of Decline," in *Plan B 3.0* (New York: W.W. Norton & Company, 2009), http://www.earth-policy.org/Books/PB3/PB3ch6_ss4.htm.

Chapter Two: Why Not a Non-Profit Economy?

1. Lester R. Brown, *Plan B 2.0: Rescuing a Planet Under Stress and a Civilization in Trouble.* (New York: W.W. Norton, 2006), 49.

2. Faith Popcorn's Brain Reserve, Leading Future-Focused Trend Consultancy Brain Reserve sees 2009 as a year marked by unprecedented fear, anxiety, and uncertainty, http://www.faithpopcorn.com/.

3. David Korten, "The Speech President Obama Should Deliver But Won't," January 19, 2009, http://www.greenbiz.com/blog/2009/01/19/speech-obama-wont-deliver.

4. Robert Reich, *Supercapitalism: The Transformation of Business, Democracy, and Everyday Life.* (New York: Alfred A. Knopf, 2007), 213.

5. Daniel Gorman, *Ecological Intelligence.* (New York: Broadway Books, 2009), 196.

6. Frances Moore Lappé, *Democracy's Edge.* (San Francisco, Jossey-Bass, 2006), 144.

7. Marco Visscher and Janet Paskin, "A Sustainable Alternative to the Financial Meltdown," *Ode* (December 2008) http://www.odemagazine.com/doc/59/a-sustainable-alternative-to-the-financial-meltdown/2/.

8. Patrick Mitchell, "Socially Responsible Investing Assets In U.S Surged 18 Percent From 2005 To 2007, Outpacing Broader Managed Assets," *Social Investment Forum* Web site, 28, http://www.socialinvest.org/news/releases/pressrelease.cfm?id=108.

9. Lester R. Brown, *Plan B 4.0.* (New York: W.W. Norton & Company, 2009), 52.

10. Jared Diamond, *Collapse: How Societies Choose to Fail or Succeed.* (New York: Viking, 2005), 233.

11. Stefan Lovgren, "Costa Rica Aims to Be 1st Carbon-Neutral Country," March 7, 2008, *National Geographic News*, http://news.nationalgeographic.com/news/2008/03/080307-costa-rica.html.

12. Robert Reich, *Supercapitalism: The Transformation of Business, Democracy, and Everyday Life.* (New York: Alfred A. Knopf, 2007), 115.

13. Kurt Andersen, *Reset*. (New York: Random House, 2009), 3–5.

14. Editorial staff "Just the Facts," *YES!* (Fall 2007), 23.

15. David Korten, "Better Than Money," *YES!* (Fall 2007), 37–41.

16. Van Jones with Ariane Conrads, *The Green Collar Economy*. (New York: HarperOne, 2008), 110.

17. David Korten, "Why This Crisis May Be Our Best Chance to Build a New Economy," *YES!* (June 19, 2009) http://www.yesmagazine.org/issues/the-new-economy/why-this-crisis-may-be-our-best-chance-to-build-a-new-economy.

18. Tracy Fernandez Rysavy & Prianjali, "Financing Hope," *YES!* (Winter, 2007), 41–43

19. Ibid., 41–43.

20. Marco Visscher and Janet Paskin, "A Sustainable Alternative to the Financial Meltdown," *Ode* (December 2008) http://www.odemagazine.com/doc/59/a-sustainable-alternative-to-the-financial-meltdown/2.

21. Carmel Wroth, "Michelle Chan: "Fighting for sustainability in the bank sector," *Ode* (January/February 2009) http://www.odemagazine.com/doc/60/michelle-chan-fighting-for-sustainability-in-the-bank-sector/.

22. Wikipedia, http://en.wikipedia.org/wiki/Ethical_banking

23. Liz Pulliam Weston, "Ditch Your Bank for a Credit Union," April 9, 2009, http://articles.moneycentral.msn.com/Banking/BetterBanking/DitchYourBankForACreditUnion.aspx.

24. Janet Paskin, "Think Outside the Bank," *Ode* (December 2007), 3–42.

25. Monica Davey, "States Barter Fish and Bullets to Save Money," *New York Times*, May 23, 2009, http://www.nytimes.com/2009/05/23/us/23share.html?_r=1&th&emc=th.

26. Marco Visscher and Janet Paskin, "A Sustainable Alternative to the Financial Meltdown, *Ode* (December 2008) http://www.odemagazine.com/doc/59/a-sustainable-alternative-to-the-financial-meltdown/all.

27. Judy Wicks, in conversation with author, July 25, 2009.

28. Michael Shuman, *The Small-Mart Revolution*. (San Francisco: Berrett-Koehler, 2001), 65.

29. Ibid.

30. Judy Wicks, in conversation with author, July 25, 2009.

31. Inscription at the Jefferson Memorial, Washington, D.C.

32. Charles Siegel, *The Politics of Simple Living*. (Berkeley, California: Preservation Institute, 2008), 7.

33. Victor Lebow, quoted in Michael F. Jacobson and Laurie Ann Mazur, *Marketing Madness: A Survival Guide for a Consumer Society*. (Boulder, Colorado: Westview Press, 1995), 191.

34. *Crossroads Magazine* http://crossroadsmag.eu/2006/11/high-labour-participation-rate-but-many-part-time-workers-in-the-netherlands/)

35. Charles Siegel, *The Politics of Simple Living*. (Berkeley, California: Preservation Institute, 2008), 7

36. George Lakoff, "7 Reasons Why Obama's Speeches Are So Powerful," *AlterNet* (March 3, 2009) http://www.alternet.org/story/128629/

37. Thomas L. Friedman, "Are We Home Alone?" *New York Times*, March 22, 2009 http://www.nytimes.com/2009/03/22/opinion/22friedman.html?th=&emc=th&pagewanted=print

38. Devin T. Stewart, "Is Ethical Capitalism Possible?" *Policy Innovations* (January 28, 2009) http://www.enn.com/top_stories/article/39189)

39. Editorial Staff, *MSN Money,* "What Does it Cost to Drop 30 Pounds?" December 26, 2008 http://articles.moneycentral.msn.com/SavingandDebt/Consumer ActionGuide/WhatDoesItCostToDrop30Pounds.aspx

40. Hilary Smith, *MSN Money,* "The High Costs of Smoking," September 3, 2008 http://articles.moneycentral.msn.com/Insurance/InsureYourHealth/HighCostOfSmok ing.aspx?page=all

41. Michael Shuman, *The Small-Mart Revolution,* (San Francisco: Berrett-Koehler, 2001), 73.

42. Michael Pollan, "Big Food vs. Big Insurance," *New York Times,* September 9, 2009 http://www.nytimes.com/2009/09/10/opinion/10pollan.html

43. David Brooks, "Let's Get Fundamental," *New York Times,* September 3, 2009 http://www.nytimes.com/2009/09/04/opinion/04brooks.html?_r=1)

44. Pollan, Michael, "Big Food vs. Big Insurance," *New York Times,* September 10, 2009 http://www.nytimes.com/2009/09/10/opinion/10pollan.html)

45. Lester R. Brown, "Mobilizing to Save Civilization" Earth Policy Institute Web site, http://www.earth-policy.org/Books/PB2/PB2ch13_ss4.htm)

46. Joseph Stiglitz and Linda J. Blimes, *The Three Trillion Dollar War: The True Cost of the Iraq Conflict.* (New York: W.W. Norton, 2008), 127.

47. Dr Andrew Dlugolecki, Chartered Insurance Institute, February 25, 2009 http://www.epolitix.com/latestnews/article-detail/newsarticle/dr-andrew-dlugolecki-chartered-insurance-institute/

48. Joe Romm, "It's Easy Being Green: A New Military Mission: Clean Energy," Center for American Progress, March 4, 2009, http://www.americanprogress.org/issues/2009/03/green_military.html

Chapter Three: Overfed but Undernourished

1. Wendell Berry "One thing to do about food," *The Nation,* September 11, 2006, 14.

2. Alice Waters, "Slow Food Nation," *The Nation,* September 11, 2006, 13.

3. Ibid.

4. "Still No Free Lunch," Brian Halweil, Organic Center, September 2007, 5–10. http://www.organic-center.org/reportfiles/Yield_Nutrient_Density_Final.pdf

5. Andrew Schneider, "Taste, Nutrients Decline As Size of Crops Grows," *Seattle-Post Intelligencer,* September 12, 2007. http://www.seattlepi.com/national/331421_bigfood13.html

6. Ibid.

7. Jon Mooallem, "Twelve Easy Pieces," February 12, 2006. http://www.nytimes.com/2006/02/12/magazine/12apples.html?_r=2&th=&adxnnl=1&emc=th&pagewanted=print&adxnnlx=1139756454-bn69uaR39wLdefMXyDfbLg)

8. Michael Pollan, "Unhappy Meals," *New York Times,* January 28, 2007. http://www.nytimes.com/2007/01/28/magazine/28nutritionism.t.html?_r=2&pagewanted=all

9. Douglas J. Lisle and Alan Goldhamer, *The Pleasure Trap: Mastering the Hidden Force that Undermines Health and Happiness.* (Summertown, Tennessee: Health Living Publications, 2003), 114.

10. Martin Lindstrom, *Buyology: Truth and Lies About Why We Buy.* (New York: Random House, 2008), 128.

11. Bill McKibben, *Deep Economy: The Wealth of Communities and the Durable Future*. (New York: Henry Holt and Company, 2007), 90.

12. Michael Grunwald, "Why Our Farm Policy is Failing," *Time*, November 12, 2007. http://www.time.com/time/magazine/article/0,9171,1680139,00.html

13. Jim Motavelli and E Magazine Staff, "The Passionate Palate," in *Green Living*. (New York: Plume Books, 2005), 8.

14. American Cancer Society Web site, September 8, 1999. http://www.cancer.org/docroot/NWS/content/NWS_1_1x_Farming_May_Be_Linked_to_Increased_Prostate_Cancer_Risk.asp)

15. Susan Lang, Cornell University, July 13, 2005. http://www.news.cornell.edu/stories/July05/organic.farm.vs.other.ssl.html

16. "Just the Facts: When Corporations Rule Our Food," *YES!* Spring 2009, Issue 49, 24.

17. "GO LOCAL! "10 Ways to a Human-Scale Economy," *YES*, Winter 2007 http://yesmagazinc.org/article.asp?ID=1571

18. Kim Severson, "A Locally Grown Diet With Fuss but No Muss," *New York Times*, http://www.nytimes.com/2008/07/22/dining/22local.html July 22, 2008 NYT)

19. Roger Bybee, "Growing Power in an Urban Food Desert," *YES!* Spring 2009. http://www.yesmagazine.org/article.asp?id=3328&utm_source=mar09&utm_medium=email&utm_campaign=f11_Alln

20. Mark Winne, "Fresh from . . . the City," *YES!* (Spring 2009), 23

21. Farm-to-school.org http://www.farmtoschool.org/aboutus.php

22. Food Security.org http://www.foodsecurity.org/NourishingtheNation-One-TrayataTime.pdf

23. Michael Pollan, "Farmer in Chief," *New York Times*, October 12, 2008, http://www.nytimes.com/2008/10/12/magazine/12policy-t.html?fta=y&pagewanted=print

24. Ibid.

25. Op cit.

26. Jimmy Carter, "Subsidies' Harvest of Misery," *The Washington Post*, December 12, 2007. http://www.washingtonpost.com/wp-dyn/content/article/2007 . . . 120900911.html?nav=rss_opinions/outlook?nav=slate

27. Michael Grunwald, "Down on the Farm," *Time*, November 12, 2007, 26–36.

28. Lester R. Brown, *Plan B 3.0: Mobilizing to Save Civilization*. (New York: W.W. Norton and Company, 2008.)

29. "Urban Agriculture: An Abbreviated List of References and Resources," USDA, 2000 http://www.nal.usda.gov/afsic/AFSIC_pubs/urbanag.htm

30. Jason Mark, "Growing it Alone," *Earth Island Journal*. http://www.earthisland.org/journal/index.php/eij/article/growing_it_alone/)

31. "World's Largest Urban Farm Planned for Detroit," *Restaurant News*, http://www.qsrmagazine.com/articles/news/story.phtml?id=8405 2009-04-02.

32. Roger Bybee, "Growing Power in an Urban Food Desert," *YES*, February 13, 2009. http://www.yesmagazine.org/article.asp?id=3328&utm_source=mar09&utm_medium=email&utm_campaign=f11_Alln

33. Ibid.

34. Roger Doiron, "What's a Home Garden Worth?" *Kitchen Gardeners International* http://www.kitchengardeners.org/2009/03/whats_a_home_garden_worth.html

35. Heather Cobum, "Don't Be Wasted on Grass!" *Cascadia Food Not Lawns* Web site http://www.foodnotlawns.com/lawns_to_gardens.html

36. John Jeavons, in conversation with author, May 20, 2008.

37. Elisabeth Rosenthal, "As More Eat Meat, a Bid to Cut Emissions," *New York Times* December 4, 2008, http://www.nytimes.com/2008/12/04/science/earth/04meat.html

Chapter Four: Getting Carbon Out of Our Systems

1. Christopher Flavin, "Building a Low-Carbon Economy," Chapter 4 in *State of the World: Innovations for a Sustainable Economy*, 2008, (New York: Worldwatch Institute, W.W. Norton & Company, 2008), 89.

2. Earth Policy Institute "New Energy Economy Emerging in the United States," http://www.earthpolicy.org/Updates/2008/Update77.htm.

3. American Wind Energy Association, *Annual Wind Industry Report, Year Ending 2008*, 9–10.

4. Christopher Flavin, "Building a Low-Carbon Economy," Chapter 4 in *State of the World: Innovations for a Sustainable Economy*, (New York: Worldwatch Institute, W.W. Norton & Company, 2008), 83.

5. Ben Block, "Study Finds Rich U.S. Energy Potential," Worldwatch Institute, July 31, 2009 http://www.worldwatch.org/node/6212

6. Worldwatch Institute, "American Energy: The Renewable Path to Energy Security," http://www.worldwatch.org/files/pdf/AmericanEnergy.pdf, 12.

7. Michael Grunwald, "Dream On!," Time Magazine, November 2, 2009, 27-32

8. White House Press Release, Barack Obama, Earth Day, April 22, 2009 talk in Newton, Iowa http://www.whitehouse.gov/the_press_office/remarks-by-the-president-in-Newton-IA/.

9. GTM research website, May, 2010, http://www.gtmresearch.com/report/2010-global-pv-demand-analysis-and-forecast.

10. Amory Lovins, *Soft Energy Paths: Toward a Durable Peace*, (New York: Harpercollins, 1979).

11. Amory B. Lovins, "More Profit With Less Carbon," Scientific American, September 2005, http://features.csmonitor.com/environment/2009/10/08/why-arent-we-harnessing-waste-heat/.

12. Kamal Patel, "Paul Hawken Shares His Thoughts with Worldchanging About Optimism, Doomers and What's Next," From the 2009 Sustainable Industries: Economic Forum. Seattle, Washington, http://www.worldchanging.com/archives/010556.html.

13. Christopher Flavin, "Building a Low-Carbon Economy," Chapter 4 in *State of the World: Innovations for a Sustainable Economy*, 2008, (New York: Worldwatch Institute, W.W. Norton & Company, 2008), 89.

14. Ken Livingstone, BBC News, "Mayor Unveils Climate Change Plan," 2007, http://news.bbc.co.uk/2/hi/uk_news/england/london/6399639.stm.

15. Wikipedia, Major uses Energy in the United States, http://en.wikipedia.org/wiki/Energy_in_the_United_States#cite_note-7.

16. Moises Velasquez-Manoff, "Why aren't we harnessing waste heat?" October 8, 2009 http://features.csmonitor.com/environment/2009/10/08/why-arent-we-harnessing-waste-heat/.

17. Lester R. Brown, "Restructuring the U.S. Transport System: The Potential of High-Speed Rail" February 03, 2009 http://www.earth-policy.org/index.php?/book_bytes/2009/pb3ch11_ss5.

18. Eric, "High Speed Rail Stimulus Grants Announced," January 28, 2010, Trans Bay Blog http://transbayblog.com/2010/01/28/high-speed-rail-stimulus-grants-announced/.

19. Alan S. Drake, "A 10% Reduction in America's Oil Use in Ten to Twelve Years," Light Rail Now, October 2006, http://www.lightrailnow.org/features/f_lrt_2006-05a.htm.

20. Eviana Hartman, "A Promising Oil Alternative: Algae Energy," http://www.washingtonpost.com/wp-dyn/content/article/2008/01/03/AR2008010303907.html.

21. Murphy, Pat Plan C: Community Survival Strategies for Peak Oil and Climate Change (Gabriola Island, British Columbia, Canada) New Society Press, 2008, 162.

22. Lester R. Brown, "U.S. Headed for Massive Decline in Carbon Emissions," Plan B Updates, October 14, 2009, http://www.earth-policy.org/index.php?/plan_b_updates/2009/update83.

23. Ibid.

24. Sharon Ho, "Energy efficiency fails to cut consumption: study, November 27, 2007," http://www.reuters.com/article/environmentNews/idUSN2749536620071127.

25. Lisa Takeuchi Cullen, "Going Green at the Office," Time Magazine, June 7, 2007, http://www.time.com/time/magazine/article/0,9171,1630552,00.html.

Chapter Five: Living Wealth: Restoring the Economies of Nature

1. Ricardo Banyon, "Banking on Biodiversity," in State of the World 2008: Innovations for a Sustainable Economy, ed. Linda Starke (New York: Worldwatch Institute W.W. Norton, 2008), 123–24.

2. Gretchen Daily, Paul Ehrlich, et al., "Ecosystem Services: Benefits Supplied to Human Societies by Natural Ecosystems," http://www.ecology.org/biod/value/EcosystemServices.html.

3. Juliet Eilperin, "25% of Wild Mammal Species Face Extinction," Washington Post, October 6, 2008, http://www.washingtonpost.com/wp-dyn/content/article/2008/10/06/AR2008100600641.html.

4. G. A. Bradshaw et al., "Elephant Breakdown," Nature, February 24, 2005, http://74.125.45.132/search?q=cache:ZR7qkSnBeHsJ:www.elephants.com/pdf/PTSD.pdf+Elephant+Breakdown&cd=1&hl=en&ct=clnk&gl=us&client=firefox-a.

5. Ibid.; Charles Siebert, "An Elephant Crackup," New York Times, October 8, 2006, http://www.nytimes.com/2006/10/08/magazine/08elephant.html.

6. Banyon, "Banking on Biodiversity," 136.

7. Thomas Friedman, "(No) Drill, Baby, Drill," New York Times, April 12, 2009, http://www.nytimes.com/2009/04/12/opinion/12friedman.html?th&emc=th.

8. Rik Langendoen, "Forests Win Protection," Yes! (Spring 2004), http://www.yesmagazine.org/issues/a-conspiracy-of-hope/718.

9. Andrew Simms, Ecological Debt (London: Pluto Press, 2005), 63.

10. Storm Cunningham, Restoration Economy: The Greatest New Growth Frontier (San Francisco: Berrett-Koehler, 2002), 59.

11. Molly Reid, "Wetlands Restoration Touted at Panel Discussion on Climate

Change," *New Orleans Times-Picayune*, April 16, 2009, http://www.nola.com/business/index.ssf/2009/04/wetlands_restoration_touted_at.html.

12. Banyon, "Banking on Biodiversity," 123–24.

13. Cunningham, *Restoration Economy*, 59.

14. Max Christern, "Willie Smits: Hanging Around with Orangutans," *Ode* (January/Feb. 2009) http://www.odemagazine.com/doc/60/willie-smits-hanging-around-with-orangutans/.

15. "Lester Brown in online book excerpt Shifting Subsidies, *Plan B: Rising to the Challenge,* http://www.earth-policy.org/Books/PB/PBch11_ss6.htm.

16. Lester Brown, online book excerpt "Planting Trees and Managing Soils to Sequester Carbon," http://www.earthpolicy.org/Books/Seg/PB3ch08_ss6.htm.

17. Menominee Tribal Enterprise Web site, http://mtewood.com/.

18. Brown, *Plan B 3.0,* 168.

19. Brown, "Planting Trees and Managing Soils to Sequester Carbon."

20. Michael Perry, "Untouched Forests Store 3 Times More Carbon: Study", Reuters, http://www.enn.com/ecosystems/article/37839.

21. Tanya Mohn, "Family Forestry" *New York Times,* June 14, 2007, http://www.wflccenter.org/news_pdf/244_pdf.pdf.

22. Sara J. Scherr and Sajal Sthapit, "Farming and Land Use to Cool the Planet," in *State of the World 2009,* ed. Linda Starke (New York: Worldwatch Institute, W.W. Norton, 2009), 35.

23. *Brown, Plan B 3.0,* 163.

24. Ibid.

25. Ibid.

26. John Sutter, "Ocean Trash Problem 'Far from Being Solved,' U.N. Says," CNN, June 8, 2009, http://www.cnn.com/2009/TECH/science/06/08/ocean.trash.report/index.html.

27. "The Price of Quenching Our Thirst," Worldwatch Institute Web site, http://www.worldwatch.org/node/1479.

28. Ibid., http://www.worldwatch.org/node/1497.

29. Douglas W. Tallamy, and Rick Darke, *Bringing Nature Home* (Portland, Oregon: Timber Press, 2009), 9.

30. David Sobel, *Beyond Ecophobia: Reclaiming the Heart in Nature Education* (Great Barrington; Massachusetts: Orion Society and the Myrin Institute, 1996), 39.

31. Marla Cone, "A Greener Future, Part 1: Products derived from Natural Non-Toxic Ingredients—once seen as fringe—are now mainstream" *Los Angeles Times,* September 14, 2008, http://www.safecosmetics.org/article.php?id=311.

32. David Wann, *Deep Design: Pathways to a Livable Future* (Washington, D.C.: Island Press, 1996), 63–66.

33. "California Passes Nation's First 'Green Chemistry' Law," Environmental News Networks October 2, 2008, http://www.enn.com/pollution/article/38318.

34. Michigan Sate University press release, http://news.msu.edu/story/6258/.

35. Brown, *Plan B 3.0,* 90.

36. Emily Sohn, Discovery News April 6, 2009 http://dsc.discovery.com/news/2009/04/06/bottled-water.html.

37. "Bottled Water Carries Hidden Cost to Earth" ("The Water Is Someone's

Home, syndicated Global Citizen column, May 23, 1996, archived on the Sustainability Institute Web site, http://www.sustainabilityinstitute.org/dhm_archive/)

38. Teril L. Shorb, "Climate Change and Creature Comforts," in *Thoreau's Legacy*, Union of Concerned Scientists, http://www.ucsusa.org/americanstories/.

Chapter Six: Where We Live to Consume, or Where We Come to Life?

1. Peter Calthorpe, in conversation with author, October 2004.

2. Richard Jackson, in conversation with author, May 2003.

3. Solomon, Shay. *Little House on a Small Planet*. (Guilford, Connecticut: Lyons Press, 2006), 5.

4. Susanka, Sarah. *The Not So Big House: A Blueprint for the Way We Really Live*. (Newton, Connecticut: Taunton Press, 2009.)

5. Heisler, Gordon. Computer Simulation for Optimization, Windbreak Placements. http://www.sfrc.ufl.edu/forestry/resources/PDFdownloads/Heissler

6. Steve Cramer, in conversation with author, June 2005.

7. Donald Chen, in conversation with author, October 2005.

8. John Wolff, in conversation with author, August 2004.

9. John de Graaf, in conversation with author, October 2008.

10. John de Graaf, research compiled from data from OECD (Organization for Economic Cooperation and Development).

11. David Johnston, in conversation with author, September 2006.

12. Alex Wilson, in conversation with author, November, 2008.

13. James Kunstler, in conversation with author, May 2008.

Chapter Seven: Revolt of the Munchkins: Value, Not Volume in the Market

1. Jon Moolallem, "The Self-Storage Self," *New York Times Magazine*, September 6, 2009, MM24'

2. Erik Assadourian, "The Rise and Fall of Consumer Cultures," in *State of the World 2010: Transforming Cultures*. (New York: W.W. Norton, 2010), 7.

3. Beringer Founders' Estate "5 to 9" Web site http://www.living5to9.com/5to9/page/time_truths.jsp

4. Daniel Goleman, *Ecological Intelligence: How Knowing the Hidden Impacts of What We Buy Can Change Everything*. (New York: Broadway Books, 2009), 191–194.

5. Ibid, 182–186.

6. Edward Bernays, *Propaganda*. (New York: Horace Liveright Press, 1928), 14.

7. Linda Starke and Lisa Mastry, eds, *State of the World 2010: Transforming Cultures*. (New York: W.W. Norton, 2010), 77.

8. Patrick Purcell, "Congressional Research Service Retirement Savings and Household Wealth in 2007," April 8, 2009 http://www.globalaging.org/pension/us/2009/retire.pdf.

9. Matt Richtel, "Even At Megastores, Hagglers Find No Price Set in Stone," *New York Times*, March 23, 2008, http://www.nytimes.com/2008/03/23/business/23haggle.html.

10. Michael Braungart and William McDonough, *Cradle to Cradle: Remaking the Way We Make Things*. (New York: North Point Press, 2002), 113.

11. Ibid.

12. Op cit.

13. Jeffrey Masters, "The Skeptics vs. the Ozone Hole," Weather Underground Web site http://www.wunderground.com/education/ozone_skeptics.asp?MR=1.

14. Ibid.

15. William and Michael Braungart, "Transforming the Textile Industry," 2002 http://www.mcdonough.com/writings/transforming_textile.htm.

16. Keith Bradsher, "Earth-Friendly Elements, Mined Destructively," *New York Times* December 26, 2009, http://www.nytimes.com/2009/12/26/business/global/26rare.html.

17. Ethan Watters, "Product Design, Nature's Way, *Business 2.0 Magazine*, June 12, 2007 http://money.cnn.com/magazines/business2/business2_archive/2007/06/01/100050991/index.htm

18. Andy Isaacson, "Mimicking Mother Nature," *Utne*, March-April, 2006, http://www.utne.com/2006-03-01/mimicking-mother-nature.aspx

Chapter Eight: Social Alchemy: Creating a New Normal

1. Gyorgy Doczi, *The Power of Limits: Proportional Harmonies in Nature, Art, and Architecture*. (Boston: Shambhala Press, 2005), 33.

2. Donella H. Meadows, Dennis Meadows, and Jorgen Randers, *Beyond the Limits*. (Post Mills, Vermont: Chelsea Green, 1992), 56.

3. Ray Anderson, Mona Amodeo, and Jim Hartzfeld, "Changing Business Culture From Within," in *State of the World 2010: Transforming Cultures*, (New York: Worldwatch Institute, W.W. Norton, 2010), 97–100.

4. Amanda Hirsch, Remotely Connected Blog, September 3, 2008 http://www.pbs.org/remotelyconnected/2008/09/stress_portrait_of_a_killer.html.

5. Lester Brown, *Plan B 4.0 Rescuing a Planet Under Stress and a Civilization in Trouble*. (New York: W.W. Norton, 2009.)

6. Lester Brown, "U.S. Car Fleet Shrinks by Four Million in 2009," Earth Policy Institute update, http://www.earthpolicy.org/index.php?/plan_b_updates/2010/update87.

7. Amanda Ripley, "Ten Things You Can Like About $4 Gas," *Time* July 2, 2008, http://www.time.com/time/specials/packages/article/0,28804,1819594_1819592,00.html#ixzz0c8GbnZVo.

8. Donella Meadows, Sustainability Institute, 1999, Hartford, Vermont: www.sustainer.org/pubs/leverage-points.pdf

9. David Kestenbaum, "Debate: Do Smart Meters Curb Energy Use?" January 8, 2010, "Morning Edition," National Public Radio, http://www.npr.org/templates/story/story.php?storyId=122350735.

Recommended Readings

Ausubel, Kenny, with J. C. Harpignies. *Nature's Operating Instructions: The True Biotechnologies*. (San Francisco: Sierra Club Books, 2004).

Benyus, Janine M. *Biomimicry: Innovation Inspired by Nature*. (New York: Harper Perennial, 2002.)

Braudel, Fernand. *A History of Civilizations*. (New York: Penguin, 2005.)

———. *The Structures of Everyday Life : the Limits of the Possible*. (New York: Harper & Row, 1982.)

Brown, Lester. *Plan B 4.0: Mobilizing to Save Civilization*. (New York: W.W. Norton, 2009.)

Calthorpe, Peter, and Sim Van der Ryn. *Sustainable Communities: A New Design Synthesis for Cities, Suburbs, and Towns*. (Gabrida Island, British Columbia, Canada: New Catalyst, 2008.)

Daley, Herman E. *Beyond Growth: The Economics of Sustainable Development*. (Boston: Beacon Press, 1996.)

Diamond, Jared. *Collapse: How Societies Choose to Fail or Succeed*. (New York: Viking, 2005.)

Gladwell, Malcolm. *Outliers: The Story of Success*. (New York: Little, Brown, 2008.)

Goleman, Daniel. *Ecological Intelligence: How Knowing the Impacts of What We Buy Can Change Everything*. (New York: Broadway Books, 2009.)

Hawken, Paul, Amory Lovins, and Hunter Lovins. *Natural Capitalism*. (New York: Little, Brown, 1999.)

Heinberg, Richard. *Peak Everything: Waking Up to the Century of Declines*. (Gabriola Island, British Columbia, Canada: New Society, 2007.)

Hopkins, Rob. *The Transition Handbook*. (White River Junction, Vermont: Chelsea Green, 2008.)

Jones, Van, with Ariane Conrad. *The Green Collar Economy: How One Solution Can Fix Our Two Biggest Problems*. (New York: HarperOne, 2008.)

Korten, David C. *The Great Turning: From Empire to Earth Community*. (Oakland, California: Kumarian Press/Berrett-Koehler, 2006.)

Kuntsler, James Howard. *The Long Emergency: Surviving the Converging Catastrophes of the Twenty-First Century*. (New York: Grove Press, 2006.)

Lindstrom, Martin. *Buyology: Truth and Lies About Why We Buy.* (New York: Doubleday, 2008.)

McDonough, William, and Michael Braungart. *Cradle to Cradle : Remaking the Way We Make Things.* (San Francisco: North Point Press, 1992.)

McKenzie-Mohr, Doug. *Fostering Sustainable Behavior: An Introduction to Community-Based Social Marketing.* (Gabriola Island, British Columbia, Canada: New Society, 1999.)

Meadows, Donella H., Dennis Meadows, and Jorgen Randers. *Beyond the Limits.* (White River Junction, Vermont: Chelsea Green, 1992.)

Mumford, Lewis. *Technics and Human Development.* (New York: Harcourt, Brace, Jovanovich, 1967.)

Murphy, Pat. *Plan C: Community Survival Strategies for Peak Oil and Climate Change.* (Gabriola Island, British Columbia, Canada: New Society Publishers, 2008.)

Pollan, Michael. *In Defense of Food: An Eater's Manifesto.* (New York: Penguin, 2009.)

Reich, Robert. *Supercapitalism: The Transformation of Business, Democracy, and Everyday Life.* (New York: Alfred A. Knopf, 2007.)

Rubens, Jim. *OverSuccess: Healing the American Obsession with Wealth, Fame, Power, and Perfection.* (Austin, Texas: Greenleaf Books, 2009.)

Sachs, Jeffrey D. *Common Wealth: Economics for a Crowded Planet.* (New York: Penguin Press, 2008.)

Shuman, Michael. *The Small-Mart Revolution: How Local Businesses Are Beating the Global Competition.* (Oakland, California: Berrett-Koehler, 2006.)

Siegel, Charles. *The Politics of Simple Living.* (Berkeley, California: Preservation Institute, 2008.)

Sperling, Daniel, with Deborah Gordon. *Two Billion Cars: Driving Toward Sustainability.* (New York: Oxford University Press, 2008.)

Starke, Linda, ed. *State of the World 2008: Innovations for a Sustainable Economy,* (New York: Worldwatch Institute, W.W. Norton, 2008.)

———. *State of the World 2009: Into a Warming World.* (Worldwatch Institute New York: W.W. Norton, 2009.)

Starke, Linda, and Lisa Mastny, eds. *State of the World 2010: Transforming Cultures.* (New York: Worldwatch Institute, W.W. Norton, 2010.)

Wansink, Brian. *Mindless Eating: Why We Eat More Than We Think.* (New York: Bantam Books, 2006.)

Weisman, Alan. *The World Without Us.* (New York: Picador, 2008.)

Williamson, Marianne, ed. *Imagine: What America Could Be in the 21st Century.* (New York: St. Martin's Press, 2000.)

Wilson, Edward O. *The Diversity of Life.* (Cambridge, Massachusetts: Harvard University, 1992.)

Index